LANGUAGE AND LITERACY SERIES
Dorothy S. Strickland and Celia Genishi, SERIES EDITORS

WHOLE LANGUAGE ACROSS THE CURRICULUM

GRADES 1, 2, 3

Edited by

SHIRLEY C. RAINES

Foreword by Dorothy S. Strickland

International
Reading
Association

Teachers College
Columbia University
New York and London

Published simultaneously by Teachers College Press, 1234 Amsterdam Avenue, New York, NY 10027 and The International Reading Association, 800 Barksdale Rd., Newark, DE 19714

Library of Congress Cataloging-in-Publication Data

Whole language across the curriculum: grades 1, 2, 3/edited by Shirley
  C. Raines; foreword by Dorothy S. Strickland.
      p.   cm.—(Language and literacy series)
    Includes bibliographical references and index.
    ISBN 0-8077-3446-2 (pbk. : acid-free paper)
    1. Language arts (Primary)—United States. 2. Language arts—
Correlation with content subjects—United States.
3. Interdisciplinary approach in education—United States.
I. Raines, Shirley C. II. Series: Language and literacy series (New
York, N. Y.)
LB1529.U5W46   1995
372.6—dc20   94-48696

ISBN: 0-8077-3446-2 (paper)
IRA Inventory Control Number 156

Printed on acid-free paper
Manufactured in the United States of America
02 01 00 99 98 97 96 95   8 7 6 5 4 3 2 1

Contents

Foreword

No matter where I travel throughout the United States and beyond, I encounter educators who are carefully reexamining their literacy programs. They are rethinking old assumptions about how children learn to read and write and how teachers and parents can best help them. Among the changes I see are these: more attention is paid to writing and its relationship to reading, even at the very earliest years of schooling; increased use is made of quality children's literature throughout the curriculum; greater choice is offered to students in the materials they read and the topics about which they write; and genuine attempts are made to truly integrate the language arts across the curriculum through inquiry around topics of interest and importance to children. In many ways, it is the most exciting and hopeful time in my more than three decades as a literacy educator.

Most would agree that the theoretical perspective and professional movement known as *whole language* is largely responsible for these new directions in literacy education, and that children in the early years of schooling have benefited most from the new knowledge and practice. Teachers of these children are apt to be aware of the principles of child growth and development central to whole language. Yet, even for many of these professionals, adapting to new practice often presents a real challenge. It is for that reason that *Whole Language Across the Curriculum: Grades 1, 2, 3* is such a welcome addition to the professional literature.

In addition to being well versed in whole language theory, the contributors to this volume are aware of the key areas of concern for teachers and administrators who attempt to modify and strengthen curriculum at the primary grade levels. Throughout the book, the voices of classroom teachers who are effectively "doing it" are heard. Rich descriptions are offered for how these classrooms look, and for the planning required to make learning happen.

Whole language advocates have sometimes been admonished for being vague or "fuzzy" about what they mean by whole language, and about what it should look like. *Whole Language Across the Curriculum: Grades 1, 2, 3* is an excellent answer to these critics. It offers sufficient detail without being prescriptive. Indeed, it is a rich resource of good ideas for the classroom—an excellent example of whole language theory *in practice.*

Dorothy S. Strickland
State of New Jersey Professor of Reading
Rutgers University

Preface

Choosing the title that will help a book reach the intended audience is a difficult matter. After struggling with the title of this book, the editors, contributors, and I chose *Whole Language Across the Curriculum: Grades 1, 2, 3*. Realizing that the term *whole language* has become over-used and little understood, we flirted with titles that included terms such as *integrated curriculum, integrated language arts, literature and language-rich,* and *emergent and beginning literacy*. It was also recommended that we use *active learning* or *interactive learning* in the title. We tried titles with other words and phrases, such as *constructivism, socially constructed knowledge, psycholinguistic,* and *sociolinguistic precepts in primary classrooms*. The book is, indeed, about all of these mutually supportive constructs found in "good" primary whole language classrooms. In the end, we decided to keep the title *Whole Language Across the Curriculum: Grades 1, 2, 3*. We believe that readers who know about whole language will make the above associations, and for others who want to learn about whole language, the title is direct.

Titles of books have a special significance to me. One particular book title became for me a statement of my philosophy of what it means to be a teacher. In 1967, when I was a senior in college and about to begin my teaching career, I owned a book entitled *Perceiving, Behaving, Becoming* (Combs, 1962). In fact, I owned it more than once. Faced with dwindling funds in my senior year, I sold my books to pay for graduation fees. Soon after graduation, I took a job in the college bookstore and bought back the very same book I had sold to them. The book contained chapters by Earl Kelley, Carl Rogers, Abraham Maslow, and Arthur Combs. Now, many years later, I have forgotten the exact contents of each of the chapters, but I have retained the title as a guiding philosophy for me as a teacher and as a teacher educator. I believe that we must first perceive our roles as teacher, then behave as the best examples of our profession, and continue the life-long process of becoming better teachers.

The subtitle for *Whole Language Across the Curriculum: Grades 1, 2, 3* could have been "Perceiving, Behaving, and Becoming a Whole Language Teacher." The purpose of this book is to help the reader perceive the whole language perspective, to invite the reader into whole language classrooms to see how a teacher with this philosophy behaves, and to start the process of becoming a whole language teacher.

DESCRIPTION OF THE BOOK

You will read about classrooms alive with activity where teachers are creating what it means to help learners become literate in the complex and dynamic world of a living classroom and curriculum. We trust teachers' interpretations of their lives as professionals, so you will read about them as people. The contributing authors who write about the classrooms have been collaborators with individual teachers over time and with groups of teachers, as entire schools moved to whole language. The writers are insightful, reflective teacher educators. They are knowledgeable and care deeply about children and teachers.

The authors who contributed chapters were chosen for their expertise, their ability to communicate, and their strengths in building connections. To make the curriculum connections "real" for the reader, the writers build connections between who the children are as learners, what the curricular subject areas require of children in order for them to be constructors and users of that information, how classrooms can be organized, and ways in which teachers relate to learners. The writers are "meaning makers." I have asked them to share the salient points, the connections to whole language, and the glimpses inside classrooms where these ideas are alive. These expert meaning makers will be our guides through the classroom doors, leading the reader to construct her or his own interpretations.

The rationale for what is happening in the classroom is established in Chapter 1. This chapter introduces what we mean by whole language, uncovers some of the roots of the meaning of the term, and illuminates major connections between theory and several position papers on classroom practices from professional organizations that have similar views of the learner and the curriculum. Readers interested in finding further guidance for classroom practices are referred to the position paper from the International Reading Association (IRA), *Literacy Development and Early Childhood (Preschool through Grade 3)* (Early Childhood Committee and Literacy Development Committee, 1991).

Chapters 2, 3, and 4 are about teachers and their process of change as they become whole language teachers. In Chapter 2 we meet Terri, who had been teaching first grade for a few years before she was transferred to a school where whole language is accepted practice. In Chapter 3 we are introduced to Carol and Jolene. Carol is a veteran second grade teacher who changes her approach to writing instruction after her experience in an Area Writing Project. Jolene is a third grade teacher who has been reassigned from first grade and decides that she likes the challenge of using whole language in social studies and science. In Chapter 4 we encounter the many decisions Lynn makes as she becomes a whole language teacher in a continuous progress (or multiage) classroom.

The second section of the book, Chapters 5 through 8, was written to help the reader understand that whole language has implications across the curriculum. Chapter 5, by Linda Leonard Lamme, is entitled "Dance! Chant! Discuss! Write! Responses to Literature in the Primary Grades." In Chapter 6, Joan Isenberg writes about "Whole Language in Play and the Expressive Arts." In Chapter 7, Carol Seefeldt helps us understand how whole language and the social studies curriculum are mutually supportive. The authors of Chapter 8, Rosalind Charlesworth and Karen Lind, help the reader understand "Whole Language and Primary Grades Mathematics and Science: Keeping in Step with National Standards." They reference and discuss the connections between whole language and the standards of both the National Council of Teachers of Mathematics and the National Science Teachers Association. In Chapter 9, Gary and Maryann Manning write about "Whole Language Portfolios: Assessment and Evaluation to Inform Children, Parents, and Educators."

Chapter 10, "Epilogue: Challenges for Whole Language Primary Teachers," helps the reader to answer some evaluative questions about the state of professional development, and to discover where a whole language view of practice might lead us as educators.

Whole Language Across the Curriculum: Grades 1, 2, 3 is a continuation of *The Whole Language Kindergarten* (Raines & Canady, 1990). After publishing this volume, Robert Canady and myself were often asked by first grade teachers when we planned to write "The Whole Language First Grade." Second grade teachers asked about second grade, and third grade teachers wanted a third grade book. Then, after working with teachers in a nongraded, continuous progress school, I was asked about a whole language book that focused on *their* needs. While we have chosen not to continue a grade-by-grade review of whole language, we do believe that a need exists among primary teachers for descriptions of how whole language relates to the total curriculum. We hope that *Whole Language Across the Curriculum: Grades 1, 2, 3* helps fulfill that need.

I wish to express appreciation to Dorothy Strickland, for her thoughtful reflections in the Foreword; to the contributors for their perceptions, insights, and belief in the value of our book; to the teachers who inspired us to write about them; to the children whose work we reproduced; and to those who assisted in the preparation of the manuscript, especially Christine Miranda at the University of South Florida. The editors at Teachers College Press who made this book possible deserve much credit, and I wish to thank Sarah Biondello and Susan Liddicoat for continuing to pursue another book from me, and Carol Collins for her excellent, consistent, and persistent editing and for copyediting. Thank you.

Shirley C. Raines

REFERENCES

Combs, A. W. (Ed.) (1962). *Perceiving, behaving, becoming.* Washington, DC: Association for Supervision and Curriculum Development.

Early Childhood Committee and Literacy Development Committee (1990). *Literacy Development and Early Childhood (Preschool through Grade 3).* Newark, Delaware: International Reading Association.

Raines, S. C., & Canady, R. J. (1990). *The whole language kindergarten.* New York: Teachers College Press.

1

Introduction: Reflecting on Whole Language

SHIRLEY C. RAINES

In the preface to this book, change was described as a series of steps in "perceiving, behaving, and becoming." For many positive reasons, teachers perceive that changes in their teaching are necessary. Reflective practitioners make changes in their teaching because of a state of disequilibrium. Perhaps the teacher's state of disequilibrium is caused by struggles to help one particular child, or by comparing one's own teaching to a wonderful lesson conducted by a colleague, or by reading an article about some new strategies. Perceiving that they want to change, teachers then begin behaving differently as they experiment with organizational patterns, strategies, and relationships with their students. While in the process of experimenting with their teaching, they also reflect, or participate in "reflection in action" (Dewey, 1904; Schon, 1983). As reflective practitioners, whole language teachers are in the process of change, of becoming teachers who perceive their students, the curriculum, and themselves differently.

Whole Language Across the Curriculum: Grades 1, 2, 3 is a book about teachers who are becoming whole language educators. For some the steps are small and for others the leaps are gigantic but each primary grade teacher who is described and each classroom visited provides insights into the process of change.

WHAT IS WHOLE LANGUAGE?

Whole language is being created by teachers in their classrooms based on an amalgamation of findings from psycholinguists, sociolinguists, researchers, and practitioners. The meaning of whole language is interpreted differently across the country, even throughout the world, because it is a perspective, not a prescribed set of practices. The whole language perspective is based on the literacy processes; it is not a method of instruction but a view of literacy learning that is compatible with psycholinguistic and sociolinguistic theory and research. Altwerger, Edelsky, and Flores (1987) have said: "It must be practice, but it is not practice itself" (p. 145). As Dorothy Watson (1987) has pointed out, whole language should in no way be used to develop future step-by-step literacy instruction programs. Teachers who have a whole language perspective operate their classrooms with an abundance of children's literature, use a writing process approach, usually organize the curriculum in integrated, thematic units, teach strategies approaches to inquiry, and find authentic, meaningful ways for children to communicate about their lives and what they are learning.

Influences from Psycholinguistic Research

In the late 1960s and early 1970s, teachers who wanted to learn more about whole language were directed to the research and writing of Kenneth S. Goodman. Although the foundations of whole language do not begin with Goodman's contributions, he is recognized as one of the most significant figures in the establishment and development of the whole language movement. In this section, we will review the research and theories that form the foundation of whole language education and refer to contributions made by Kenneth Goodman's research and the work of some of his colleagues. (Readers are referred to the sources cited in this chapter, and listed in the references, for additional information.)

One of the most significant research studies in the evolution of whole language education was conducted by Kenneth Goodman in the mid-1960s. Influenced strongly by the earlier works of Piaget (Piaget & Inhelder, 1969), Vygotsky (1978), and Dewey (1904), Goodman wanted to learn more about the process of reading. While past reading research can be characterized as studies of various methods of teaching reading, Goodman was more interested in the relationship between thought (psycho) and language (linguistics) as it applied to the reading process. For his research, hundreds of readers from various parts of the country read passages in natural classroom settings and were asked to tell about the story. Comprehension was measured by their retelling of the story and by their reading errors, referred to as *miscues*, which were analyzed to determine why children skipped, substituted, or added words.

The Goodman research resulted in the construction of the Goodman Model of Reading, and in a totally new way to evaluate reading called *miscue analysis* (K. S. Goodman, 1969). Goodman's original findings, published in 1968 in his book, *The Psycholinguistic Nature of the Reading Process*, caused traditional reading instruction to be questioned and, along with the research that followed, suggested that reading was not the letter-by-letter, step-by-step decoding process that it appeared to be. Rather, Goodman found that readers skipped, substituted, and made logical guesses as they attempted to construct meaning from the print before them. His research further suggested that counting the number of mistakes a reader makes reveals very little about the reader (Y. M. Goodman, Watson, & Burke, 1987). Goodman found that readers have logical reasons for their mistakes, or miscues, and that readers' miscues must be analyzed if reading performance is to be evaluated.

Psycholinguistic research grew rapidly in the 70s and 80s, verifying and adding to Goodman's initial studies (Clay, 1972; Ferreiro, 1986; Y. M. Goodman, 1986; Harste, Woodward, & Burke, 1984; Taylor, 1983, just to mention a few). As the findings from psycholinguistic research became available to teacher educators and classroom teachers, many made major changes in their classrooms, especially in teaching reading and writing. The information concerning the nature of the reading process only verified what many inquiring teachers had already suspected. Reading is a thought/language process, and instructional materials must contain language that is whole and meaningful to the learner. Thus, the term *whole language* was coined to describe a perspective on reading and writing instruction. Because of its positive effects on learning, the whole language perspective on reading and writing is now being applied across the curriculum as teachers reflect on the question, "If I am a whole language teacher, how will I teach the other areas of the curriculum differently?"

The whole language perspective is a view of instruction that is compatible with psycholinguistic research, and it is now applied to the thinking processes. Whole language education requires that the teacher's perspective reflect the information being gathered about literacy processes from psycholinguistic and sociolinguistic research.

Influences from Sociolinguistic Research

Kenneth Goodman has often stated that he did not found whole language but that whole language found him (1992). He is quick to recognize those who have influenced his own thinking and broadened his knowledge concerning the thought/language process. In an article published in *Language Arts* (1992), Goodman notes that Lev Vygotsky's research (1978) revealed the social nature of learning itself and that Vygotsky's theory concerning the internalization of social language has helped whole language teachers understand the importance of language interactions in the classroom.

Sociolinguistic researchers have studied the social contexts within which language is used and their work has extended the view of language learning established by M. A. K. Halliday (1978). Halliday found that as children learn how to use language, they also learn how to "mean." Halliday's research has been interpreted to mean that there is a need for language-rich learning environments to support all areas of the curriculum.

Sociolinguistic research has helped whole language educators understand the importance of accepting children's personal language in the learning environment. As Feldman (1980) points out, intended meaning cannot be understood without examining the communication intentions of language users, and communication intentions cannot be examined without looking at the social context in which they occur.

The social nature of learning, and in particular of learning about reading and writing, means that children are listeners, talkers, and conceptualizers. The interrelatedness of learning how to construct print and how to read the print that others have constructed is a highly social event. Like the young child who figures out that knowing what the print is about "gets you something," the primary grade child determines that "figuring out" the literacy system gets you admitted to the "literacy club" (Smith, 1988). Those who do poorly have less status. Frank Smith talks about inviting children into the "literacy club." Children figure out that joining the club created by the teacher in the social context of the classroom—and by their families in the social context of home and community—is a high priority in our society.

Findings from Literacy Research

For many teachers, one of the most difficult aspects to accept about whole language education is the idea that reading and writing "emerge" as a natural part of a child's growth and development. Parents and teachers alike have accepted as fact that in a verbal environment, children will emerge as listeners and speakers without specific instruction, but that reading and writing must be taught. Many teachers hold the view that children enter school unable to read and write and that sequential-skills reading programs are necessary for the development of successful readers.

Literacy research has left little doubt that reading and writing, like listening and speaking, are processes that have begun in all children long before they enter school. Teale and Sulzby (1986) credit Marie Clay with the concept of emergent literacy. Clay's studies appeared in New Zealand in the 1960s and in the United States in the 1970s. The term *emergent literacy* embodies the concept of literacy as a process. Yetta Goodman (1986) characterized the process as "like the roots of a growing tree." The roots of literacy lie in the relationships the child constructs between the print and the meaning. In studies of young children's print awareness, researchers (Canady, 1982; Clay, 1975; K. S.Goodman, 1986) point out the social nature of how children come to know about print. In a literate society, children grow up surrounded by print and become aware of the ways it functions in their environments. Whether it is noticing the special toy in a fast food packaged meal, or reading the signs and logos in shopping malls or on cereal boxes in grocery stores, young children learn that print "gets you things" (Canady, 1982; Raines & Canady, 1990, p. 4).

Information gathered by *emergent literacy* researchers is not only important to teachers of young children entering school but to all primary grade teachers. Teachers who understand the emergent nature of the literacy process are more concerned with their first, second, and third graders' continuing literacy development rather than with a standardized test to determine grade level. The need to interact in a language-rich environment does not end at kindergarten. The various stages children go through as they develop as readers and writers continue through the primary grades.

THE LEARNING/READING/WRITING PROCESSES

Constructivism (Piaget, 1977; Vygotsky, 1962) is the theory of learning that is most compatible with whole language education. According to Piaget, learning takes place through assimilation and accommodation. Learners make predictions by sampling information, then confirming or rejecting their predictions. If the learners' predictions are confirmed or verified, the information is assimilated and they continue sampling. If their predictions are rejected, they must either abandon or adjust their predictions and sample for additional information. New information may cause learners to organize their thinking into new constructs or schemata, indicating a process of accommodation. The depth of the learning will be determined by the quality of the predictions, the samples of information, and the prior knowledge of the learners.

The Reading Process

Whole language teachers view reading as a process of constructing meaning from interacting with the print and relating the information to what one already knows. The process is one of assimilation and accommodation. First, the reader scans or samples the print and predicts meaning. Then the reader samples the print to confirm or reject the predicted meaning. If the prediction is confirmed, the reader moves on to the next sample. If the prediction is rejected, the reader either abandons or adjusts the prediction and continues on. Going through the text, sampling, predicting, confirming, and continuing the process, the reader integrates the information with previous knowledge. The depth of understanding or comprehending is determined by the quality of the reader's predictions, by the print samples, and by prior knowledge. Frank Smith (1985) has said that "children do not learn to read in order to make sense of print. They strive to make sense of print and as a consequence they learn to read" (p. 120). The process of reading is thus an interactive one, with the child interacting with the print to actively construct meaning.

Young children begin figuring out how print works and over time develop their concepts of print. Readers in the primary grades are refining their knowledge of and use of print and of the literacy processes. Their concepts of the constructs of print also relate to the problem of organization of different types of texts and literacy for different contexts.

The teacher's role becomes one of interacting with the primary grade children about print and, through these interactions and mediations, the child is helped in the construction process. As teachers begin to view children as "constructors" of the process, the ways in which they teach children differ (Atkins, 1984; Ferreiro, 1986). Brian Cambourne (1988) has argued that "Learning to become literate ought to be as uncomplicated and barrier-free as possible" (p. 4). Whole language teachers plan interactions with a variety of texts, experiences, and activities in a classroom atmosphere that supports literacy development.

The Writing Process

The view of "children as constructors of meaning" is also an appropriate view of their development as writers. Writers select a thought to be expressed and choose words and print symbols they know to convey their thoughts. The writer then constructs a sample of print and examines it to confirm the meaning. If meaning is confirmed, the writer continues; if meaning is not confirmed, the writer adjusts the print. Whether the author is a mature writer or a beginning writer struggling to invent a way to spell, the process is one of thinking of what is to be communicated, using whatever writing knowledge one can bring to bear on the task, and keeping on writing. The variety of types of writing, the purposes for writing, and the opportunities for constructing print are best practiced in classrooms where children are supported in a nonthreatening environment, where they can be risk takers.

Perhaps the most visible impact of whole language education has been in the area of writing. Writing, long thought of as a skill to be learned after children were fluent readers, has now been fully recognized as an essential activity in the total learning process. Writing centers and independent writing activities are now found in many primary grade classrooms, whether or not whole language is the dominant emphasis in instruction.

Two researchers who have had an enormous impact on writing instruction in the whole language classroom are Marie Clay (1975) and Donald Graves (1983). Clay's research with beginning writers revealed that even before children are able to read, they are already using whatever knowledge they possess of how print functions to construct meaning. Graves studied the early writings of children and established a developmental sequence of invented spelling. In the primary grade classrooms where Graves and colleagues conducted their research, the composing process was examined and the steps labeled. From writing research conducted in classrooms, whole language teachers have discovered the importance of writing across all areas of the curriculum. They have found that independent writing can serve as a vehicle for primary grade children to practice the "basic skills" of reading, writing, and spelling in a meaningful way. Whole language teachers have also learned that, like reading, writing is not learned by filling out workbooks or through isolated skills lessons. Writing is learned by active involvement with meaningful writing activities.

The relationships of reading to writing and of writing to reading continue to be sources of investigation. The information from whole language classrooms is that children engaged in the process of becoming literate are influenced by their concepts of what it means to be a reader and a writer. As Frank Smith (1982) has discussed, learning to read and write is complicated, but it is no more difficult a process than that by which children learn to talk or learn the difference between a dog and a cat.

Martha King (1991) discusses children's symbolism and the representations they construct as they attempt to gain control of the way language works in print. Learning "to mean" in print, and to figure out what others mean in print, is a highly abstract experience. Primary grade school children need firsthand experience with the experience of abstracting and of constructing the symbols and representations our culture has devised to form a record of our lives. Whole language programs use children's own language, employ activities and materials that are meaningful to the children, and give them opportunities to develop, refine, further develop, and further refine their language, respecting them as constructors of concepts.

TRANSLATING PRACTICE INTO RESEARCH AND RESEARCH INTO PRACTICE

In many aspects of education, it appears that practice usually follows theory and research. An example would be the swing back and forth from an emphasis on phonics to an emphasis on sight words in reading instruction. When the results of a reputable research project indicated that children scored higher on a reading test after receiving phonics-based instruction, an emphasis on phonics was soon apparent in the classroom. When other research studies indicated that scores were higher after children were given whole word instruction, reading programs tended to swing back to a word emphasis. Still other research suggested various combinations of the two approaches, and large numbers of reading programs were labeled "eclectic." If this "musical chairs" approach to reading instruction is confusing to educators, imagine what it is like for the children and their parents.

It is not surprising that many educators and parents believe that whole language is just another swing of the educational pendulum. Nothing could be farther from the truth. Whole language is founded on an entirely different theoretical base than are the instructional programs that have preceded it.

Child-Centered, Developmentally Appropriate Practice Teachers

Teachers who plan their literacy programs around the individual needs of their children are probably already involved in the kinds of learning activities that would be considered whole language. A child-centered teacher, rather than a materials or an instructional program teacher, knows that children construct knowledge based on what they already know and want to find out. Whether or not child-centered teachers can articulate a particular theory of learning, they have little difficulty in recognizing and creating whole language classrooms, as they are described in this book. The teacher's perspective is a developmental one, in which children are expected to develop over time and move from gross approximations toward refinement.

Skills-Based Teachers

There is a myth that whole language teachers do not teach skills and refuting this myth is part of the function of the chapters which follow on reading and writing in real classrooms. The teacher who labels himself or herself as a "skills" teacher often requires that learners must master a set of reading and writing skills in a sequential order. These teachers, who treat children as passive learners, are not likely to be successful whole language teachers. However, if skills-based teachers visit strong, whole language teachers' classrooms, they will find children learning skills but practicing them in more meaningful ways. Primary grade children remember the skills of reading and writing, or the individual aspects of any subject matter, because those skills were acquired and practiced in meaningful contexts.

Reconciliation of Research and Concerns

Whole language teachers accept the constructivist theory of learning, the Goodman Model of Reading, and the writing process approach, and then adapt their classrooms accordingly. Conversely, as Victor Froese has pointed out in *Whole-Language: Practice and Theory* (1991), some teachers change their instruction first and then accept the theory behind it.

Whole language is a puzzling term to many teachers, but the emphasis on teaching the whole is not. For example, primary grade teachers use stories, songs, and poems for entertainment, for inspiration, for information, and for teaching concepts. When teachers present a new song, they introduce it by singing the whole song first, then the children sing along. Teachers may pause at a later rendition of the song to point out a special word, note, or phrasing, but in the initial singing, the children hear the song through from start to finish, to have a sense of the whole, of what they are expected to learn. "It would never occur to . . . teachers to emphasize the individual words or letters of a song until the whole song was learned" (Martin, 1988) word-by-word. Teachers of songs do not break the language into such small pieces that meaning is lost for the child. In a whole language classroom, the basic skills of language are learned without destroying the song.

Where Do We Begin?

Probably the best place to begin for any teacher wanting to create a whole language classroom is by observing other whole language teachers. In some areas, the teachers and district leaders have "customized" their own names: literacy process approach, literacy and literature learning, or integrated language arts. However, whole language means the perspective of the child as a constructor of knowledge. The teacher's acceptance of the whole language perspective means he or she operates the classroom in ways that promote these views. Even though there are no set guidelines for a whole language classroom, or criteria for what it means to be a whole language teacher, teachers must have a commitment to the basic philosophy of whole language education.

Whole language primary grade teachers agree with the following basic principles:

- Meaning is constructed by the learner.
- Reading and writing are thought/language processes.
- Reading and writing are evaluated through authentic assessment processes.

- Subject matter is best learned through teaching that promotes concept understanding, often through integrated thematic unit teaching.
- Choices of topics, learning activities, materials, and experiences promote interest, construction of concepts, and investment in the learning processes.
- Whole, meaningful, functional language should be used across the curriculum.

KEY ELEMENTS FOR WHOLE LANGUAGE
PRIMARY GRADE CLASSROOMS

Based on pyscholinguistic and sociolinguistic theory and research, as well as on research in existing whole language classrooms, several key elements guide whole language teachers' instructional practices. They include:

- Immersion—immerse children in a rich language and literacy environment
- Opportunities and resources—provide time, materials, space, and activities to be listeners, speakers, readers, and writers
- Meaningful communication—focus on the whole because the mind makes sense of, or constructs meaning from experiences— whether the experiences are spoken, or listened to, or read, or written about—when they are communicated as wholes
- Modeling—act as a communication role model in listening, speaking, reading, writing, so that instruction, function, and purpose are meaningful
- Acceptance—accept young children as readers and writers capable of whole, and thus meaningful communication
- Expectancy—create an atmosphere of expectancy, an affective, attitudinal climate that is encouraging and supportive, where children are expected to continue in their literacy development.

Immersion in Language and Print

Whole language classrooms are noisy places, but it is good noise. They bustle with activity, pause for group reflection, and churn with energy as learners work industriously on their goals of finding out about our physical and social world. When the learning environment is one in which children are constructors of language in its spoken and print forms, they are immersed in the process. They listen, speak, draw, perform, read, write, dramatize, present, chart, graph, measure, synthesize, extrapolate, infer, interpret, and apply information. They are learning the processes of literacy and practicing what they have learned within the whole context of the curriculum.

Opportunities and Resources

The time, space, materials, and opportunities for activities are resources provided by the teacher. The underlying organizational structure is usually one of large blocks of time during which children can work as individuals, in small groups, and in whole class. The materials are abundant because when choice is a guiding principle, then learners must have a variety of materials, rather than the "one size (or one basal) fits all" approach. Whole language classrooms are filled with interesting books, magazines, newspapers, access to expanded data bases, even choices of papers, pens, art supplies, and construction materials for projects. The open-endedness of materials is the difference. Rather than fill-in-the-blank photocopy sheets or workbooks, children have paper, pencils, art supplies, chart paper, and materials for making displays.

Meaningful Communication

Meaningful communication has been described as "authentic." Children want to communicate—in writing, discussion, and through their play and expressive arts—what they are learning. They make discoveries, uncover interesting facts, pose more questions, and simply enjoy the human need to socialize and to be with others. Children are "meaning makers" (Wells, 1986) and, in that role, they need ways to represent what they have learned. As children seek to (re)present what they are learning and are struggling to figure out, they become more representationally competent (Raines, 1986).

Teacher as Communication Role Model

At one time, the idea of the teacher as a communication role model was concerned for the most part with the teacher as a user of standard spoken "school English." Later, we expanded that view. Teachers were requested to read their own books when they asked children to have silent reading time, or to write some of their own writing when all the children were involved in uninterrupted, sustained writing. Today, the idea of the teacher as a communication role model encompasses both interpretations and is expanding to include the teacher as a communicator of his or her thinking about the process of communicating.

　　Teachers become effective communication role models in the living community of the classroom by reading aloud well, by pointing out their deliberations about book selections, by informing children of the decision-making processes they went through as they developed a unit, organized a field trip, or worked with the school office to solve a problem. Children should be involved with the life of the classroom and of the school; composing thank-you notes to school personnel, helping to complete order forms for supplies, and, most importantly, figuring out ways to share with others what they have learned about topics. The teacher as a communication role model in the primary grades means teachers read, write, and think aloud, helping to make apparent the metacognitive processes one uses to think about literacy, to think through decisions.

Acceptance of Children as Readers and Writers

The developmental model of children as readers and writers builds on children's strengths. In the past, teachers often began every analysis of the child's work by stating what he or she did not know. Instead, whole language teachers accept that children are readers and writers now, and are using what they know.

Wholeness refers to the child's communication as whole. The first grader who draws a picture of a piece of chocolate cake and places it in the refrigerator communicates that he took the cake. The drawing told much more than the sum of its lines. We accept that children are communicating whole thoughts and messages even when their skills for communicating are limited developmentally. As children progress through the primary grades at various stages of literacy development, we accept them as learners and build on strengths. Brian Cambourne (1988), in his discussion of approximations, provides additional insights into the developmental versus the deficit view of children's learning.

Attitude of Expectancy

Perhaps the one defining element of whole language classrooms is the attitude of expectancy. We expect children to succeed, to flourish as readers and writers. The "community of learners" approach is one in which we celebrate everyone's learning. As children tell us about where they are stuck in writing and how they got "unstuck" to go on to the next part, as they figure out a way to make a record of the temperature for a month, as they sort through hundreds of articles on the CD-Rom encyclopedia, as they create text and recreate their lives through play, we have the attitude of expectancy, that as learners they will make great strides.

When children write a few letters to convey a whole story, we accept that as a representation of what they know and we expect that as they observe, participate, and live and learn in the classroom, they will get better at the writing process. We will provide the opportunities, not just the expectations. The attitude of expectancy is the balm of the community of learners. Children and teachers gather in a classroom for the purpose of absorbing interesting, meaningful information that guides their inquiries, their sense of community.

RECOMMENDATIONS FROM EDUCATIONAL LEADERS

Teachers moving in the direction of whole language who decide to restructure their classrooms or refine their teaching can take comfort in knowing their changes are compatible with the views of leaders of professional organizations. In their position papers and developmental practice statements, literacy organizations, child-centered teacher groups, and other subject area associations offer similar proposals. Two documents that will guide our recommendations are the International Reading Association's (IRA) *Literacy Development and Early Childhood (Preschool through Grade 3)* (Early Childhood Committee and Literacy Development Committee, 1990) and the National Association for the Education of Young Children's (NAEYC) document, *NAEYC Position Statement on Developmentally Appropriate Practices* (Bredekamp, 1987). These two documents have been endorsed by numerous other professional organizations, such as the Association for Childhood Education International, the Association for Supervision and Curriculum Development, the National Association of Elementary School Principals, and the National Council of Teachers of English, to name a few.

The recommendations of the IRA position paper *Literacy Development and Early Childhood* are as follows:

1. Build instruction on what the child already knows about oral language, reading, and writing. Focus on meaningful language rather than merely isolated skill development.
2. Respect the language the child brings to school, and use it as a base for language and literacy activities.
3. Ensure feelings of success for all children, helping them see themselves as people who can enjoy exploring oral and written language.
4. Provide reading experiences as an integrated part of the broader communication process, which includes speaking, listening, and writing, as well as other communication systems, such as art, math, and music.
5. Encourage children's first attempts at writing, without concern for the proper formation of letters or correct conventional spelling.
6. Encourage risk-taking in first attempts at reading and writing, and accept what appear to be errors as part of children's natural patterns of growth and development.

7. Use materials for instruction that are familiar, such as well-known stories, because they provide the child with a sense of control and confidence in their ability to learn.
8. Present a model for students to emulate. In the classroom, teachers should use language appropriately, listen and respond to children's talk, and engage in their own reading and writing.
9. Take time regularly to read to children from a wide variety of poetry, fiction, and nonfiction.
10. Provide time regularly for children's independent reading and writing.
11. Foster children's affective and cognitive development by providing opportunities to communicate what they know, think, and feel.
12. Use developmentally and culturally appropriate procedures for evaluation, ones that are based on the objectives of the program and that consider each child's total development.
13. Make parents aware of the reasons for a broader language program at school and provide them with ideas for activities to carry out at home.
14. Alert parents to the limitations of formal assessments and standardized tests of pre-first graders' reading and writing skills.
15. Encourage children to be active participants in the learning process rather than passive recipients, by using activities that allow for experimentation with talking, listening, writing, and reading (pp. 6, 7).

IRA's 15 recommendations are consistent with our current knowledge from research and from whole language classroom practice.

Whole Language Across the Curriculum: Grades 1, 2, 3 is also consistent with the recommendation of NAEYC's *Developmentally Appropriate Practice* (Bredekamp, 1987). The literacy processes are examined in light of their developmental nature, and the whole language classroom is organized and orchestrated to support young children's development. The practice of whole language is developmentally appropriate.

SUMMARY

The foundations of whole language in theory and key research positions were examined. Whole language perspectives are derived from psycholinguistic and sociolinguistic theory and research. Translating theory, research, and practice into better, more effective practice means teachers reflect on their work. Some begin by changing practice and figuring out what these changes imply. Others begin with theory and sort out the implications for their practice. There are not neat packages of what is theory and what is practice, but rather there is a dynamic sphere of interactions and a place where these become reality—the whole language classroom.

Teachers can be guided in their process of "perceiving, behaving, and becoming" whole language teachers by using the key elements listed above. They can be confident of the directions they are taking because of the widespread support for the whole language perspective among educators, among learning theorists, and among school and supervisory personnel. Primary grade teachers can be assured that, indeed, whole language is developmentally appropriate practice.

REFERENCES

Altwerger, D., Edelsky, C., & Flores, B. M. (1987). Whole language: What's new? *The Reading Teacher, 41* (2), 145–154.

Atkins, C. (1984). Writing: Doing something constructive. *Young Children, 40*(1), 3–7.

Bredekamp, S. (Ed.) (1987). *National Association for the Education of Young Children (NAEYC) position statement on developmentally appropriate practices.* Washington, DC: National Association for the Education of Young Children.

Cambourne, B. (1988). *The whole story: Natural learning and the acquisition of literacy in the classroom.* New Zealand: Ashton Scholastic.

Canady, R. J. (1982,). Young children's use of environmental print to construct meaning. Paper presented at Catskills Reading Conference, Oneonta, NY.

Canady, R. J. (1983). Beginning reading programs: How can we begin what has already begun? In S. Raines (Ed.), *The Wesleyan papers: Keeping the child in childhood* (pp. 19–28). Rocky Mount, NC: North Carolina Wesleyan Press.

Clay, M. M. (1972). *Reading: The patterning of complex behavior.* London: Heinemann.

Clay, M. M. (1975). *What did I write?* Auckland, New Zealand: Heinemann.

Dewey, J. (1904). The relationship of theory to practice in education. In C. McMurray (Ed.), *The relation of theory and practice in the education of teachers* (Third Yearbook of the National Society for the Scientific Study of Education, Part I, pp. 9–30). Chicago: University of Chicago Press.

Early Childhood Committee and Literacy Development Committee (1990). *Literacy Development and Early Childhood (Preschool through Grade 3).* Newark, Delaware: International Reading Association.

Feldman, C. (1980). Two functions of language. In M. Wolf, M. K. McQuillan, & E. Radwin (Eds.), *Thought & language/language & reading* (pp. 59–125). Norwood, NJ: Ablex.

Ferreiro, E. (1986). The innerplay between information and assimilation in beginning literacy. In W. H. Teale and E. Sulzby (Eds.) *Emergent literacy: Writing and reading* (pp. 15–49). Norwood, NJ: Ablex.

Froese, V. (1991). *Whole-language: Practice and theory.* Boston: Allyn and Bacon.

Goodman, K. S. (1968). The psycholinguistic nature of the reading process. In K. S. Goodman (Ed.), *The psycholinguistic nature of the reading process* (pp.

13–26). Detroit: Wayne State University.

Goodman, K. S. (1969). Analysis of oral reading miscues: Applied psycholinguistics. *Reading Research Quarterly, 5* (1), 9–30.

Goodman, K. S. (1986). *What's whole in whole language?* Portsmouth, NH: Heinemann.

Goodman, K. S. (1992). Why whole language is today's agenda in education. *Language Arts, 69* (5), pp. 354–363.

Goodman, Y. M. (1978). Kid watching: An alternative to testing. *National Elementary School Principal, 57* (1), 41–45.

Goodman, Y. M. (1986). Children coming to know literacy. In W. H. Teale & E. Sulzby (Eds.), *Emergent literacy: Writing and reading* (pp. 1–14). Norwood, NJ: Ablex.

Goodman, Y. M., Watson, D. J., & Burke, C. L. (1987). *Reading miscue inventory: Alternative procedures.* New York: Richard C. Owens.

Graves, D. H. (1983). *Writing: Teachers & children at work.* Exeter, NH: Heinemann.

Halliday, M. A. K. (1978). *Learning how to mean: Explorations in the development of language.* London: Edward Arnold.

Harste, J., Woodword, V., & Burke, C. (1984). *Language stories and literacy lessons.* Portsmouth, NH: Heinemann.

King, M. (1991). Viewpoint: Martha L. King—behind and beyond whole language. In K. S. Goodman, L. B. Bird, & Y. M. Goodman (Eds.) *The Whole Language Catalogue* (p. 16). Santa Rosa, CA: American School Publishers.

Martin, B. (1988, April). *Language, literature, and reading.* Keynote address at the Children's Literature Conference, George Mason University, Fairfax, VA.

Piaget, J. (1977). *The development of thought: Equilibration of cognitive structures.* New York: Viking.

Piaget, J., & Inhelder, B. (1969). *The psychology of the child.* New York: Basic Books.

Raines, S. C., & Canady, R. J. (1990). *The whole language kindergarten.* New York: Teachers College Press.

Rosenblatt, L. M. (1938). *Literature as exploration.* New York: Noble and Noble.

Schon, D. (1983). *The reflective practitioner.* San Francisco: Jossey-Bass.

Smith, F. (1988). *Joining the literacy club: Further essays into education.* Portsmouth, NH: Heinemann.

Taylor, D. (1983). *Family literacy: Young children learn to read and write.* Exeter, NH: Heinemann.

Teale, W. H., & Sulzby, E. (1986). Introduction: Emergent literacy as a perspective for examining how young children become writers and readers. In W. H. Teale & E. Sulzby (Eds.), *Emergent literacy: Writing and reading* (pp. vii–xxv). Norwood, NJ: Ablex.

Vygotksy, L. S. (1962). *Thought and language.* Cambridge, MA: MIT Press.

Vygotsky, L. S. (1978). *Mind in society.* Cambridge, MA: Harvard University Press.

Watson, D. J. (Ed.) (1987). *Ideas and insights: Language arts in the elementary school.* Urbana, IL: National Council of Teachers of English.

Wells, G. (1986). *The meaning makers.* Portsmouth, NH: Heinemann.

PART I

TEACHERS IMPLEMENTING WHOLE LANGUAGE

2

A First Grade Teacher Becomes a Whole Language Teacher

SHIRLEY C. RAINES

Few tasks are more daunting than that of a first grade teacher. Terri, the young woman we meet in this chapter, stated that her reason for wanting to be a first grade teacher was this: so she could look back on her life and think of all the children she had taught to read. Even in the case of such a dedicated young teacher as Terri, whole language changed her views of herself as a reading teacher. In this chapter, we explore the changes she made in her classroom and in her views.[1] At the end of the chapter, the validity of Terri's classroom as a whole language learning environment is tested by comparing how well the key elements described in Chapter 1 are met:

1. Immersion—immerse children in a rich language and literacy environment.
2. Opportunities and resources—provide time, materials, space, and activities to be listeners, speakers, readers, and writers.
3. Meaningful communication—focus on the whole because the mind makes sense of, or constructs meaning from experiences—whether the experiences are spoken, or listened to, or read, or written about—when they are communicated as wholes.
4. Modeling—act as a communication role model in listening, speaking, reading, writing, so that instruction, function, and purpose are meaningful.
5. Acceptance—accept young children as readers and writers capable of whole, and thus meaningful communication.

6. Expectancy—create an atmosphere of expectancy, an affective, attitudinal climate that is encouraging and supportive, where children are expected to continue in their literacy development.

Teachers like Terri can find support for changing their classrooms into whole language learning environments from the official position papers of professional associations. All these position papers, professional organization benchmarks, and recommendations for improving teaching share a basic premise—one that accounts for the striking similarity of recommendations across the following chapters on science, mathematics, social studies, and creative expressions. The premise is that teachers should make learning opportunities relevant to the learners, interactive, and respectful of the child as a strategic learner; and that the teacher should help the child understand the interrelatedness of the various areas of the curriculum.

Many teachers find the position papers reassuring because they support the type of teaching in which they are already engaged. As teachers assess their current practices related to literacy, the next steps are to decide what needs to be added, modified, or eliminated.

As mentioned in the Preface, the journey of change is one of perceiving, behaving, and becoming. One must perceive what it means to be a whole language teacher, behave as do the best teachers who practice whole language, and realize that becoming a whole language teacher is a process. This chapter is about Terri, who is engaged in that process. Terri is a first grade teacher who had been teaching for three years before being transferred to another school.

Meet Terri, a First Grade Teacher

Terri was a determined first grade teacher who took her work very seriously. At first, when she learned she was one of the teachers to be transferred to another school, she was upset. Then, as the principal explained she was to be transferred to a school that was nearer her own home, Terri was relieved. The district had redrawn school boundary lines to help with overcrowding at one school and underenrollment at another. After she learned the name and location of the new school, she became excited. Teaching at the new school offered her a class of greater diversity; there were students from many different ethnic and racial backgrounds. Terri also thought this might be a good time to put into practice more of the whole language strategies she had been learning.

Terri's decision to work toward becoming a whole language teacher had been influenced by a kindergarten teacher's success with the five- and six-year-olds who were promoted into Terri's first grade. Over the three years that Terri had been teaching, an increasing proportion of kindergarten children came into first grade knowing about print and reading. Curious about the changes in her entering first graders, Terri began looking at what the kindergarten teacher was doing in literacy instruction. Sharing information back and forth was a natural, since the two teachers were just across the hall from one another. However, the curriculum and instruction decisions for first grade were usually guided by the grade level teams' decisions.

Schools are often organized by teams. All the first grade teachers are part of the first grade team, and so on. Principals who organize their schools along grade lines tell us that grade-level assignments mean that some groups of teachers become powerful social and political voices in school decision making. While Terri's team at her old school had not been receptive to whole language, it was reported that at the new school, teachers were not organized by grade level teams but by pod areas, and so they were encouraged to be more innovative.

In each "pod"—an arrangement of classrooms around an open-space area—there was a kindergarten, first, second, and third grade teacher. These "across-grade-level" or "pod teams" worked together, and some were using whole language. Terri hoped she would be assigned to a whole language pod.

At the first meeting of the pod teachers, Terri was excited by the warm welcome she received. She introduced herself by saying that she was eager to bring with her into first grade the things she had learned from the kindergarten teacher at her old school.

The principal and teachers talked about their views of individual teacher accountability. If teachers knew their grade level well (as they assumed Terri would after three years of teaching experience) and if they could explain what they were doing and why to the other members of the team and to the parents, the teachers would be treated as professionals, accountable for professional decisions. The principal quickly pointed out, however, that the reading specialist for the school would provide a check. Selected children from Terri's classroom would be tested near the mid-year holiday break to be certain they were making adequate progress in reading and writing.

After the welcoming meeting, Terri was a bit shaken by the thought that the children were going to be tested by the reading specialist to make sure the children were on grade level; she wondered if they really trusted her professional decision making. For a few days, she considered whether or not she should keep the basal reader series she knew well until she had proven herself at the school, and then make the change. However, after being reassured by other teachers on the pod team and by the reading specialist, Terri decided to become more of a whole language teacher.

PERCEIVING, BEHAVING, BECOMING
A FIRST GRADE, WHOLE LANGUAGE TEACHER

The first step in becoming a whole language teacher is to make the decision and then to assess what one must do differently. Terri made a list of all the things she wanted to change in first grade at her new school. She wrote:

> More children's literature
> Big books
> Children writing more
> Integration of writing throughout the day

As she reread the list, Terri realized that each item inferred changes in how she viewed the literacy learning of her first graders.

Changed Views of Literacy Learning

As described in Chapter 1, the constructivist view of literacy learning means that the child constructs meaning from print. With an adult helping to mediate the process, as the child interacts with print, he or she constructs strategies of how to read and write. From watching readers and writers, from strategy modeling, and from recognizing the functions of print, learners construct their own interpretations of the "conventions of written language," or of how print functions. They learn the symbols of the alphabet and their relationship to the sounds of language. They construct their interpretations of the structural conventions of the language, such as how spelling works, where words and sentences break, and how information is organized on pages. As Galda, Cullinan, and Strickland point out in *Language, Literacy and the Child* (1993), the child also develops metalinguistic awareness, "an awareness of the processes and conventions of written language" (p. 86).

   In the past, Terri expected first graders to come to her having learned the alphabet in kindergarten and knowing little else about reading and writing. The previous year, on the first day of first grade, Terri noticed that several of the kindergarten children were already reading. While she chatted with the parents as they dropped the children off for the first day, she instructed the children to select a book and read it or look at it until everyone arrived. To her surprise, when she asked the children to put their books away and join her on the carpet circle, a boy asked if he could take his book, *Frog and Toad Are Friends* (Lobel, 1970), home with him because he was not finished with the story about Toad losing his swimsuit. "Of course you may," Terri had replied, after which several other children said they had already read that book and started telling the boy what happened in the story. The children had had a big book version of *Frog and Toad Are Friends* in their kindergarten. Their kindergarten teacher had taught them to read it through an experience she described as "shared book reading."

Shared Book Reading

Terri learned about "shared book reading" from the kindergarten teacher at her former school. At first, Terri credited the already-reading kindergarten children entirely to their teacher's use of "big books." However, after some lengthy discussions with the teacher, Terri soon learned that being a whole language teacher is more than just using big books. She learned that an effective use of shared reading experience provides a model for looking at children's interactions with print.

Don Holdaway (1979) wrote about the "shared book experience" in *The Foundations of Literacy*. Shared book experience is meant to approximate the experience of lap reading. When a child sits on the lap of an adult, he or she experiences print and the illustrations through a close-up view of the print. The adult often points out key features of the print and of the pictures. "See, that word starts with an 'R,' just like your name, 'Robert.' That's an 'R.' " Or the adult might say: "Show me where to start reading," or "What do you think this page might be about?" Each of these interjections into the story helps the child get a grasp of how the print works and how to make sense of this combination of print and pictures that tell a story.

Many children are bereft of literacy experiences because adults have seldom, in some cases never, taken them into their lap to read with them. Even those who are fortunate to have an adult read to them may not have an adult who is tuned in to the child's attempts to make sense of the print. The adult may think of reading only as entertainment, or as a transition into a quiet bedtime, both worthy reasons for reading. Holdaway began making "big books," enlarged versions of printed books, as a means to approximate the lap-reading experience. In the last decade, the popularity of commercially made big books has soared, and every major book publisher republishes favorite children's books in big book format.

The advantage of the big book format is that it allows a group of children to see the illustrations and print easily, and to make associations between the rate of reading and the print as it is being pointed out to the reader (Raines & Canady, 1990). According to Andrea Butler (1988), choosing the right big book is key to the success of the shared-book experience. She identified the following selection guidelines:

Good story line
Characters or situations the children can identify with
Quality illustrations
Humor or warmth

Terri noticed that many of the big books read by the kindergarten teacher were of the "predictable" book type, or "patterned language" books. They used rhyme, rhythm, and repetition. Predictable books are ones in which the child can predict what will come next because a pattern has been established in the story. For example, at the end of each scene, the children know that the words, "Run, run as fast as you can, you can't catch me, I'm the gingerbread man" *(The Gingerbread Boy,* Galdone, 1975), will appear in the story. As the phrase is repeated, they begin to read it.

Presenting big books to her first graders was something Terri looked forward to doing. She had had several successful experiences with big books in the previous year in her teaching. Her approach was to present the big book on two different occasions. First, she would read the book to the children just as if it were any other story. She began by having the children look at the illustrations on the cover of the book and predict what the story might be about. Then, she would have them look through the illustrations in the book and determine, from these additional samples of meaning, whether or not their predictions were on target. The next step would be to read the story or the text to the children.

During her first few attempts at big book reading, Terri almost reverted to her old first grade teacher habits, and pointed to each word of the text on a word-for-word basis, but she remembered seeing the kindergarten teacher simply reading the text straight through without pausing. When she thought of the big book as a children's literature book, rather than a basal reading lesson, Terri found herself relaxing and enjoying the big book for the sake of the story first, and then for reading instruction purposes.

The second presentation of the big book should be at another time during the day, or on another day. Terri invited the readers to join her in reading any of the repeated or recurring phrases, and used a pointer to move along under the print so that the children could begin making an association with the natural or fluent rate of reading. If the story has repeated phrases, such as those in *The Gingerbread Boy,* the teacher concentrates on having the children join her for those phrases. In addition, the second presentation is a good time for focusing on some aspect of language study, such as high frequency words, conventions of language in spelling, grammar, punctuation, and sound/symbol relationships (Raines & Isbell, 1994).

Thinking about the big book format and about her presentation of big books, Terri also revisited the slogan she had seen in one of the reading workshops she attended: "Reading = predicting, sampling, confirming, integrating." Only later, in her reading following the workshop, did Terri realize that the slogan was a drastic oversimplification of the steps of the Goodman Model of Reading (Goodman, 1969). She planned to teach her students with big books and to have them use the reading process steps of predicting, sampling, confirming, and integrating information. These steps in the reading process are based on the view that reading can be defined as "the reader actively constructing meaning."

Prior Knowledge: Respecting What the Child Already Knows

In studying the modeling of the kindergarten teacher on how to teach a reading lesson using big books, Terri was struck by how much the children enjoyed reading the familiar books, and by how often they requested to read them again and again. After watching another big book lesson, Terri realized how skillful the teacher was in introducing the book. As Terri thought about the ways in which the teacher interacted with the children about the stories they were about to read, she remembered the basal reader approach, which often included introducing the new vocabulary words, teaching them in isolation from the text, and then plunging right into reading the story, first silently, then orally, but never reading more than a few pages at a time.

In discussions with the reading specialist at her new school, Terri was encouraged to conduct all her literature read-alouds much as she did the reading of big books. She asked herself: What is this book about? What questions can I ask that will help the children think about the main idea of the story? What experiences have my students had that are similar? Whether she was reading aloud to them, reading in a circle of readers who chose the same children's literature book, or reading a big book, she planned to make more use of the children's prior knowledge. The emphasis in whole language is on making meaning from print. The children already know a lot about the content of the print, as well as the print forms and structures.

BEFORE, DURING, AND AFTER READING STEPS. The reading specialist suggested that Terri think of the reading lesson in three parts: before, during, and after reading. *Before* reading, the teacher introduced the topic of the book. For example, before reading *Ira Says Goodbye* (Waber, 1988), the children discussed how they felt when a friend moved away. After the children expressed their feelings and told about the incidents that precipitated the feelings, the teacher began reading the book. The children's prior knowledge helped them identify with Ira's dilemma and feelings of rejection when Reggie moved. *During* the reading, the teacher paused at key points for the children to predict what they thought might happen next,

and confirmed or rejected some of their earlier predictions. *After* reading
Ira Says Goodbye, the children discussed their feelings, the changes, the sur-
prises, and the longing each felt for his or her friend. The emphasis in
before, during, and after reading was on reading for meaning.

When Terri first began the three phases of reading, she was tempted to
stop often during the story and ask questions. Her old structure, learned
well from the basals, was to read a page or two and stop and ask a question,
and not to allow the children to read ahead. Now, she read the whole story
to the first graders, then had them go back and read short sections of their
own choosing, rather than go through the entire book again. The practice
was for practice sake, and even then, she asked the children to select a passage in the story that they wanted to learn to read. She also called attention to some of the ways in which the author pointed out dialogue, by
using quotation marks.

Using the three-phased approach to a reading lesson and concentrating on reading for meaning became Terri's means of organizing her reading instruction. She felt she was taking advantage of the children's prior
knowledge and respecting what the children already knew.

K-W-L CHARTS.   Another means of taking advantage of the children's prior
knowledge is the K-W-L chart (Ogle, 1986). *K* means "what we already
know," *W* means "what we *want* to know," and *L* means "what we
learned." Constructing a K-W-L chart allows the teacher to take advantage
of the child's prior knowledge and focus the instruction at the children's
levels of understanding. For example, in a science unit on "Where Animals
Live," Terri planned to read *Spoonbill Swamp* (Guiberson, 1992). The
main idea of the book is that the mother alligator and the mother spoonbill must share the same habitats and protect their young.

Figure 2.1 is a K-W-L chart of *Spoonbill Swamp* from some first
graders, answering the questions: "What do we know about swamps; what
do we want to know; and what did we learn?"

A Changed View of Language Experience Approach

Reading the enlarged texts and constructing the K-W-L charts, which she
saw other whole language teachers using, reminded Terri of the "dictated
experience charts," a part of the Language Experience Approach to teaching reading. Language Experience had always been a part of Terri's teaching. The cooperating teacher in her student teaching experience had
required that she write at least one language experience story per day with
one of the reading groups. The practice was one Terri had continued during her three years of teaching.

Each day, she had a small group of children (one of three groups in her class) dictate a story to her. Sometimes it was about a topic the children were studying for the theme of the unit she was teaching. One of the first graders' favorite topics was "Families." She always enjoyed the families experience chart because it let the children learn more about one another. Figure 2.2 is a language experience chart on families from some of Terri's first graders.

As each child in the group dictated a sentence, Terri wrote the words on a large sheet of lined chart paper while the child repeated them. As she

Figure 2.1. *K-W-L chart about swamps.*

K   What we know about swamps
      Swamps are scary places.
      There are snakes in swamps.
      The trees grow funny in swamps.
      Swamps smell dirty.

W   What we want to know about swamps
      What animals live in swamps?
      Why do trees grow funny in swamps?
      Are there any swamps near us?
      Are the plants dying in the swamps?

L   What we learned about swamps
      Lots of things live in swamps: alligators, roseate spoonbills, otters,
          pelicans, blue herons, minnows, sailfin mollies, raccoons.
      Some plants that grow in the swamps are duckweed, cattails, mangroves,
          and water lilies.
      Plants live and die in the swamps just like they do other places.
      There are a lot of insects in the swamp: mosquitoes, crickets, waterbugs,
          grasshoppers.
      Alligators eat spoonbills.
      Spoonbills put their beaks in the water and scoop until they get a minnow,
          then they hold their beaks up and swallow the fish.

Figure 2.2. *First graders' language experience chart on "families."*

My family is just me and Mama.
My family is all of us and Granddaddy, too.
My family's got seven: Mama, Dad, and five kids. I'm the baby.
My family lives in two houses. Mother and me stay at Grandmother's and I
    stay with my Dad on the weekends.
My family goes to this school, except for Mama and Daddy.

wrote, Terri would also read each word, and then at the end she would read the whole sentence. After composing the chart, the children read the entire dictated experience chart together while Terri used the pointer to keep the rhythm of the reading at the right rate.

The dictated experience chart was also the source of special words the teacher wanted to emphasize, such as the compound word, "Granddaddy," or high frequency words, such as "my," "the," "is." The children often copied their sentences as practice in writing and took them home to read to their families. This procedure was repeated each day on a different topic, rotating among the three groups.

Another dictation exercise that has a long-standing tradition among first grade teachers is the dictated story. Instead of a group of children dictating an experience chart, individual children dictate a story, which the teacher writes down. At the beginning of the year, the dictations are usually just short captions or titles for the children's drawings. As the year progresses, they begin dictating stories to accompany their drawings.

Strategies Approach to Instruction

Thus far, Terri had changed the materials she used to teach reading by switching to big books and to children's literature selections. Many of the literature selections are folktales and favorite authors for beginning readers. She had begun concentrating on reading for meaning, thus emphasizing the semantics cues.

Given her early success with emergent literacy, and her experience of the kindergarten teacher's modeling of lessons, Terri's confidence began to grow. She found the *cloze procedure* helpful in group presentations and in helping first graders decide how to read the print. In this procedure, the teacher reads part of the sentence or phrase and the child finishes it. Cloze emphasizes "making meaning." The cloze procedure is often used with big books: the teacher will be reading along, then stops, and the child completes the sentence. For example, the teacher might read: "Run, run," and the child completes the phrase, "as fast as you can, you can't catch me, I'm the gingerbread man." Cloze procedure can also be used with unfamiliar texts because, as the readers hear more stories, they develop a text vocabulary, rely on the natural syntactical structure of the language, and develop insights into the message the author is trying to convey. The child predicts what the print conveys by using meaning cues and syntactic cues.

Another strategy Terri teaches beginning readers is to say the word "blank" when they do not know a word and just keep on reading. Don Holdaway calls this process, "read-ons" (Holdaway, 1979). Eventually, when the child encounters the word later in the text, he or she may know the word or, if it is a word of little consequence in the meaning of the story, it can be skipped. Some children just "hum" instead of saying the word "blank."

A third strategy Terri teaches her children is using beginning-letter sounds. This strategy is one she uses after the child has read through the text and needs to revisit a word because it is a significant word for the meaning of the story. For example, in *Frog and Toad Are Friends,* the word "porch" was used. The child said "blank" the first time he saw the word, and the second time he skipped it. At the end of the story, Terri asked the child, "Now that you have finished the story, is there a word you want to know?" The boy pointed to "porch." The teacher read the sentence first, "Frog and Toad sat on the 'blank,' feeling sad together." The child looked at the picture and said, "stoop." Then he said, "No it can't be stoop, it doesn't start with 's'; it's a 'p.' " Then the teacher read the sentence a second time and the child filled in the word "porch."

Terri's first graders fall along a continuum of reading behaviors. Some readers in the emergent stages use reading-like behaviors approximating the language of the book, self-correct to make sense, and repeat recurring phrases from the text. The advanced early readers use many different clues to determine the words: first meaning and context clues, then beginning letter-sound associations to confirm their predictions. Holdaway details the "stages of development in a first-year programme" in the section, "Teaching Basic Strategies," in *The Foundations of Literacy* (1979), a relevant book written more than fifteen years ago.

While Terri's view of the reading process had changed—and her instructional strategies reflect these changes—her view of the writing process and the resulting changes in instruction are even more dramatic.

A CHANGED VIEW OF THE WRITING PROCESS

In previous years, the only composing that children did in Terri's first grade classroom was through dictated experience charts and dictated stories. After learning more about whole language, Terri decided to keep the dictated experience chart as a part of her whole language classroom, but to change the individual dictated stories. As she learned more about the process approach to writing, she decided she had been doing too much of the thinking for the children.

Donald Graves (1983) emphasized the composing process for young children. When Terri wrote the experience charts for her first graders, she formed the letters and words; the child composed the thoughts and spoke them aloud. However, in the writing process approach, Graves suggests that the teacher place the pen in the child's hand and the child constructs the print. The children write rather imaginatively and, indeed, "invent" ways to spell the words.

Children learn about writing in much the same way as they learn about other things in their immediate environment. They pay attention to print, inquire about what it means, recognize similarities, and begin to make associations between the print they see and what they already know. Children learn to write their names first and then they go on to use the letters that have significance for them, i.e., a "T," because "T" is the first letter in a friend's name—Tim.

The teacher's instructional role in the writing process is to:

1. Observe and infer meaning from the children's writing forms
2. Recognize their construction of print in various stages and contexts
3. Value their compositions and refinements of print forms (Raines & Canady, 1990)

Writing Is Meant to Be Read

On the very first day of first grade, Terri asked the children to write something about themselves and to read it to her. She told them they could also draw a picture. Each of the first graders drew first, then wrote a sentence. Some of the first graders complained, "I don't know how to spell," but Terri replied, "Spell it the way you think it should look or how it sounds." As the children finished their first written compositions for first grade, she had each person read his or her composition. Reading the writing helped the children know she understood and accepted the writing, whatever the form. Every child was complimented on what he or she had written. The emphasis was on the content of the composition. Gradually, as the children learned more letter forms and wrote more words and sentences, she called attention to their successes.

Steps in the Writing Process

Constructing print or composing is a difficult process for young children. It is an excellent indicator of the child's understanding of how print works. Some children begin by stringing letters together with no spaces between to separate words or phrases, and without (or with very few) sound/symbol relationships. For example, in Figure 2.3, Jon writes a string of letters and numbers as his first writing sample.

Jon was taught the writing process through seeing the writing process modeled. Because the teacher provided time each day for writing, there was an expectation that every child would write. Just as children learn to read

ⓑТА Rʒ Ѣ ρ ı ∩ Ϸ Ϧ Ρ G ⸁ ∩ ⸁ Н ∩ ⸁

Figure 2.3. *Jon's string of letters, first of the year writing.*

by reading, they learn to write by writing. The process approach to teaching writing is called *writing workshop* in some whole language classrooms. The stages of the writing process, as described by Donald Graves (1983), include prewriting, first draft and reading one's own writing, drafting and revising, and sharing the writing.

Prewriting can be thinking of topics to write about. Young children are often inspired by stories their friends write, and will exhibit what one teacher called "contagious behavior." If one child writes a pet story, there will be five or six pet stories. Brainstorming topics is an excellent way to help first graders get started writing.

WRITING FOLDERS. Keeping track of the children's progress as writers was much easier for Terri once she began using *writing folders*. From the first day of the children's writing, she had them place their writing in a folder. After the mid-year holiday break, she started a two-folder system. Because the children were writing longer stories, and because they often continued writing the same story over several days, she needed one folder for writing in progress and one for completed writing. After the children completed a few longer pieces, she helped them edit their work, page it, illustrate it, and finally have their writing made into a bound book.

PUBLISHING CHILDREN'S WRITING. Publishing can take many forms in the first grade classroom. Some include: displaying writing on a classroom bulletin board; adding a poem to the school newspaper; publishing one's writing on an electronic bulletin board or in a bound book. The excitement is the same. All writers, including young ones, like to see their name in print.

There is disagreement among teachers about the need to edit children's published writing. Many teachers edit only if the piece is to be published; others prefer not to edit at all. Tompkins (1990) reports that many teachers ask if they should "overwrite" or "print the correct spelling, grammar, or punctuation, under the child's invented text." To do this, some teachers write what the child reads back to them, interpreting their first attempts at writing by printing the child's text (using standard spelling and letter formation) under the child's writing. Others use "Post-it" notes and write what the child says on the note. But many teachers feel it demeans the child's writing to have the adult write what the child has already written (Raines & Isbell, 1994). Terri decided to overwrite the pieces of writing she planned to keep for assessment purposes, but not to edit the children's writing otherwise.

Since revising drafts and editing are part of the writing process, Terri modeled these steps as well for the children. She often took a dictated story from a previous day and rewrote it with the group's help on another day. After modeling the revising process, Terri began asking the children to revise as well.

By the end of first grade, Jon was writing stories, spelling more words correctly, and even editing them. At the teacher's request for a longer story, Jon complied, though with a less than enthusiastic expansion of the story line. See his story, "Jon and the Cats," and the requested second page of it, in Figures 2.4 and 2.5.

Becoming a published author is a favorite stage of the writing process for first graders. In a year-long visit with first and second graders who were learning to be readers and writers, this author observed the power of the published book as a motivator for writing (Raines, 1986). The children found it difficult to edit during the first semester of the first grade because they were struggling so much just to gain control of the letters and the sound/symbol relationships. As they made progress in reading and writing, however, they wrote longer pieces and were then ready for the rewriting and drafting process.

Helping young children rewrite means facilitating their desire to change the story to make it better. Terri accomplished this by modeling writing and rewriting experience charts, as described in the next section. In addition, she used a modification of Donald Graves' (1983) recommendation for a "writing conference." The usual process for a writing conference is for the child to finish a piece of writing, then call for listeners among the children in the class to hear his or her writing and suggest changes. The teacher tried this process on numerous occasions, with less than favorable results. The first graders in the class were either too critical—with the result that the writer left in tears, thinking no one liked the writing—or the praise was so lavish that the writer left exuberant, thinking his or her writing was perfect, and reasoning perhaps that there was no need to bother to revise it.

Finally, the teacher decided to call the conferences *listening* conferences. The children were given three instructions: they were not allowed to criticize; they were not allowed to praise; but they *were* allowed to ask questions. The teacher modeled the process. The child read and then asked if there were any questions. At first, the questions were directed to the story itself: "When did this happen?" "How did you feel?" "Who gave you the toy?" Later, the questions became more directed toward the writing: "Could you explain more about what happened when your father forgot

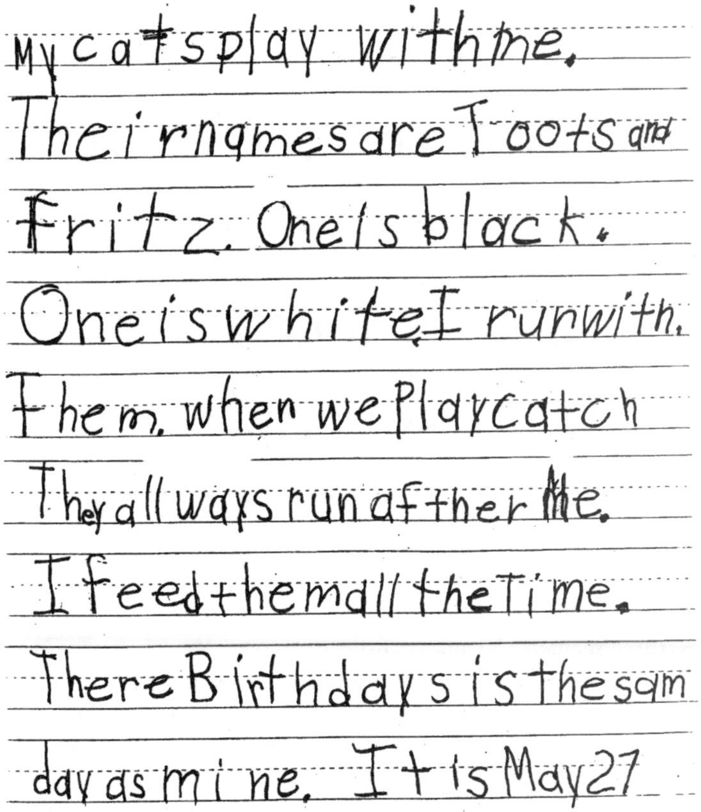

My cats play with me.
Their names are Toots and
Fritz. One is black.
One is white. I run with.
them. when we Play catch
They all ways run after me.
I feed them all the Time.
There Birthdays is the sam
day as mine. It is May27

Figure 2.4. *Jon's first draft of "Jon and the Cats."*

to pick you up at school?" or "I would like to know more about the part where you and your brother sneaked out and slept in the back yard; were you scared?" The listening conference appeared to be a safe first grade adaptation of the writing conference.

The listening conferences lead to the children feeling more confident about revising and changing their stories to make them more publishable. At first, Terri was hesitant to insist that the children revisit their stories, because these children were writing so much more than any of her first graders from previous years. However, after a session of group writing and editing, in which Terri edited to final book form and published under the group's name, the children became enthusiastic about editing because they knew it would lead to a published book. The rule of thumb for the class was that no story would be published unless it had been edited with listening conferences at least three times. Three times were required because that was

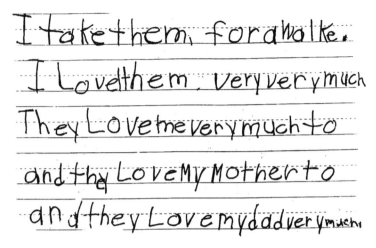

Figure 2.5. *Jon's second page, added to "Jon and the Cats."*

how many times the teacher had used. Later, Terri hoped the children would understand that one edits until satisfied with the work, but for first graders, three seemed like an expansive process.

Binding books for publishing is an excellent task for class volunteers, but even without them, if a simple method of binding books is used, the process is worth the effort. Quality binding means the book will last and will become a child's and a family's treasure.

The first graders shared their published writings at a special time of the day, called "author's chair," another writing suggestion from Donald Graves. Terri decorated the rocking chair in the library corner with red cushions and hung an oaktag sign across the back with the word "author" in large print. After a child finished writing, and his or her book was in published form, the author sat in the chair and read it aloud to the class. After the reading, the children stood and applauded the author.

MODELING WRITING AND THINKING ALOUD.   Terri's decision to keep the dictated experience chart for group compositions proved to be a wise one. The group experience chart allowed her to model writing. She added another dimension to the modeling by thinking aloud and telling the children what she was trying to decide, such as: "Where should I put the quotation marks?" "Does this sentence need a question mark?"

Writing the experience chart was also a way to begin modeling functional writing. Terri wrote huge thank-you notes on the experience chart, thanking some of the special "cleaner-uppers," as she called the children who had done a good job of straightening and cleaning up the room. She wrote chart-sized invitations for another first grade class to visit their classroom and see the flea market set up there. Sometimes the writing was an announcement of a special event, such as a puppet show or a musical performance by one of the children's older brothers or sisters. Whatever the occasion, the teacher used it as a time for modeling writing.

INVENTED SPELLING. Invented spelling was a controversial subject at Terri's former school. The idea that the children should be allowed to spell a word in any way they wanted was a problem for many teachers. Even the term *invented spelling* was indicative of a different focus in writing. Children were asked to construct print using whatever they knew at the time, with the expectation that they would get better and move toward standard spelling.

Terri decided that she would ask the first graders every day to write a caption for their drawings and to write something at the writing center. At the beginning of the year, she prompted their writing by making suggestions, such as, "Tell me about playing games with your friends." After the children became accustomed to writing every day, she no longer suggested topics but encouraged them to write about a variety of topics of their own choosing. Soon the writing center became so crowded that Terri began a daily writing workshop and left the writing center as a "choice" area, where children could choose to go and write on their own. (For more variations on the writing process workshop, see Chapter 3.)

One of Terri's students, Amy, wrote the caption for a drawing of her house with the spelling, "My Hows." In the past, Terri would have considered how Amy's writing reflected that she did not know how to spell "house," but after observing the composing process, where young children are figuring out how to spell and constructing print on their own, Terri now appreciated the level of sophistication of Amy's writing. Amy knew the high frequency word "my," and she had all the sounds in the word "house." She simply did not spell it the way it is spelled in books.

Children who are asked to write and spell words the way they think it sounds are sometimes frustrated at the beginning because they are not sure that the adult will accept "kid spelling." Terri had noticed that, when the children of the kindergarten teacher from her previous school first came to her first grade, they had talked about both "kid spelling" and "book spelling."

Terri was a bit nervous about accepting "invented spelling" but she decided that, since there were so few words the children were supposed to know how to spell in first grade, she would let the second and third grade teachers worry more about spelling.

GLIMPSES INTO TERRI'S FIRST GRADE CLASSROOM

Visitors to whole language classrooms want to know about room arrangements, schedules, and interaction patterns. A visitor to Terri's first grade classroom would be surprised to see the room arrangements, since they seem to change from month to month. The first graders have become "decorators." They like making things to go along with the units they are studying. Some weeks their classroom is hanging with vines to simulate the rain forest; other times, it is set up like a grocery store, a nursery, or a flea market.

Similarly, the schedule for Terri's day has also changed. She used to plan in small segments of time; almost every 15 minutes, the children were changing activities. Now, since becoming a whole language teacher, she uses blocks of time more effectively. (Figure 2.6 provides an example of a daily schedule from a first grade whole language classroom.) For example, she begins the day with a time of activity. Since the children (bus riders and those who walk to school) arrive sporadically over a 30-minute period, Terri invites them to come into the classroom as they arrive and to get a book or a game from the library and have "partner time." They read to one another, play games, or record what they have done together in their activity logs.

When all the children are gathered, Terri uses the next 30 minutes as "circle time." She seats the children in a circle on a rug and reviews the social studies or science unit topic, emphasizes main concepts, then reads a book related to the theme and announces special activities, such as *story s-t-r-e-t-c-h-e-r-s,* ways to take the ideas from the story and stretch them into other areas of the curriculum. For example, for the unit on families, Terri read *Family Pictures. Cuadros de familia,* a bilingual book by Carmen Lomas Garza (1990). The children then drew their own family pictures and wrote a caption for their pictures using either English or Spanish.

The hour immediately after the opening, or circle time, is reading and writing workshop. The children are expected to read at least one children's literature book, write the title in their reading log, and write at least one story. At the beginning of the year, of course, the children are often just looking at the pictures when they read their stories, and their writing ranges from simple, one-line captions to long stories.

After a period of outside play or time in the gym, Terri reads a book associated with the theme of the unit she is teaching, or rereads a favorite book the children enjoy. On some days this slot is allotted to singing time, with the words printed on large chart tablets. After lunch, the class reviews the morning activities briefly and celebrates one of the children's writings by having "author's chair." The afternoon also begins with a brief forecast of the afternoon's activities.

Mathematics and science are taught through projects that involve real problem solving. The data from the projects are also another reading and

Fig. 2.6. *First grade whole language teacher's schedule.*

8:30	Signing in: Choice of reading or games with partner (Partners reassigned each week.)
9:00	Opening at circle time rug
9:30	Reading and writing workshop. Children read on their own, write on their own, and participate in a literature circle of approximately 20 minutes per group. Groups change each week based on the children's literature selections, with children choosing their groups.
	Children have snacks between 9:30 and 10:30, depending on when they finish their literature group.
10:45	Outside play or gym
11:15	Read-aloud selection: Washing up for lunch
11:30	Lunch
12:00	Review of morning activities; Author's chair; Plan for the afternoon.
12:30	Mathematics and science investigations
1:15	Science or social studies unit projects
2:00	School specialists: art, music, or library
2:30	Clean-up, organize materials; Prepare for departure
2:40	Highlights of the day; Teacher reading a favorite book
3:00	Dismissal

writing exercise. (See Chapter 8 for additional insights into how teachers handle this portion of the day.)

Writing and reading are also integral to the teaching of science and social studies lessons for first graders. One way Terri keeps track of their progress is through a learning log. Each day the children write something they have learned. One of the most successful units Terri taught was entitled "Growing Things." The children planted lima bean seeds in plastic baggies into which they had placed a wet paper towel. They clothes-pinned the baggies onto a line stretched across the windows, then they watched daily for signs of the lima beans sprouting. And finally, after six days, they planted them; over the next six days, they watched the sprouts as they burst forth into plants and added leaves. The children recorded their observations by making a little book with twelve sheets of paper stapled together. Each day they observed their plant, drew what they saw, and wrote a sentence recording their observations.

At approximately 2:00 PM each day, one of the school specialists arrives to either take the children to a special classroom for art, music, or the library, or to work with the children in the classroom. Each special teacher tries to connect his or her lessons with what is going on in the classroom. Terri provides each special teacher with a list of the units she has planned for the semester and lets them know if changes have been made in the schedule.

After a very busy day, dismissal needs to be a calm and reassuring time to look back at the day's activities and to decide what the highlights are. The children are encouraged to speak about, or "tell" anything they like. Sometimes Terri writes down what they say and on other days they just enjoy the chat. If there is a book that the children want to hear again, then they reread a favorite. Some of the most requested "rereads" are the big books, the very items that brought Terri to ask some questions of her teaching, and to learn from a kindergarten teacher about what it means to become a whole language teacher.

REASSESSMENT OF TERRI'S FIRST GRADE

At the beginning of this chapter, we stated that the validity of Terri's whole language classroom would be tested by examining the key elements of the whole language environment that are listed there: immersion, opportunities and resources, meaningful communication, modeling, acceptance, and expectancy. Certainly, these first graders were immersed in a rich language and literacy environment. From the descriptions of the shared book experiences, reading selections to accompany the thematic units, and children's samples of writing, it is clear Terri provides a language and literacy immersion environment.

Terri also provides numerous opportunities, time, and ample resources for the children to be listeners, speakers, readers, and writers. Terri's emphasis on meaningful communication is apparent by the modeling of writing the functional notes, thank-you letters, and invitations. Similarly, her encouragement of the children to write about topics that interest them is another indication of meaningfulness. However, the most important facet of meaningful communication is that the emphasis in her reading instruction is on reading for meaning. The first graders are meaning makers.

As a communication role model, Terri is an excellent example. Not only does she act as an effective model of reading and writing, but she also listens well and speaks clearly and correctly. Reading and writing instruction in Terri's classroom has become more meaningful for the children. They write to communicate and they read to understand.

Few teachers are more accepting and appreciative of young children's reading and writing, and the complexity of the task to teach them, than is this first grade teacher. From the children's first day in the classroom she accepts them as readers and writers, reassuring them that they already know a lot about reading and writing and that they will get even better. She keeps tapes of children from the previous year and has the children listen to how the first graders sounded at the beginning of the year and how they read later. She also shows the children samples of writing from the previous year's children, and their improvements throughout the year.

Lastly, Terri is one of those teachers who believes in children and always has a sense of "expectancy." Rather than expecting children to fail, or concentrating on their weaknesses, she focuses on what the children have learned and projects a sense that new breakthroughs are just around the corner. Terri has become a whole language teacher.

ACKNOWLEDGMENT

The author is indebted to April Phillips, whose teaching of first graders and reflective practice inspire those who observe her.

NOTES

1. Terri is a fictitious name. Terri's case was derived from the author's work with teachers in the Literacy Forum of C.A.R.D., the Center for Applied Research and Development, at George Mason University in Fairfax, Virginia.

REFERENCES

Butler, A. (1988). *Shared book experience*. Crystal Lake, IL: Rigby.

Galda, L., Cullinan, B. E., & Strickland, D. S. (1993). *Language, literacy and the child*. Fort Worth: Harcourt Brace Jovanovich College Publishers.

Goodman, K. S. (1968). The psycholinguistic nature of the reading process. In K. S. Goodman (Ed.), *The psycholinguistic nature of the writing process* (pp. 13–26). Detroit: Wayne State University.

Graves, D. H. (1983). *Writing: Teachers and children at work*. Exeter, NH: Heinemann.

Holdaway, D. (1979). *The foundations of literacy*. Sydney: Ashton Scholastic.

Ogle, D. (1986). The K-W-L: A teaching model that develops active reading of expository text. *The Reading Teacher, 39* (6), 564–570.

Raines, S. C. (1986). Teacher educator learns from first and second grade readers and writers. *Childhood Education, 62* (4), 260–264.

Raines, S. C., & Canady, R. J. (1990). *The whole language kindergarten*. New York: Teachers College Press.

Raines, S. C., & Isbell, R. T. (1994). *Stories: Children's literature in early education*. Albany, NY: Delmar.

Tompkins, G. (1990). *Teaching writing: balancing process and product*. Columbus, OH: Merrill.

Children's Book References

Galdone, P. (1975). *The Gingerbread Boy*. New York: Clarion.

Garza, C. L. (1990). *Family pictures. Cuadros de familia*. San Francisco: Children's Book Press.

Guiberson, B. (1992). *Spoonbill swamp*. Illustrated by M. Lloyd. New York: Henry Holt and Company.

Lobel, A. (1970). *Frog and Toad are friends*. New York: Harper & Row.

Waber, B. (1988). *Ira says goodbye*. Boston: Houghton Mifflin.

3

Second and Third Grade Teachers
Implement Whole Language
in Their Classrooms

SHIRLEY C. RAINES

The title of our book is *Whole Language Across the Curriculum: Grades 1, 2, 3,* and we want to continue providing the reader with views of the classroom from the inside. Realizing that no one can fully understand the multitude of decisions primary grade teachers must make throughout the day, we have focused on key aspects of each classroom, on experiences that influenced teachers to make changes, and on the results of their efforts. In Chapter 2 you met Terri, a first grade teacher, who made dramatic changes in her classroom and who concentrated on reading instruction derived from children's literature, from the student's own writing, and from the teacher's modeling of strategies. In Chapter 3 you will meet Carol, a veteran second grade teacher, and Jolene, a third grade teacher reassigned from first grade.[1]

MEET CAROL, A SECOND GRADE TEACHER

Carol is a veteran second grade teacher. On the information card the professor passed around for the Area Writing Project course Carol had elected to attend, she wrote in huge numerals "19," indicating her years of teaching experience, all at the elementary school level. In response to the question "Why are you applying for the writing workshop and enrolling in this course," she replied, "The school is moving to whole language and I don't know enough to do it."

The teachers in the course were going to study the writing process through first-hand experience. The aim was to make them into writers through experiencing the writing process. It was felt that, through this process, they would become better teachers of writing for children. At first, many of the teachers wanted to transfer their learning immediately to the classroom. During the first days of the month-long course, many of the questions they asked began with, "But, how would you do this with young children?" The professor would not answer the question. She continued to insist that first they must become writers and then, at the end, they would know the answers, because they were experienced teachers who would figure out the answers.

The application form for membership in the Area Writing Project class required statements from the school principal to the effect that the school would implement the writing process and that the teacher involved possessed strong teaching abilities. It was an honor to be selected for the class. However, the class was one that Carol approached with much trepidation.

Carol had always considered herself a good basic-skills teacher. When her second graders left her class for third grade, they could all spell the most common words in the spelling book, use periods and question marks, and write capital letters at the beginnings of their sentences. She checked all these items regularly in the response to the spelling exercise in the spelling series the county school district had adopted some years before. She also included daily handwriting exercises in her classes, and most of her students, with the exception of the learning disabilities (LD) children, left her classroom with fairly legible handwriting.

In her earlier years of teaching she had been more creative and had included much more drama, music, and art in her classroom. However, when the school district began achievement tests at every grade level—leaving no doubt that every teacher would be evaluated on the basis of the results—Carol found herself concentrating more on direct instruction and less on the creative expression she enjoyed. She had never thought of second graders as being capable of creative writing. She thought they still had too many basic skills to learn just to be able to form good sentences, to spell words correctly, and to punctuate at a minimum level. When she did ask the children to write sentences of their own composition, as in the spelling book exercises, they seemed so trite, always following a simplistic pattern: "I like pizza." If she encouraged them to write more, the next sentence would be something like, "I like ice cream." All the words, however, were spelled correctly, the "I" was capitalized, and there was a period at the end of the sentence.

Carol Learns to Teach Writing by Becoming a Writer

Interestingly, the professor moved the class outside for the first morning of writing instruction. She asked the students to go to some far corner of the campus, to sit and observe the passersby, and to write down their impressions about the people they saw and where those people might be going. She asked them to describe what the people looked like, how they acted, and then fantasize about their destinations. It was an enjoyable exercise, much like sitting in an airport surrounded by unknown people, indulging in people-watching.

At the appointed time, Carol returned to the group, a bit anxious about what she had written. But when the professor called for volunteers to share some snippet of their writing they considered good, Carol raised her hand. When her classmates gave her specific praise about what they liked about her writing, and the professor smiled and applauded, Carol was hooked on writing. Knowing that the professor's first objective for the first day of the class was to make everyone feel successful did not daunt Carol's enthusiasm. She truly felt successful, and began thinking of herself as a writer. Another aspect of the course was to keep a journal about the experience of becoming a writer. The only sentences Carol wrote in the journal that first day were: "I think I'm going to like this. I guess I am a writer."

The course had its own designated classroom space for the entire month. The class met all day, every day, for three weeks. In the last week, the teachers said they had the impression that they met all day and all night because they stayed there long after the class was supposed to be over, to continue working on their compositions. One teacher described the experience as "summer camp for teachers." The writing project classroom was personalized with the writers' work in much the same way that teachers display children's work in their elementary school classrooms. The walls were decorated with teachers' finished pieces of writing, with banners, posters, "congratulation" balloons, an author's chair, and many writing instruments—fancy papers and pens, legal pads, note pads, scratch pads, and computers with word processing software. The printers were hooked up to another office so that the noise would not bother the writers.

The teachers wrote using the writing process steps of prewriting, writing, drafting, redrafting, and publishing. They published poetry, a class newspaper, and finally a literary journal of their favorite pieces. At the end of the course, the professor asked the teachers to construct some guidelines for beginning the writing process in their classrooms. They were to review their journals, think about the community of writers that had developed in the class, and write guidelines for writing for use in their elementary school classrooms based on what they had experienced in the writing project class.

Each teacher was to come to class with a list reflecting his or her own experiences as writers, and to join a small group for discussion of the lists. The professor purposefully structured the groups so that different grade levels were represented in each.

Each group then developed a composite list. Carol's group included the following in its list:

1. Find a way to make everyone feel like a writer.
2. Give specific praise about the writing piece, not just that it was good.
3. Celebrate breakthroughs and successful completions.
4. Write using whatever instruments and papers are comfortable for you.
5. Emphasize the content, not the form.
6. Use the writing process: prewrite, write, redraft and revise, publish.
7. Write every day.
8. Remember writing is meant to be read. Be an audience and find audiences.
9. Display and publish works.

The follow-up to this course included regular reunions. Each month during that school year, the teachers met and discussed what they were doing in their elementary classrooms. They brought samples of their students' writing and problem-solved around actual pieces of children's writing or dilemmas they faced as teachers. They casually networked a support system for one another that crossed school and district lines. The following year, these teachers were entitled to enroll in another course in which they taught writing at a children's writing camp in morning and afternoon sessions and, afterwards, met and worked together on improving their teaching of writing strategies. All the teachers from Carol's class applied for it, and Carol was one of the first chosen.

Basic Skills Teacher Becomes a Writing Process Teacher

After she had attended her first writing workshop course, Carol was asked by her principal to report on her training; after all, the school district had paid for her to attend. Carol decided to precede her presentation of the report with an article written for the district's school newspaper. The tentative title was "Basic Skills Teacher Becomes a Writing Process Teacher."

Carol asked the principal if the faculty meeting where she would make her report could be held in her classroom. At the meeting, Carol was congratulated for having her article accepted at the district newspaper. No other teacher from the school had ever been featured in this large, metropolitan district's publication. When Carol began to speak, her voice quivered, and after a short interval, she said: "This was a writing workshop, not a speaking workshop, I attended last summer." At that point, the faculty broke into applause and everyone relaxed. On each table in the classroom was a sample of Carol's writing from the summer, application forms for the next writing workshop course at the Area Writing Project, and samples of her children's writing.

The teachers were delighted with Carol's writing, and some of them took the application forms home, but most of the questions the teachers at the meeting asked revolved around the second graders' writing. (See Figures 3.1 and 3.2.) The papers did not look like the ones Carol's students displayed on the outside hall bulletin board when she taught basic skills. There were some examples of children's writing that were filled with misspelled words and grammar errors, others which used no punctuation, and many that were written without capital letters. Granted, these were the first writing samples of the year, but the teachers were surprised that Carol would praise her children's writing when all these problems existed.

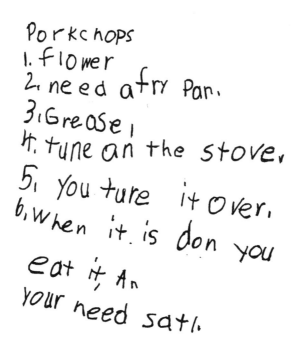

Figure 3.1. *Patricia's writing: "Cooking Pork Chops."*

Carol asked them to read some of the other things the children had written, from the samples collected in writing folders marked *Work in Progress* and *Completed Work*. One teacher laughed: "I can't do this, my children wouldn't even know what the folders mean." Carol listened to their concerns and recalled her own dilemmas. She did not purport to have all the answers, but she shared with them what the writing workshop had been like for her, and what she was now doing differently in her classroom.

A few teachers stayed afterward to ask more questions, to get a list of books to read on their own, and to quiz Carol on what the principal and assistant principal thought about the changes she was making in her classroom. One teacher was particularly fascinated by the contents of Patricia's writing folder.

CAROL'S WRITING INSTRUCTION DILEMMAS

Over the course of the year, Carol had faced many dilemmas about how to work with her second graders to improve their writing and to enjoy the revising process. Meanwhile, the teachers at her school had been

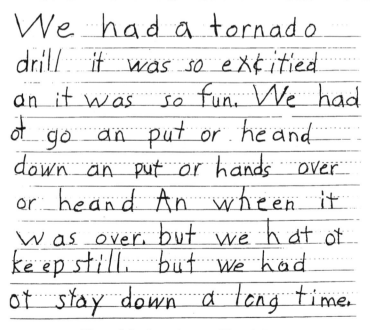

Figure 3.2. *Patricia's writing: "Tornado Drill."*

most interested in how she organized her instruction. Basically, the writing instruction dilemmas Carol faced could be grouped into five categories: scheduling, getting started, spelling, conferencing, and documenting progress.[2]

Scheduling

Carol knew, after returning from the writing workshop course, that one of her first chores was to revise her schedule to include more writing. The district language arts supervisor had been suggesting to teachers that they should have at least an hour and a half of language arts instruction each morning. Carol had never given over such a large block of time to one area of instruction; however, language arts was a large area when one considered listening, speaking, reading, and writing. But Carol's major interest was writing.

After consulting with an experienced writing teacher who had been a guest speaker in the summer workshop, Carol began a writing workshop for her class with the following time guidelines. As soon as they arrived each morning for school, each child would be asked to come into the classroom, find his or her Work in Progress folder, and begin writing. For approximately 30 minutes, while the children wrote on their own, Carol would circulate among them, assisting where needed, encouraging, and listening to writers read their compositions. In the second period, also approximately 30 minutes, she planned to have writing conferences in which groups of four or five children would sit in a circle and listen to one another read what they had written that day. During the last 30-minute period, the writers would have the choice of continuing with their writing (if they were near the end of a piece) or of reading a book from the classroom library that Carol had collected over her 19 years of teaching.

Satisfied that this sounded like a workable plan, she put it into practice. The first week of school was disastrous; on the fourth day, Carol realized that her plan, modeled after the writing workshop process she had attended as an adult the previous summer, was just that: a process for adults. Her second graders needed more support at the beginning of the year.

Getting Started

One of the first things Carol noticed was that the children's writing was very controlled, much like the old spelling-book writing exercises; it seemed as if the children found little meaning in the act of writing. Carol reviewed the guidelines she remembered from the summer writing workshop and realized that she had to help her students to see themselves as writers, as risk takers. She told the children about what she wanted to do and began modeling writing, from prewriting through publishing. Working with the whole class, she brainstormed some topics about which they might like to write. She prompted the class to talk about what they liked and what they did. The list the children came up with included:

Soccer
Rollerblading or skating
Cub Scouts, Rainbow Girls

Then Carol asked, "What about your problems?" No one answered, so she tried again: "Last year, some problems the second graders had were really difficult. Some kids got into arguments, had their feelings hurt, and were blamed for things they didn't do. Has anything like this ever happened to you?"

The list the children came up with this time was more emotionally charged.

"Like the time my brother said I broke the glass on Mama's coffee
    table but he really did it."
"One time, my bike was stolen and I saw it down the street. My
    Daddy went after the kid's father and they started pushing each
    other. I told Daddy, the kid could have my bike. I was so
    scared."
"I got two best friends and sometimes they gang up on me and
    won't let me be their best friend."
"I don't like to argue cause my mother and her boyfriend argue. I
    don't argue."

Carol became a bit concerned about the emotionally charged topics the children were bringing up and asked them to also brainstorm some happy times. Their list included some of the following:

Presents and birthday parties
Trips to Disneyland

Then, the brainstorming took a new turn when Carol had the children think of everyday things that made them happy. The list included:

Waking up to the smell of blueberry pancakes
Having all my homework finished the night before
Finding my glasses without having my brother help me
Getting to stay up late
Playing at my friend's house who has computer games

Playing Pac Man at the mall

Sleeping over at my auntie's house where everything is so clean and
smells good

Not having to do anything but go swimming, play in the park, and ride
bikes all day

When Carol showed the children a book she had written over the
summer and told them she wanted to write a book with them, asking what
it should be about, the children replied, "Everything," meaning "everything on the list." Their first class book was born. The children could
choose to write about any of the topics they had brainstormed. Some
chose the safe topics, others ventured into the emotionally charged ones,
and some celebrated the happy times.

Carol's modeling of the prewriting stage was a success. The children
came away with many ideas. New struggles awaited them, however, when
they actually began writing.

"How Do I Spell _____ ?"

After the children chose their topic and began writing, hands immediately
went up and they began asking, "How do I spell _____ ?" After a while,
Carol looked around the room and saw that almost all of the children's
hands were waving in the air. All the time the children sat with their hands
in the air, they were not writing; they were waiting for her to come to them
to spell a word they didn't know. Finally, in desperation, Carol asked the
children to look around the room and notice how many people had their
hands raised. She made the observation that all the time their hands were
raised, they were not writing. What could they do?

Some children suggested asking Michael how to spell words because
he was a good speller, but then Michael's writing would be disturbed.
One child said everyone should think of the words they needed and just
remember them until the teacher came around. Not a bad suggestion,
but then the children just sat remembering the words, not writing.
Finally, someone suggested they could just guess, and asked if guessing
was allowed in spelling. "Yes," Carol assured them, guessing was
allowed.

She stopped the children writing and asked Nakisha to read what she
had written so far, and then to tell what else she was planning to write
about her bike being stolen. Carol wrote Nakisha's exact words on the
chalkboard, in the child's own spelling, then wrote the remaining sentences that Nakisha dictated. In writing out Nakisha's dictation, Carol purposefully misspelled some words according to how they sounded. She

helped the children read Nakisha's writing and told them that later, they could go back and correct the spelling, but that the most important part was to get their thoughts down on paper as quickly as possible. Some still argued that they needed help from the teacher or from Michael. Finally, the class came up with a rule: "If the teacher is near you, you can ask how to spell a word. Put your hand in the air and count to 10; if the teacher doesn't get to you by the count of 10, you have to guess-spell it."

The rule worked for most of the children, but some were still quite frustrated. After a few days, the children amended the rule to add two other possibilities: "Draw a line about the length of the word you need help to spell. Or, write the first letter of the word and draw a line."

With these three options, guess spelling, or "invented spelling," was born in Carol's classroom. With the reassurance that they could leave a blank, or just start to spell the word, the children became more comfortable at trying the word and more of them began guess spelling. However, some children drew a line under words they spelled themselves, indicating that they were confident enough to write them but still uncertain about the spelling. The lines helped Carol notice which words gave the children the most difficulty. For some children, particularly those who were very rule-bound (as many second graders are), the erasers wore out quickly as they tried many different ways to spell a word. Some of the better spellers among the children adopted other spelling strategies. They could remember seeing a word in a story they were reading and would go get the book and find the word. Some would still ask Michael how to spell a word. But for many, the freedom to write without being concerned about spelling on the first draft unleashed a storehouse of pleasurable remembrances, painful friendship problems, and exciting adventure-hero stories in their writing.

The Circulating Writing Conference

As Donald Graves recommends in his book *Writing: Teachers and Children at Work* (1983), the teacher should circulate among the writers, pausing when she or he sees a child who seems to be stuck, and ask: "Read to me what you have so far." Often, the child, hearing his or her own story read aloud, will think of something to add. This brief exchange can also be a time for the teacher to ask questions that the child might want to write the answer to, such as: "Did this happen recently or a long time ago?" "How did you feel about having to set the animal free?" "Will you tell your mother about this?"[3]

Another problem the children face after they have written and feel they have completed their stories is finding someone to listen if the teacher is still busy circulating around. After discussing the problem, the children and Carol came up with another rule: "If you need listeners, look around the room and find some kids who are drawing their illustrations; they can be editors."

During the circulating conference, Carol took notes about direct instruction lessons she needed to give to the whole class and about instruction that individual children needed. She felt that, while she could still teach her children the basic skills of spelling, punctuation, and capitalization, she need not be limited to doing it only in the old ways.

Editing Conferences Become Listening Conferences

Like Terri, the first grade teacher in Chapter 1, Carol was not as successful as Donald Graves and the teachers in New Hampshire had been with the concept of the editing conference. Carol's original plan was that four or five children would work as editing group members. They would listen to the author read his or her piece of writing, then give praise to the author and make suggestions for improvement. Like Terri's first graders, Carol's second graders were not good at receiving suggestions, and while some of the children who were friends praised one another's work, they could not bring themselves to make any suggestions for improvement.

Carol adopted Terri's methods for making the editing conference into a listening conference. The children listen to each other's compositions, then ask questions: "What else did you think about adding?" "Is this a true story or a made-up one?" "What are you going to do if this happens again?" "What happened next?" "What happened after the . . . ?"

The authors retained control of the story; they could either add the answers to the questions the other children asked or, if they thought the answers did not improve the piece, they could leave it as it was. Carol understood that the listening conferences were working in the same way as editing conferences when some of the children got stuck in their writing and asked if they could have a listening conference.

DOCUMENTING PROGRESS

The second graders were well on their way to seeing themselves as writers when Carol realized that she had to invent some system for keeping track of their writing. The suggestion from the summer writing workshop was to have the two-folder system, with one folder marked Work in Progress and the other Completed Work. During the first days of Carol's writing workshop sessions, the children put all their work into the Completed Work folders. They wrote until they finished one page of paper and then stopped. But after their brainstorming session, when the topics became livelier, the children needed more time to write and, with prompting from Carol, they began using the Work in Progress folders.

Carol also modeled this evaluation of writing by keeping her own Work in Progress folder. The children often looked in her folder to see what work she had in progress. Sometimes it was a story she was writing for them. At other times it was school reports, orders for supplies, or letters she was composing to parents to ask for volunteers. The children liked checking up on her writing.

However, documenting progress means more than just placing writing in writing folders. Again, drawing on the work of Donald Graves, and other teachers' modifications to his work, Carol revised her folder system.

Second Graders' Work in Progress Folder

As Lucy Calkins (in her book *Lessons from a Child: On the Teaching and Learning of Writing*, 1983) and other leading educators (Graves, 1983; Hall, 1989) in the process writing movement attest, the purpose of documenting progress is for the teacher to improve instruction. If the teacher can help the child become invested in the process of documenting progress, then the folder itself becomes another record of the child's writing, and another tool to improve instruction.

For the Work in Progress folder, Carol stapled a lined, blank sheet of paper onto the inside cover. The paper was entitled "What I Want to Write About." The children wrote their ideas for stories on the paper and added to the list as new ideas came to them.

Second Graders' Completed Work Folders

The Completed Work folder was organized differently, with two sheets of paper: one stapled on the outside cover, entitled "Writing I Have Completed" (where the children listed the titles of all their pieces) and one on the inside back cover of the folder, entitled "Writing Skills I Know."

After the children completed several pieces of writing, they could fill out the list of Writing Skills I Know. Carol conferenced with each child and let them tell her what they knew how to do. Often the children concentrated on the mechanics. The second step in conferencing about skills they knew was to take several pieces of writing and point out in them other accomplishments. Carol pointed out to Patricia that she was also good at writing beginnings, that she knew how to write with a sense of suspense or surprise, and that she wrote good endings.

Later in the year, when the children were more confident as writers, Carol added another sheet of paper to the inside of the front cover, divided into two columns; above the first column she printed the word "spelling" and above the second, the word "punctuation." The children made lists of their "spelling demons"—common words that were difficult for them to remember how to spell. They wrote the word out in the way that they misspelled it, then crossed through it and wrote it out correctly. Carol also helped the children pick out "high frequency" words—the ones they read, spoke, and wrote most often, as opposed to unusual words, such as *umbrella* or *Tyrannosaurus*. They also worked on punctuation, but less successfully than they did with spelling. The children used quotation marks, commas, and many exclamation points, but used them less reliably than they did periods and question marks. However, Carol was pleasantly surprised to notice that her children knew and used more punctuation marks than did most of the second graders she had taught in her 19 years.

When the children finished a piece of writing, it had to be checked against their personal spelling lists, punctuation charts, and writing skills sheets before it could be placed in their Completed Work folder. In this way, the children began functioning as their own proofreaders.

CAROL'S GROWTH AS A TEACHER OF WRITING

While there are many more details of Carol's year with her second graders to relate, suffice it to say that the children grew and Carol grew. She continued to write and to struggle with the instruction of second grade writers. None of Carol's second graders achieved extraordinary levels of writing revision. Some examples of the work they *did* accomplish include: Kevin's story, which, by the end of the year, he had revised seven times; and Nakisha's 14-page saga, which she refused to revise. Revision, like all the other areas of the children's writing, was highly dependent on both the context and the individual. Teaching writing revision, however, became a topic of interest for Carol as she worked with the children at the writing camp the following summer.

MEET JOLENE, A THIRD GRADE TEACHER

At critical junctures in teachers' lives they must make decisions that are often career turning points. Being transferred to a different school and being reassigned to a different grade level are two such turning points. Jolene, an experienced first grade teacher, asked for this juncture. She thought she was becoming stale and wanted some new challenges. She requested a reassignment to a different grade level for the following year. Anxious to keep a seasoned teacher happy, the principal agreed, and assigned her to the third grade.

At the beginning of the year, when the third grade team met, Jolene was greeted politely, but cautiously. She heard the concerns some of the teachers expressed about whether or not she would be able to teach her third graders differently than she had her first graders. Third graders needed to develop new reading strategies to get more information from content area books. The teachers emphasized the social studies and science requirements as a part of the county school district's program of studies.

Wondering if she had made the right decision, Jolene talked at length with the principal, asking for reassurances that indeed she was up to the task of teaching third graders. Jolene's own son had loved third grade, and she enjoyed his friends at that age.

The third grade teacher's team had been working on the social studies and science curriculum, with some casual division of labor. Some enjoyed science more and others social studies, so they divided the work along the lines of their strengths. Jolene had a difficult time deciding which she preferred; in first grade, she had enjoyed teaching thematic units on both subjects. At last she decided on science, since one of the teachers she particularly liked had also chosen science.

Searching for Meaningful Content Area Reading and Writing

The challenge for the third grade curriculum teams was to work on incorporating more children's literature into the science units they were teaching. The major theme for the unit Jolene and her partner were developing was "oceans," something particularly appropriate for these Florida teachers.

Jolene brought in books she had read to her first graders, as well as some books her own son had on the theme of oceans, and began a library search for other selections. Her search was productive and generated a list of a dozen titles to add to others her colleagues found.

Children's literature always inspired Jolene. She was excited when she found new authors or new releases on topics for her units, and she liked comparing the social studies and science textbooks to the writing in the children's literature books. She found the writing in children's trade books much livelier, the information more current, and also that these books genuinely aroused the children's interest.

In mapping out a strategy for planning the unit of study on the oceans, Jolene decided there were three critical steps she needed to take: (1) to assess the students' prior knowledge of the oceans; (2) to combine their study of the topic with an expansion of their reading strategies; and (3) to determine their interests.

ASSESSING STUDENTS' PRIOR KNOWLEDGE. Activating and developing prior knowledge seems especially appropriate for third graders. In *Literacy, Helping Children Construct Meaning* (1993), David Cooper discusses prior knowledge in the context of the children's accumulated experiences both inside and outside school (p. 114). He also refers to prior knowledge as both text-specific and topic-specific.

Text-specific knowledge refers to the children's understanding of narrative and expository texts. As most teachers know, narrative texts are the story forms, with the story elements easily identifiable, including plot, setting, characterization, theme, point of view, and style. Expository texts are often thought of as information books. Nonfiction books must be accurate, portray as complete a picture as possible for the intended audience, be written by someone with expertise, and be developed to convey information in an interesting and vital manner (Kobrin, 1988; Raines & Isbell, 1994; Tunnel & Jacobs, 1989). According to Cooper (1993), expository texts have several structures: description, collection, cause and effect, problem solving, and comparison.

Assessing text-specific prior knowledge was essential to Jolene's understanding of how the children constructed meaning. From her experience with first graders, Jolene knew they preferred the narrative text and enjoyed the story structures. With her own son at about third grade, she noticed his keen interest in the nonfiction book. She thought this might be his attempt at separating reality from fantasy. He often said he "wanted to read about something real."

In the context of topic-specific knowledge, discussion is often cited as one of the poorest means to determine prior knowledge, but Jolene had always been quite successful at simply asking children what they knew about a topic and keeping a written record of what they said. Then she would review her list and keep adding to it as other children were prompted by what they heard their classmates say. (See the discussion in Chapter 2 of K-W-L charts as an expansion of the answer to the question: "What do you know about . . . ?").

A second strategy that Jolene had tried with narrative texts, and planned to use with expository texts, was also a simple one: look through the book at the pictures and illustrations and make predictions about the content of the book. Often, this process peaked the interest of the youngsters and she found them deliberately waiting for her to reach the part of the book where "their" special interest picture was explained. Interestingly, many of the books she had read aloud to the first graders were now appropriate for the eight-year-olds to read on their own. She mused that perhaps the difference between first and third grade might not be as vast as she once thought.

EXPANDING READING STRATEGIES.   Jolene arrived on the first day of her unit lesson with an armload of books about oceans. The previous day, she had prepared the children by saying that there were many changes in store for the class. Her first request was that several of the children spend time categorizing the books. They were to group books which should go together. She refused to tell the children how many different categories or sets of books there should be.

Interestingly, the children's first sorting of the books was into the categories of "true" and "not true." Obviously, Bush and Paul's *The Fish Who Could Wish* (1991) was not a true story, and neither was J. Cole's *The Magic School Bus on the Ocean Floor* (1992), but there were parts of this last story that contained some facts. They also deliberated about DeSaix's *The Girl Who Danced with Dolphins* (1991). What happened to the girl was real, but the end of the story was her dream, and that was not real, or were dreams real? Real people dream. They eventually placed it in the "not true" group. They were convinced that Himmelman's story (1990) was true because the title read, *Ibis: A True Whale Story*. They had difficulty with Weller's *Riptide* (1990), the story of a dog who saved a drowning swimmer. The beautiful oil painting illustrations seemed to the children to be ones often associated with fiction stories. And the cartoon-like illustrations of Jacob's *Sam, the Sea Cow* (1979, 1991) convinced them that the story could not be true. However, after reading the back inside cover, they discovered there was a real manatee that had been named Sam by the newspapers.

The children easily decided that the photograph books were real; however, after closer examination, they found that the photographs illustrated stories that could have been real or that could have been fiction.

DETERMINING INTERESTS AND TEXT TYPES.   Simply sorting the literature selections became an invitation to read the books. The children's strategies for deciding their categories involved the *preview and predict technique.* They flipped through the book, paused to read a bit and, often finding enough clues, decided whether the books were reality or fantasy.

Several children dropped out of the sorting exercise. Some found books they wanted to read and simply started reading. Two children became engrossed in the unusual photographs of the octopus and the jellyfish in the two books by Patricia Kite, *Down in the Ocean: The Octopus* (1993) and *Down in the Ocean: The Jellyfish* (1993). The same children wondered aloud why the book on sponges, *Sponges Are Skeletons* (Esbensen, 1993), had drawings, because they would have liked to see real pictures of real ones.

Jolene certainly had captured the children's interest by bringing in information and narrative texts, but all the children seemed to be interested in *all* of the books. They enjoyed the funny stories, *The Fish Who Could Wish* and *The Magic School Bus,* but they were equally interested in the photo essays of interesting and unusual facts about animals.

Suddenly, Jolene's interest in assessing prior knowledge was less important. She had a group of anxious, eager readers who wanted to investigate the new books and who subsequently would learn about oceans from them. The instructional dilemma for her became one of learning how to organize the information and how to help the children learn from one another.

WORKING TOGETHER TO ORGANIZE INFORMATION FOR A UNIT

Jolene's dilemma was an intriguing one. She had a number of eager readers, a nice assortment of books on numerous topics, and more enthusiasm than she could control. What more could a teacher ask? She decided she needed to use some organizing structures to help her get a handle on the children's prior knowledge, their interests, and the match with the literature selections she had found for the classroom. She used a K-W-L chart (Ogle, 1986), generated categories of information, invented an interest survey, and planned a data retrieval system.

K-W-L Charts

The first organizing step for Jolene, who was eager to move on, was a whole-class exercise in assessing prior knowledge utilizing the strategy of the K-W-L chart (see Fig. 2.1). In answer to the first, or "K" question on the chart ("What do we know about the ocean?"), the children generated an extensive list that could be used as a first K-W-L chart, and afterward broke the list down into different categories. They divided the list into animals, plants, places, fishing, swimming, safety, food, and problems. Each of these headings could then be used to construct a series of smaller K-W-L charts (i.e., "What do we know about animals in the ocean," and so on).

Keenly aware of interest as a motivating factor, Jolene made up a brief survey with the intention of finding out which of the eight categories most interested the majority of children in the class. She gave each child a blank sheet of paper, then asked them to fold the sheet in half and draw a line along the fold. She wrote on the chalkboard the names of the eight categories the children had chosen as "what they already knew," and asked them to write down the four categories that interested them most on the top half of the paper and the four categories that interested them least on the bottom half. If they could not decide about a topic, they could place it on the center line. (See Kristin's survey in Figure 3.3.)

The class then made a *check-mark graph* from the interest surveys. One of the children wrote all the categories, one beneath the other, in a list on the chalkboard, and then each child put a check mark next to the four they had chosen as their favorites. They deliberated over what to do with the choices of Kristin and other children who had difficulty making a decision, and who had put one or more of the categories on the center line. In the end, the winning categories were animals, plants, food, and problems. One astute student remarked that the "fishing" category could also be part of the "getting food" category, but he was argued down by another child who said he had meant the "ocean food chain" when he chose "food," and not "people food." The class decided to keep "food" and not to exchange it for "fishing." However, in an effort not to discourage the minority vote, Jolene explained that the class as a whole would study the four winning categories, but that individuals would be free to choose any of the other topics not chosen.

Jolene's strategies helped her to organize, but they also set the stage for subsequent data retrieval exercises that would help the class get an overview of what they were learning, and teach them how to keep track of their learning. The organizing structures were just the beginning; the next steps were to find ways to encourage the children to share their information and to instruct them in how to retrieve key data.

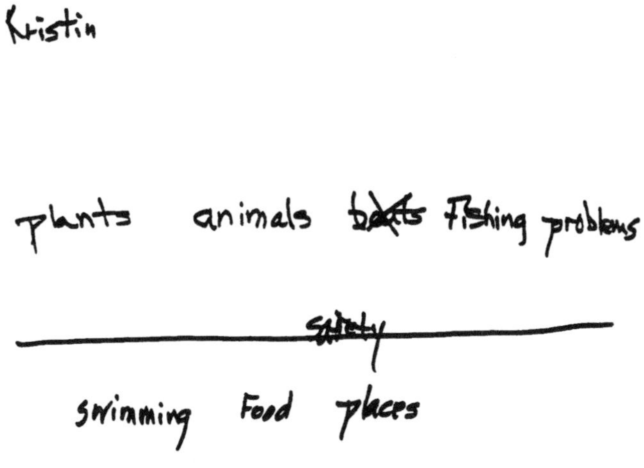

Figure 3.3. *Kristin's "Ocean Interest Survey."*

Another important step was to challenge the children to want to learn more. In a classroom already stimulated toward learning, Jolene was quick to follow the lead of the children themselves, as can be seen in the following anecdote. Certainly, most third graders are interested in animals, and these third graders seemed quite taken with sharks and whales, particularly sharks. Perhaps too many scary movies about shark attacks had invaded the classroom imagination. One day, when a small group of children seemed set on locating the scariest and meanest shark and whale pictures they could find, Jolene decided to read more material to the class about sharks.

ORGANIZING A DATA RETRIEVAL SYSTEM. The most challenging aspect of the unit of study was finding ways to keep track of all the things the children seemed to be learning. Returning to the first K-W-L chart, and to the smaller charts on ocean animals, ocean plants, ocean food, and ocean problems, the children reviewed the questions with which they had filled in the second, or "W" part of the charts (in answer to "What do we want to know about . . . ?"). As they looked for the answers to these questions by reading classroom literature selections, and other works they located in the library, they recorded what they had read in a *reading log*. Whenever someone found an answer to one of the questions, they wrote the answer on an index card and then taped the card onto the K-W-L chart under "L" section—"What we learned about . . ."

READING JOURNALS AND LEARNING LOGS. After a few days of investigations, Jolene and the children revised the charts, asked more questions, and set off on more investigations. The reading logs proved to be valuable cross references for the information they were gathering. Each child recorded the book, magazine, or CD-Rom encyclopedia article he or she had read. Since their index card answers often prompted more inquiries, the cross referencing of what each child had read helped to trace data sources.

Learning logs, another classroom strategy, also served as daily writing assignments. At the end of each day, each child was asked to write at least one new interesting fact he or she had learned, and to identify its source. Interestingly, the sources quoted most often were the smaller K-W-L charts. The children were learning from one another.

JOLENE'S TRANSITION TO WHOLE LANGUAGE TEACHER

"We didn't end the oceans unit," Jolene said, "we just paused frequently to decide what else to study." While the official class unit of study moved on to ponds, lakes, swamps, and wetlands, the children continued to be intrigued with oceans. The children compared their information about all the other water environments they studied later in the year to what they had learned about oceans.

Looking back over the course of the month-long study of oceans, Jolene realized she had accomplished her goal of helping third graders see themselves as capable users of information. They had learned how to think about knowledge, how to organize thoughts, and how to seek information: not a bad start for someone who had been teaching first graders to read and was now enjoying seeing third graders tackle some of the earth's most difficult concerns. One child asked at the end of the unit, "How can we clean up the ocean?"

SUMMARY

Through our glimpses into the classrooms of two teachers, we have continued the process of perceiving, behaving, and becoming whole language teachers. We observed both a second grade and a third grade teacher perceiving changes they needed to make to create whole language environments for their students. Carol made drastic changes, evolving from a basic-skills writing teacher into a teacher with a developmental writing approach. She prepared for the changes by learning how writers behave, and then by becoming first a writer and finally a teacher of writing. Jolene initiated the changes by asking to be reassigned to a third grade class. She brought many of the successful reading and information organization strategies she had used with first graders into her third grade classroom. She also invented a few new ways to organize information and to help the children retrieve data from their research and collection efforts. These two teachers practiced the process of perceiving, behaving, and becoming whole language teachers.

NOTES

1. Carol is a fictitious name. The information for this teacher's success story was derived in part from Dr. Kathleen Beattie, of Fairfax County Public Schools, and from Ms. April Phillips and the Literacy Forum of the Center for Applied Research and Development (C.A.R.D.) at George Mason University in Fairfax, Virginia.

Jolene is also a fictitious name. This teaching case is adapted from a case study in a course this author taught as part of the Teaching Cases Research Group at the University of South Florida, Tampa. Dr. James Paul and this author co-chaired the group.

2. Part of the brainstorming and instructional dilemmas were enhanced from my own experiences teaching in a combination first and second grade class in Rocky Mount, NC.

3. For additional insights into and examples of teachers interacting with their students on a variety of writing samples, the reader is referred to the book edited by Nigel Hall, *Writing with Reason: The Emergence of Authorship in Young Children,* 1989, Heinemann, Portsmouth, NH.

REFERENCES

Calkins, L. M. (1983). *The art of teaching writing.* Portsmouth, NH: Heinemann.
Cooper, L. D. (1993). *Literacy: Helping children construct meaning.* Boston: Houghton Mifflin.
Graves, D. H. (1983). *Writing: Teachers & children at work.* Exeter, NH: Heinemann.
Hall, N. (Ed.) (1989). *Writing with reason: The emergence of authorship in young children.* Portsmouth, NH: Heinemann.
Kobrin, B. (1988). *Eyeopeners! How to choose and use children's books about real people, places, and things.* New York: Penguin.
Ogle, D. (1986). The K-W-L: A teaching model that develops active reading of expository text. *The Reading Teacher, 39* (6), 564–570.
Raines, S. C., & Isbell, R. T. (1994). *Stories: Children's literature in early education.* Albany, NY: Delmar.
Tunnel, M. O., & Jacobs, J. S. (1989). Using "real" books: Research findings on literature based reading instruction. *The Reading Teacher, 42* (7), 470–477.
Wray, D., & Medwell, J. (1991). *Literacy and language in the primary years.* London: Routledge.

Children's Book References

Bush, J., & Paul, K. (1991). *The fish who could wish.* Brooklyn: Kane/Miller.
Cole, J. (1992). *The magic school bus on the ocean floor.* Illustrated by B. Degen. New York: Scholastic.
DeSaix, F. (1991). The girl who danced with dolphins. Illustrated by D. D. DeSaix. New York: Farrar Straus Giroux.
Esbersen, B. J. (1993). *Sponges are skeletons.* Illustrated by H. Keller. New York: Harper Collins.
Himmelman, J. (1990). *Ibis: A true whale story.* New York: Scholastic.
Jacobs, F. (1979, 1991). *Sam the sea cow.* Illustrated by L. Kelly. New York: Walker.
Kite, P. (1993). *Down in the sea: The octopus.* Morton Grove, IL: Albert Whitman.
Kite, P. (1993). *Down in the sea: The jellyfish.* Morton Grove, IL: Albert Whitman.
Weller, F. W. (1990). *Riptide.* Illustrated by Robert J. Blake. New York: Philomel.

4

Inside a Primary House:
Whole Language in
Alternatively Structured Classrooms

SHIRLEY C. RAINES

Suzanne Pippin introduced herself to the graduate school class at the University of South Florida by saying she was a "CP" teacher. Someone in the class whispered, "What's that?" and Suzanne began recounting the story of how she became a continuous progress teacher at Centennial Elementary (in Pasco County, Florida) in a school where kindergarten, first grade, and second grade children work together in the same classroom. Her listeners were immediately spellbound by Suzanne's description, and were amazed that someone could actually teach all these different grades in the same class. Suzanne explained that she does not teach *grades*, she teaches *children in a primary house*.[1]

Four of these multiage classrooms in Suzanne's school are located in a pod of the school that is called a *primary house*, a collection of four groups of children organized not by grade level but in an arrangement variously labeled *continuous progress, multiaged, nongraded,* or *family grouping*. Not all schools organize their multiage houses by grades K, 1, and 2; some combine grades 1, 2, and 3. However, the teachers at Centennial prefer not to use *any* grade-level designations. They describe the children in their primary house as emergent, beginning, and transitional learners.[2] Some describe the children simply by their ages: 5s, 6s, or 7s.

In this chapter, we will examine how continuous progress classrooms are organized and the implications of this organization for literacy instruction, as well as for other areas of the curriculum.

The curriculum model for these alternatively structured primary classrooms is *integrated thematic units.* Integrated curriculum (see Chap. 1) will be revisited in this chapter and its merits explored. The thematic unit planning will be reviewed, particularly as it relates to social studies, science, and literature units. The value of projects and the project approach will also be examined, as well as the importance of whole language in relationship to continuous progress classrooms.

CHARACTERISTICS OF CONTINUOUS PROGRESS CLASSROOMS

One-room schoolhouses in rural areas of our country, family classrooms in Europe after World War II, and multiage classrooms in Australia and New Zealand are the roots of continuous progress education. The move away from grade-level organization is enjoying a resurgence today (Anderson & Pavan, 1993; Goodlad & Anderson, 1987; Kasten & Clarke, 1993).

While the concept of continuous progress is not new, it has emerged again in the 1990s with promising results. Robert H. Anderson (1993a) points out that the new success of nongraded classrooms is due to our increased knowledge of peer tutoring, cooperative learning, and team teaching. Many whole language educators believe the resurgence of interest can also be attributed to whole language. The International Registry of Nongraded Schools (IRONS), organized by Anderson,[3] provides a checklist for "authentic nongradedness" that can be used to characterize the concept of continuous progress.

1. All of the labels and mechanisms commonly used in the Graded School for identifying the status/standing of pupils have been officially changed to labels and terms appropriate to the concept of continuous progress and nongradedness.
2. Grade-related promotion, retention, and tracking practices have been abandoned and eliminated.
3. Appropriate, essentially noncompetitive mechanisms and procedures are in place for assessing pupil progress, for maintaining records of that progress, and for reporting progress to the concerned parties without the usage of ABCDEF and S-U designations.
4. All pupil teams and/or classes include at least two age cohorts and are therefore deliberately heterogeneous.
5. Groups that are assembled for instructional purposes are sometimes "homogeneous" (e.g., with respect to levels of skill), often heterogeneous, and always non-permanent (i.e., they are frequently reconstituted or dissolved as needed).
6. The teaching staff is organized for the most part into teams or their equivalent, so that teachers have maximum opportunity to interact and collaborate.

7. As much as possible, the curriculum is presented through interdisciplinary themes or units.
8. The Board of Education (or equivalent policy group) has adopted policies and procedures that are supportive of the aforementioned seven concepts and practices, and manifests its approval of the school's improvement goals, for example, by authorizing exceptions to district-wide requirements or habits that are inconsistent with those goals. Where necessary, the Board assists in obtaining waivers for requirements and practices from the State Department of Education or other governing body. (Anderson, 1993b, p. 3)

PHILOSOPHICAL FOUNDATIONS OF CONTINUOUS PROGRESS AND WHOLE LANGUAGE

Whole language and Anderson's checklist for "authentic nongradedness" share assumptions and beliefs about children as learners. The philosophical foundation for continuous progress and whole language is the constructivist view, sometimes called the "interactionist/constructivist view." Drawing on the philosophical underpinnings of the cognitive theorists Piaget (1955, 1962) and Vygotsky (1962), the classroom is organized to take advantage of the children's stages of development. In addition, the work of Erikson (1963) as a social theorist is foundational. Both the continuous progress and the whole language literacy views incorporate the belief that children learn from one another and function socially within a shared context.

Almy (1973) and Fields and Lee (1987) have summarized the four factors that Piagetian theory emphasizes in children's concept development. Children's construction of knowledge is dependent on maturation, action on the physical environment, social interaction, and equilibration. Thus, intellectual development is fostered through the interaction of the following factors:

Growth and development, or maturity
Physically derived perceptions and manipulation of environmental materials
Social interactions with peers, parents, teachers, and others
Children's inclinations to make sense of their world, or to seek equilibration

Piaget's emphasis on the physical manipulation of materials and his descriptions of children's abilities to conserve ideas are reflected in the varied physical activities and projects that characterize the continuous progress classroom.

Vygotsky (1962) emphasized that the child's concept development can be described in stages, but that children also operate in a *zone of proximal development*. As the learner attempts to develop concepts, he or she is able to operate on the next, or proximal level of development through the assistance and mediation of adults and other children. Vygotsky's work called attention to the value of the child's own self-talk, adult–child verbal interactions, and the influence of culture and expectations on children's concept development. Socially, continuous progress classrooms are highly interactive. Given the emphasis placed by teachers in continuous progress classrooms on the idea that children must be active learners and language producers, it can be said that Erikson's social development perspective is also congruent with their beliefs (1963). Children learn to live together and to develop social competence. In primary houses, the social and emotional development of the children and their personal interactions are valued.

The teachers' and children's interaction patterns in multiage classrooms versus traditional teacher-directed, grade-level classrooms differ greatly. However, if grade-level classrooms are operated with a great deal of child autonomy, with the inclusion of the concept of large blocks of time, and with an array of developmentally appropriate centers and activities, then the interaction patterns are similar. In continuous progress classrooms, when the children become accustomed to class routines there is less need for the teacher as "supermanager" of the time, resources, and classroom behavior rules.

Nongraded classrooms also allow for greater flexibility because children can learn from a broader age range of students and from the teacher. Consequently, the children help one another more. Learning arrangements include whole-class groups, small groups, partners, and individual learners organizing and disbanding, depending on the task (Homan & Hartwig, 1993). Similarly, children are cooperatively organizing and disbanding these groups, with and without the direction of the teachers. Given the high-choice learning environment in continuous progress classrooms, with their many different activities, materials, and resources, children develop more autonomy both as learners and as socially responsible participants of the classroom.

Cooperative learning and grouping for task purposes support the sense of community that is developed when everyone is seen as a helper. The younger children have role models who help them to envision what they will become later on in their learning and the older children refine and deepen their understanding by assisting the younger ones (Kasten & Clarke, 1993). However, continuous progress teachers are quick to point out that there is no emphasis on *helping* as such in their classrooms; there is an emphasis on *learning*, and the helping occurs naturally. Helping is not an assignment but a way of life in the primary house (Raines, Hanley, & Laframboise, 1993).

ORGANIZING CONTINUOUS PROGRESS CLASSROOMS

While this chapter is not meant as a guide for how to organize a continuous progress school, it should be pointed out that moving an entire school to a new organizational pattern requires teacher ownership of the concept, district-level support, parent and community involvement, and a committed principal and school leadership team (Rine, Giella, Nielsen, & Stanfill, 1993). Teachers and administrators in Pasco County, Florida, where Suzanne's school is located, have proposed a conceptual design for restructuring the total educational system there (Nielsen, 1993).[4] The critical components of this effort have been identified by Nielsen as: "A learner-centered philosophy that emphasizes a holistic view of the child, an integrated curriculum based on specified outcomes, and a flexible organizational structure within which students and teachers will work" (p. 9). Administrators and teachers interested in continuous progress are encouraged to contact the International Registry of Nongraded Schools (see Note 3 at the end of this chapter).

After much faculty investigation of continuous progress models, Centennial Elementary decided to use the "house" approach.[5] The principal met with each teacher and discussed who might be good team members for a primary house, or pod, of four teachers. The principal was emphatic that teachers must decide the make-up of the unit.

Each teacher is responsible for 25 children, and there are four classrooms in a pod, each classroom including 5-, 6-, and 7-year-olds. The children in these classrooms remain with the same teacher for three years. Younger children are added—and older children leave the group— each year. Each teacher in the pod teaches the same integrated thematic unit, shares resources, and team teaches or team leads some activities. Approximately 100 children make their school home in the primary house with these four teachers, one teacher's aide, and many parent and family volunteers.

Planning together is often a major challenge for schools beginning continuous progress in a pod because the teachers must learn to operate as a team (Swarzman & Smith, 1993). They must recognize each other's strengths and hold each other accountable for the work to be done. Teaming is fraught with many challenges, such as group planning sessions, the supervision of aides and volunteers, and sharing and storing materials. One of the most frequent questions from teachers beginning continuous progress is: "To whom do the materials now belong?"

After several years of working together, team members at Centennial now laugh about some of the problems—but wince at others—that continue to bother the group. According to experienced continuous progress teachers, such as Suzanne, what makes the team work is that they genuinely like one another, have become more direct in stating problems, and can laugh together and at themselves. One of the major benefits of teaming is that teachers have other adults in the classroom; teacher isolation no longer exists. In fact, the opposite is true; they must make an effort to find some time to be alone to work on their individual responsibilities.

Multiage Classrooms Without Team Teaching

In their book, *The Multi-aged Classroom: A Family of Learners* (1993), Kasten and Clarke chronicle the development of one multiage classroom in an elementary school. Unlike the continuous progress model described above, which utilizes teams of teachers planning together and presenting some topics together, a multiage classroom can also exist as the only one of its kind in a school; or the entire school may be made up of multiage classrooms.

Kasten and Clarke (1993) studied one multiage classroom in Florida and examined others in New Zealand and Australia. The class in Florida began with kindergarten children who remained in the same group with the same teacher as other children of kindergarten age joined the group each year. Kasten and Clarke give the following description of this class:

> Among the current class count of 27, four grade levels, six age levels, and three ethnicities are represented. The total count will change in a few months when, for example, third grader Jesse arrives from Alabama as many migrant families return to Florida. Jesse will rejoin this class where he has been a member for three previous years, and will settle into life as usual. (p. 2)

Benefits of Continuous Progress Classrooms

To accommodate the many visitors who come to Centennial Elementary to observe continuous progress classrooms, Lori Hartwig, a former primary house teacher, has been assigned as a continuous progress resource teacher. In an interview, she reported that visitors often comment that it is difficult to distinguish the kindergarten children from the 6- and 7-year-olds. Another frequent comment is how relaxed and comfortable the children appear. Special educators ask who the learning disabilities children are, because they are not easily identifiable. School principals usually notice that there are almost no discipline problems.

Kasten and Clarke (1993), in their studies of multiage classrooms, point out the academic and social growth benefits of the concept for primary grade children. Most studies have found that students in multiage classrooms do as well or better than their age-level peers in grade-level classrooms (Anderson, 1993b; Kasten and Clarke, 1993; Pavan, 1992; Shepard & Smith, 1989). But while the academic benefits of language development—particularly vocabulary and literacy advancement—have been well-documented, the significance of children's social development in multiage classrooms has received less attention. Experienced teachers in continuous progress classrooms (Deck, 1993; Kasten & Clarke, 1993; Nielsen, 1993) point out that students are more socially interactive, more competent in their social skills, and behave more responsibly than do children they have taught in grade-level classrooms. They attribute this to the fact that the children interact with a broader range of age groups, and to the comfort they receive from established relationships with teachers.

COMMON QUESTIONS PARENTS OFTEN ASK

The model of continuous progress education adopted by Centennial Elementary School allows parents to choose either a multiage setting or a traditional grade-level setting for their children. Given the choice, parents asked many questions, attended numerous meetings, read education articles, and sought guidance from teachers in both types of classrooms. Open discussion and genuine, positive regard for parents' concerns are hallmarks of good continuous progress schools (Deck, 1993).

According to Kasten and Clarke (1993) and Deck (1993), some of the most common questions parents ask are:

1. What if my child does not get along with the teacher?
2. Will my child be bored when s/he is the oldest in the class?
3. Will my child learn the basic skills?
4. How can all the content areas be covered for all the grades?
5. When my child leaves the continuous progress class or elementary school, will s/he be able to function in a traditional classroom?

Parents' questions should be taken seriously. These concerns are shared by many teachers as well. The advantage of a continuous progress classroom, where two or more teachers are working together, is that the child has more than one teacher with whom she or he can identify. While all children in the primary house have one teacher who is assigned to them, the children also interact with the other teachers.

Boredom is almost never a problem in a continuous progress classroom. Because the curriculum and activities are organized around themes, children process the information at their own levels. For example, if the thematic unit is "Oceans," children will research their topics, read books, write stories, and create artistic representations at their own levels. The processes are open-ended and automatically adjusted to the level of the learner, because the child is in charge.

Basic-skills learning is enhanced in the continuous progress classroom. Because teachers devote more time to individual learners, the child learning to read and write is able to get more individual attention. Teachers help children develop effective strategies for reading and writing and provide time for reading real texts and writing authentic pieces, rather than using skill-and-drill worksheets. Continuous progress teachers do group children who are emergent literacy learners, to teach them specific reading strategies; however, the group is task-driven and disbands when the task is completed, rather than staying together like reading groups in traditional classrooms.

Novice continuous progress teachers report that mathematics is a difficult curriculum area in which to operate. Yet, experienced continuous progress teachers find that, like reading strategy lessons, they may group children to teach them a computational skill, then disband the group to practice problem solving. Real problems usually require many levels of mathematical computational skills and reasoning. The children can be involved in the problem at multiple levels. While parents' concerns about their children's progress are valid, research on multiage classrooms verifies that children do as well or better than their age peers (Gutierrez & Slavin, 1992).

Continuous progress teachers are knowledgeable about the basic skills and curriculum requirements for all the grades and ages represented in their classrooms. As is evident in the discussion of unit planning below, having the curriculum "covered" does not necessarily mean that the curriculum is learned. With our traditional sets of textbooks, we covered the curriculum, but children may or may not have learned from the experience. In the continuous progress classroom, the integrated thematic units are planned around themes often found in the social studies and science content areas; however, students interact with the materials and topics in more active learning ways. While there can be gaps in the curriculum if a school or a small group of teachers ignore various areas, an organized, school-wide curriculum plan can address the balanced curriculum issues.

Parents also express concern about how their children will adjust when they leave a continuous progress classroom and go to a traditional classroom. Most parents and teachers want their children to be responsible, motivated learners, and continuous progress classrooms promote these characteristics. Children who are good learners are more likely to succeed whether the arrangement is a traditional textbook-driven class or an active learning class.

BENEFITS FOR LITERACY INSTRUCTION

Teachers in primary houses often cite three major benefits for children as literacy learners: more time, relationships with other readers and writers, and less pressure. Because the adjustment time needed when children move to a new grade level with a new teacher is removed, there is more time for the children. The emergent learners who are continuing their literacy learning from their home and child-care environments have the advantage of coming into a classroom where there are proficient readers and writers. For example, in one classroom, Scott, a proficient second-grade story writer, was taking dictation from Charles, a kindergarten child with a vivid imagination. After a long period of working together, Scott was overheard imploring Charles, "just say dinosaurs, not Tyrannosaurus rex. I get tired of trying to spell all these dinosaur names."

Interestingly, at the beginning of their collaboration, Charles, the less experienced writer, listened as Scott spelled words out loud, but later he began spelling words he wanted Scott to write. Charles was functioning in Vygotsky's zone of proximal development. He was able to function at a more advanced spelling level because of his work with Scott (Raines, 1986). The example above is a clear representation of the value of the relationships between learners.

Similarly, in a unit on plants, the teacher was working on ways to help the children develop more competence at representing what they had learned (Raines, 1990). The children were asked to think of ways to show what they were learning about plants growing. Each day one younger child cut a length of construction paper as long as the plant was tall. The lengths of construction paper were sent home in an envelope and the child told her parents what they meant. A 6-year-old drew pictures of a twelve-day sequence of plant growth, detailing the seeds sprouting, and the plant adding roots and leaves. He pasted the pictures onto pages, wrote captions for each page, and called his book, "Bean Sprouts in Baggies." A third child measured the growth of the stems in fractions of inches and centimeters by cutting lengths of string the same length as the sprouts and then stretching the string out on a ruler to determine the length, and adding and subtracting to calculate how much longer the sprouts were each day. The children all participated in the same *experience,* but they represented their learnings according to their knowledge and skills. Continuous progress teachers become adept at arranging for rich learning activities but allowing the children themselves to construct ways in which to represent what they have learned.

A continuous progress classroom is a community of learners who gain more knowledge and become more competent at representing what they are learning because of the quality of the learning and because of the social relationships. There is always someone close by who is experiencing the activity at a higher and deeper level. Since the relationship with other learners is one of helping, teaching, and sharing a sense of community, there is an excitement expressed, not in the form of pressure and peer competition, but in the form of a broad cooperation among learners. Similarly, since the teachers know they will have their students for three years, they do not feel the end-of-the-year pressures to get the children ready for a new grade level and a new teacher. At the beginning of their second year in the class, the children are comfortable and the teacher already knows them and their abilities.

INTEGRATED CURRICULUM REVISITED

In continuous progress classrooms, the curriculum is usually planned around integrated thematic units. Jarolimek and Foster (1989) describe this kind of unit teaching as a "coordinated series of learning activities planned around a broad topic that will involve the whole class in a comprehensive study" (p. 54). Integrated thematic units are enjoying a resurgence of interest, propelled by whole language. With the move toward using whole pieces of literature, building connections among curricular areas, and viewing the child as a meaning-maker, integrated thematic units make more sense than do isolated bits of lessons and concepts taught in a disjunctive fashion.

Many elementary teachers have been operating their self-contained classrooms using integrated thematic units for social studies and science. Some early childhood educators in preschool through third grade often plan an entire, integrated day organized around the children's interests. Heidi Hayes Jacobs (1989) reviewed the design and implementation of interdisciplinary units and developed a continuum of options for content design. Continuous progress teachers, like most elementary and early childhood teachers, tend to utilize interdisciplinary units; some extend throughout the entire day. The elementary grade teacher who conducts literacy workshops in the morning, teaches mathematics in the early afternoon, and plans social studies and science units can make the day a more integrated experience by shifting the subject emphasis of the unit topics throughout the day, rather than changing topics with each subject area; i.e., during reading and writing workshops, children can read and write about the topics of the social studies or science units.

The Project Approach

Katz and Chard (1990) describe another approach to integration of curriculum—the *project approach*. Project is defined as "an in-depth study of a particular topic that one or more children undertake" (p. 2). As an attempt to move away from the "mindless" activities many primary children are asked to do, the project approach is to "cultivate the life of the young child's mind" (p.3). Seen as an accompaniment to curriculum units, and to children's desires to pursue their own interests through play, projects allow children freedom while applying what they are learning.

Again, many elementary and early childhood teachers feel comfortable with the project approach because they have been using variations of it for many years. Teachers who use the project approach value the child's interests. In the early childhood arena, a developmentally appropriate curriculum is one which reflects the children's developmental needs at their particular age and stage of maturity, but one which also respects the individual learner (Bredekamp & Rosegrant, 1992). The project approach has the capacity to function for individual children or for groups of children and children in multiaged groups.

A popular project in many primary classrooms is recycling. Society's concerns about environmental issues have prompted teachers to design recycling projects appropriate for children. As one teacher pointed out, you do not just start a recycling project and end it at the end of the month. What the children learn is that recycling is important work and that it continues even into the next unit, on "Growing things," where the students began composting food wastes. Some children become more engrossed in a project than do others and their individual interests should be encouraged.

Meaningful, important learning takes place when children "adopt" a project, such as the recycling project, and make it their own. Often, the teacher may stimulate interest in the topic, or even conduct an integrated thematic unit on it, but when the children "adopt" a project, they conceive, design, and carry it out themselves.

The Reggio Emilia Influence on Projects and Symbolization

The Reggio Emilia approach to early childhood education goes far beyond what we once thought young children were capable of doing in project approaches (Edwards, Gandini, & Forman, 1994).

Harvard professor Howard Gardner (1982) states that Loris Malaguzzi, the founder of a city-run, early childhood program in Reggio Emilia, Italy, deserves to have his name mentioned in the same breath with Froebel, Montessori, Dewey, and Piaget. To what can we attribute such bold praise? In Malaguzzi's Reggio Emilia school, children's thinking is treated very seriously (Katz, 1994). There, young children who are not yet readers and writers are seen as much more capable learners than they typically are in schools in the United States. In Reggio Emilia, the children's art is seen as a representation, both realistic and imaginative, of what they are learning. The children and the teachers are engrossed in projects in great depth, and the children represent what they are learning through many different artistic expressions.

The time dimension is an important point of comparison between traditional classrooms in this country and the Reggio Emilia approach. Like continuous progress classrooms here, Reggio Emilia children stay together for three years, "coming to know each other as members of an extended family" (New, 1994). As Rebecca New points out, the time variable also differs in regard to curriculum planning and projects. "With a firm conviction in young children's abilities to concentrate on and remain involved with topics of interest for extended periods, there is no anticipated time of closure for a project once it has begun" (p. 220).

In the age-old curriculum debate of process versus product, Reggio Emilio teachers (and many authentic instruction and authentic assessment educators in this country) have begun to question the strongly held emphasis on process, with correspondingly little attention to children's products (Forman, Lee, Wrisley, & Langley, 1993; Gardner, 1982; Schirrmacher, 1986). George Forman, an interpreter of the Reggio Emilia approach, worked with a group of Massachusetts teachers to carry out a project similar to one he had witnessed at Reggio Emilia, which the Italians had called "how the city and the people in the city change when it rains." Here he describes that project:

> The project in Reggio Emilia continued for many weeks, including such activities as making audiotapes of the rain sounds on different surfaces and then making a graphic rendering of these sounds, going into the city filled with questions that had been raised from the classroom drawings, drawing machines that could make rain, drawing a system of water works that brings the rain water from the sky to the ground to pipes to homes, using a sequence of photographs that show a changing sky and then drawing these changes on paper, drawing a city before and during a rainfall, and drawing many more examples of multisymbolic learning. (Forman et al., 1993, p. 234)

Forman and a group of three classroom teachers from Marks Meadow Elementary in Amherst, Massachusetts, carried out a similar multisymbolic project on snow with their 5- through 7-year-olds. Reading about the projects at Reggio Emilia and at Marks Meadow, this author was struck by the "cycles of symbolization," or the ways the children reflected on what they knew and were trying to communicate, and by how they redrew their pictures or symbols again and again to reflect new understandings, new depths of knowledge.

APPROPRIATE PROJECTS AND TOPICS

Projects should help the curriculum come to life in meaningful, active learning ways. For example, because of a growing interest in community life and a concern for the environment, many of our schools have begun long-term projects that have resulted in clearing local bodies of water, in studies of endangered species, and in novel recycling efforts. *Come Back, Salmon* (Cone & Wheelwright, 1992) is a children's book that chronicles the story of Jackson Elementary School in Everett, Washington, as they cleaned up Pigeon Creek so that the salmon could spawn there. Projects can also be associated with special holidays, such as "Earth Day," or "African American History Month," or with local events, like fairs and neighborhood celebrations.

Selecting appropriate projects and topics for units, however, is a challenge. Not all teachers and schools are up to the ambitious undertaking of cleaning up a local creek. One effective approach is to check with school curriculum guides and teacher resource books for social studies and science topics. Groups of teachers can then get together and brainstorm possibilities from these topics (Raines, 1994).

Theme Development Process

Continuous progress teams of teachers at Centennial Elementary in Pasco County plan themes using a process developed by Pasco County Schools (Dubendorfer, 1993). Teachers plan three different types of themes: literature centered; topic centered; and problem/question/issue/project centered (see Figure 4.1). Literature-centered themes are organized around various literary genre, a particular author's works, or a group of similar books. Topic-centered themes often involve social studies units, such as families and communities, or science units, such as plant and animal life. Projects usually center around a problem, question, or issue, such as "recycling at home and at school."

After selecting the type of unit, teachers brainstorm possible topics, then evaluate the topics using a list of criteria they have developed. All the evaluation points in the list are important. They include statements addressing developmental appropriateness, topics or concepts with natural links to the curricula, topics that encourage inquiry and choice, and topics that have meaningful connections to the children's lives. (See Figure 4.2, particularly numbers 4, 7, 8, 9, 10, and 13.)

Susan Dubendorfer (1993), one of the developers of the Pasco County Schools process, points out how important it is that the teaching team find the theme interesting. Teachers must find the topic stimulating enough to engage their interest over a long period of study. Children sense their teachers' excitement for a topic or project, and are guided by their teachers' interests.

Figure 4.1. *Types of themes.*

Literature Centered
   Organized around various genres, works of a particular
   author or illustrator, or core books
   Generally focused on developing literary understandings

Topic Centered
   Organized around a topic, generally from social studies,
   science, health
   Generally focused on developing content understandings

Problem/Question/Issue/Project Centered
   Organized around a problem, question, or issue that
   students have a need to answer or resolve
   Often current topics
   Generally focused on research and problem-solving skills

After the teachers have brainstormed ideas for theme topics and evaluated them using the criteria listed in Figure 4.2, they begin thinking about the topic they have chosen and deciding what they want their students to know and be able to do as a result of engaging in this study. The next step is to inventory resources in the school and community. After the resource inventory, teachers begin developing learning experiences, usually thinking of how they will engage the students' interests through some introductory activity. Teachers try to map out a series of broad phases for the unit development. As the thematic unit is being taught, teachers develop more specific plans for center activities, strategy lessons, and ways to expand the unit. Teachers are quick to point out that they spend a great deal of time in collection of resources and making broad plans for the unit, but they leave enough flexibility so that the children's inquiries can take them in directions they may not have planned. Each unit has some type of culminating activity that draws together what they have learned in ways in which it can be communicated to others, such as displays, presentations to other classes, school newspaper articles, or special celebrations. The culminating activity is designed to bring closure to the unit.

Figure 4.2. *Criteria to judge the quality of themes.*

The following criteria should be used as the basis for choosing powerful themes.

1. The concepts and experiences are developmentally appropriate for the students.
2. There is an abundance of literature for multiage groups and printed material such as trade books, songs, and poems (both narrative and expository) to support the theme. Also, other resources and necessary materials are readily available.
3. The theme is important for providing balance to the curriculum over the semester or year.
4. The central idea of the theme is valuable to the development of the whole child: his/her social, emotional, aesthetic, physical as well as cognitive growth. The theme will be able to offer opportunities for growth in all of these areas.
5. The theme strongly reinforces the strand and performance roles under which it will be implemented.
6. The theme is broad enough to address a large number of student outcomes.
7. The main topics or concepts provide natural links to many areas of the curriculum. Intregration of the subjects will occur easily and will be meaningful rather than contrived.
8. The theme discloses fundamental patterns and important concepts that will be useful to the students throughout their lives. For example, it reveals similarities and contrasts, e.g., cycles. It does not rely on incidental relationships. Topics are important and timely.
9. The concepts foster critical and creative thinking. Students will engage in learning experiences that truly stretch and challenge them.
10. The theme creates a climate that encourages inquiry and choice. It offers several opportunities for children to find some aspect in which they are truly interested.
11. The theme fascinates the students.
12. The teaching team finds the theme interesting.
13. The theme makes meaningful connections to children's lives. Children feel ownership because of their previous experience with the topic. This allows them to make a contribution and feel they are a part of the community of learners.
14. The theme is free of gender, racial, cultural, or other biases.

Evaluating Thematic Units

The same criteria the teachers use to evaluate and select unit topics can serve as a guide for evaluating their work when the unit is over. Another appropriate way to evaluate the quality of a unit is to find out if it meets the *human impulses test* (Raines & Canady, 1990). Dewey (1902) described a child-centered and experience-centered curriculum as one that incites the human impulses to socialize, to construct, to inquire, to question, to experiment, and to express, or to create artistically.

Broad-based curriculum units and projects provide opportunities for children to fulfill these human impulses. The power of integrated units of study is not new to primary teachers. The extensive team planning and preparation needed to conduct a successful unit are rewarded when teachers see children using new equipment and materials, connecting prior knowledge to new information, building associations, exploring new possibilities, solving problems, and constructing creative representations of what they have learned (Raines, 1990).

WHOLE LANGUAGE AND THE INTEGRATED THEMATIC UNIT

In an article for *The Whole Language Catalog,* Brian Cambourne (1991) challenged teachers to create classrooms where students function at a level of language learning that supports their thinking. Quoting Gregory Bateson (1979), Cambourne theorizes that for children to truly understand, they must construct the "patterns that connect" and develop "knowing through understanding." Cambourne pleads for appropriate texts, demonstration teaching, and a policy of allowing children to decide what they will read, write, speak, and listen to. He notes that teachers must have high expectations for children who are maturing as literacy users. He goes on to emphasize the importance of "knowledgeable others" who support children's construction of meaning. None of these aims can be achieved, he asserts, if children are not given the time and opportunity to reflect on what they are learning and to "make explicit both how and what they learn" (p. 17).

Integrated thematic units and project approaches provide many opportunities for children to become deeply involved with appropriate texts because they are seeking to find answers to questions that concern them, topics that intrigue them, and projects that engage them. Teachers can demonstrate reading, writing, research, and thinking processes within the context of the topic that is being studied. Continuous progress classrooms emphasize the relationships of learners in a community in which everyone, including the teacher, values the learning. The "knowledgeable others" are the teachers, outside resource people, colleagues on the team, and the children's own classmates.

Continuous progress classrooms provide children with the time and the vast range of opportunities necessary to become truly engaged in the processes of reading and writing, which promote critical and creative thinking. They also provide time and a vast number of opportunities for children to make "explicit," or represent what they are learning. Children read, write, listen, speak, draw, dance, and sing what they are learning. Continuous progress classrooms with integrated thematic units provide the supportive learning environment for children that Dewey (1902) described as human impulses:

- To socialize
- To construct
- To inquire
- To question
- To experiment
- To create artistically

NOTES

1. Other members of the primary house team at Centennial Elementary are Deborah Berg, Rose Mary Culp, Wendy Guynn, and Carol Hatfield. Ms. Pippin's remarks were directed to students undertaking a Continuous Progress education course offered by the University of South Florida and taught by Drs. Patricia Hanley, Katherine Laframboise, and this author.

2. The categories of emergent, beginning, and transitional were devised by Pasco County Schools, Florida. They closely parallel Piaget's stages of preoperational and transition to concrete operations.

3. For information about how individual schools can participate in the International Registry of Nongraded Schools, contact the IRONS Project, P.O. Box 271669, Tampa, FL 33688-1669.

4. For information on this reform effort, the author is also indebted to members of the Design Team of the Centennial Academy, a Florida Academy for Excellence in Teaching. The Centennial Academy is funded by the Florida State Department of Education, Altha Manning, Deputy Commissioner of Human Resource Development. Members of the Design Team include Pasco County Schools' personnel: Dr. Mary Giella, Assistant Superintendent for Curriculum and Instruction; Dr. Myndall Stanfill, Assistant Superintendent for Human Resources Development; Ms. Susan Rine, Principal, Centennial Elementary; Ms. Madonna Wise, Assistant Principal, Centennial; Dr. Lore Nielsen, Director, Department of Basic Education; Ms. Sue Dubendorfer, Coordinator Continuous Progress; and Ms. Jennifer Smith, Director Staff Development and Communications. The Design Team also includes University of South Florida members: Dean William

Katzenmeyer, College of Education; Dr. Susan Homan, Professor, Child-hood/Language Arts/Reading; and Dr. Joyce Swarzman, Director, Sun Coast Area Teacher Training Program.

5. Other Centennial Elementary Teachers who allowed the author to talk with them about their work through the Centennial Academy project were: Cathy Bean, Beverly Bryant, Jan Ellsworth, Lori Hartwig, Karen Kelley, Emily Keene, Nina Klymenko, Wendy Larsen, Ellen Malone, Jan Peters, Paula Powell, Michelle Travis, Jill Warfel; and Media Specialist, Brooks Marshall.

REFERENCES

Almy, M. (1973). *Young children's thinking*. New York: Teachers College Press.

Anderson, R. H. (1993a). The return of the nongraded classroom. *Principal 72* (3), 9–12.

Anderson, R. H. (February, 1993b). Selected readings on nongradedness and related topics. *IRONS Project*. Tampa, FL: IRONS.

Anderson, R. H., & Pavan, B. N. (1993). *Nongradedness: Helping it to happen*. Lancaster, PA: Technomic.

Bateson, G. (1979). *Mind and nature: A necessary unity*. London: Wildwood House.

Bredekamp, S., & Rosegrant, T. (1992). *Reaching potentials: Appropriate curriculum and assessment for young children*. Washington, DC: NAEYC.

Cambourne, B. (1991). Helping students seek the patterns which connect: A view of literacy education from down under. In K. S. Goodman, L. B. Bird, & Y. M. Goodman (Eds.). *The whole language catalog* (p. 17). Santa Rosa, CA: American School Publishers.

Deck, J. (1993). Common questions from parents. Class report for Continuous Progress in Early Childhood and Elementary Education Course. Tampa: University of South Florida.

Dewey, J. (1902). *The child and the curriculum*. Chicago: University of Chicago Press.

Dubendorfer, S. (1993). Theme development process in continuous progress classrooms. *The Florida academy for excellence in teaching*. Tampa, FL: University of South Florida and Pasco County Schools.

Edwards, C., Gandini, L., & Forman, G. (Eds.) (1994). *The hundred languages of children: The Reggio Emilia approach to early childhood education*. Norwood, NJ: Ablex.

Erikson, E. H. (1963). *Childhood and society*. New York: Norton.

Fields, M., & Lee, D. (1987). *Let's begin reading right*. Columbus, OH: Merrill.

Forman, G., Lee, M., Wrisley, L., & Langley, J. (1993). The city in the snow: Applying the multisymbolic approach in Massachusetts. In C. Edwards, L. Gandini, & G. Forman (Eds.), *The hundred languages of children: The Reggio Emilia approach to early childhood education* (pp. 233–250). Norwood, NJ: Ablex.

Gardner, H. (1982). *Art, mind & brain: A cognitive approach to creativity*. New York: Basic Books.

Goodlad, J., & Anderson, R. (1987). *The non-graded elementary school.* New York: Teachers College Press.

Gutierrez, R., & Slavin, R. E. (1992). Achievement effects of the nongraded elementary school: A best evidence synthesis. *Journal of Educational Research, 62* (4), 333–376.

Homan, S., & Hartwig, L. (1993). Grouping and interaction patterns in continuous progress classrooms. *The Florida academy for excellence in teaching.* Tampa, FL: University of South Florida and Pasco County Schools.

Jacobs, H. H. (1989). Design options for an integrated curriculum. In H. H. Jacobs (Ed.). *Interdisciplinary curriculum: Design and implementation.* Alexandria, VA: Association for Supervision and Curriculum Development.

Jarolimek, J., & Foster, C. D. (1989). *Teaching and learning in the elementary school.* New York: Macmillan.

Kasten, W., & Clarke, B. (1993). *The multi-age classroom: A family of learners.* Katonah, NY: Richard C. Owen.

Katz, L. G. (1994). What can we learn from Reggio Emilia? In C. Edwards, L. Gandini, & G. Forman (Eds.), *The hundred languages of children: The Reggio Emilia approach to early childhood education* (pp. 19–37). Norwood, NJ: Ablex.

Katz, L. G., & Chard, S. (1990). *The project approach: Engaging children's minds.* Norwood, NJ: Ablex.

New, R. (1994). Challenges to theory and practice. In C. Edwards, L. Gandini, & G. Forman (Eds.). *The hundred languages of childhood: The Reggio Emilia approach to early childhood education.* (p. 218). Norwood, NJ: Ablex.

Nielsen, L. (1993). Core components of continuous progress training. *The Florida academy for excellence in teaching.* Tampa, FL: University of South Florida and Pasco County Schools.

Pavan, B. N. (1992). The benefits of nongraded schools. *Educational Leadership 50* (2), 22–25.

Piaget, J. (1955). *Language and thought of the child* (M. Gabian, Trans.). Cleveland: World Publishing. (Original work published in 1926. Cleveland, Meridian Press.)

Piaget, J. (1962). *Play, dreams, and imitation in childhood.* New York: Norton.

Raines, S. C. (1986). Teacher educator learns from first and second grade readers and writers. *Childhood Education, 62* (4), 260–264.

Raines, S. C. (1990). Representation competence: (*Re*) presenting experience through words, actions, and images. *Childhood Education, 66* (3), 139–144.

Raines, S. C. (1994). *More story s-t-r-e-t-c-h-e-r-s for the primary grades: Activities to expand children's favorite books.* Mt. Rainier, MD: Gryphon House.

Raines, S. C., Hanley, P., & Laframboise, K. (1993). Continuous progress teaching cases and interviews. Tampa, FL: Childhood/Language Arts/Reading Department, University of South Florida.

Raines, S. C., & Canady, R. J. (1990). *The whole language kindergarten.* New York: Teachers College Press.

Rine, S., Giella, M., Nielsen, L., & Stanfill, M. (1993). Administrative perspectives. *The Florida academy for excellence in teaching.* Tampa, FL: University of South Florida and Pasco County Schools.

Schirrmacher, R. (1986). Talking with young children about their art. *Young children, 41* (5), 3–7.

Shepard, L. A., & Smith, M. A. (Eds.) (1989). *Flunking grades: Research and policies on retention*. London: Falmer.

Swarzman, J., & Smith, J. (1993). Team processes in continuous progress schools. *The Florida academy for excellence in teaching*. Tampa, FL: University of South Florida and Pasco County Schools.

Vygotsky, L. (1962). *Thought and language*. Cambridge, MA: M.I.T. Press.

Children's Book Reference

Cone, M., & Wheelwright, S. (1992). *Come back, salmon*. San Francisco: Sierra Club Books for Children.

PART

CURRICULUM CONNECTIONS AND PORTFOLIO ASSESSMENT

5

Dance! Chant! Discuss! Write! Responses to Literature in the Primary Grades

LINDA LEONARD LAMME[1]

Melissa Isaacson, a graduate student completing a practicum experience in a public school library/media center, wrote the following account of her experience.

Assisting a school media specialist allowed me the opportunity for a lot of keen observation. Each day, different classes filed into the library, listened to a story, selected books for checkout, and filed back out of the library. The individual classes all complete these same tasks, but in many different ways. In essence, it is the way in which they interact with the library itself that is different.

For example, Teresa Carter's first grade class came into the library one day, and like a fly on the wall, I tried to listen to their conversations, especially while they looked for books. I heard students go up to Mrs. Carter and discuss their selections: "I found a book by Don and Audrey Wood"; "I'm looking for an Eric Carle book"; and "I found *Bentley & Egg*" [Joyce, 1992]. "This is a good book, isn't it?"

The students were talking about books and authors with each other and with their teacher. They were also carefully selecting books. They flipped through the pages and looked at the pictures. They acted like choosy adults in an expensive bookstore, making important decisions carefully because every penny counts. They appeared to be making informed choices. And, as they lined up to leave, they received a friendly reminder from their teacher: "How many hands do we use to hold our library books?" "Two, that's right, so we can protect them better."

Another first grade class, on the other hand, came in, listened to storytime, walked over to the shelf, picked up books and carried them to the checkout counter. The only discussion I heard was chatter about cartoons and after school activities. There was no talk about book selection; there was no literary dialogue. Do teaching and modeling book selection strategies, in the library and in the classroom, have an impact on students and their conversations with books? You be the judge.

WHY A RESPONSE TO A LITERATURE PROGRAM?

As the students in Teresa Carter's first grade class made their literature selections it was apparent that Ms. Carter had taught them about literature, and that their responses were far more advanced than were those of the students whose teacher emphasized the skills of reading rather than the joy of reading.

Historical Perspectives

In the recent past, reading programs focused on skills in a bottom-up approach to building reading ability. Skills approaches were driven by multiple choice, standardized tests, and children were given a lot of practice in skill packs and worksheets for test questions. The goal was high test scores.

Gradually we began to notice—and tests began to show—that children could be highly skilled in answering test questions yet not be able to comprehend texts, and this was the impetus for the *comprehension* movement. Still in existence today, comprehension models ask children questions when they finish reading a text to determine if they gleaned meaning from their reading. The assumption behind comprehension programs is that there is one right way of comprehending a text.

We then realized that children could be highly skilled and comprehend texts, but still not enjoy reading or be avid readers. Since the more we practice, the better we perform, it became obvious that we needed programs that emphasized actual reading. Response-oriented programs grew out of earlier research that demonstrated that "reading" means more than only comprehending what an author wrote; it is a transactional process in which the reader brings his or her past experiences and past encounters with literature to the reading to create an all new interpretation of the message (Rosenblatt, 1978). Readers who actively construct meaning from texts transcend texts by reading far more deeply than is required merely to remember the plot of the story. Rosenblatt distinguishes between *aesthetic* reading, for enjoyment, and *efferent* reading, to remember information. Responses to each type of literature are different. To encourage children to transcend texts, we develop opportunities for them to respond to literature in ways that are personal, imaginative, informative, and meaningful (Barone, 1990). Response goes beyond summarizing and recalling facts. Peterson and Eeds (1990) suggest that "interpretation is the result of a transactional process in which readers bring meaning *to* as well as take meaning *from* a text" (p. 6).

Theoretical Perspectives

A *literature-response*-oriented program is the outgrowth of the realization that teaching children how to read is not an adequate goal for schools. Adults who can read but do not are often no better informed on important issues that directly affect their lives than are adults who cannot read. Our country needs to create life-long learners whose reading makes them informed citizens. Since reading is a transactional process involving an interaction between each reader and the text (Rosenblatt, 1978), children's experiences with literature need to be *personal, empowering,* and *authentic* in order to develop in them the ability to be avid readers. These experiences are a radical departure from textbook-based instruction in which all children read the same texts and are guided to respond to the literature in the same ways.

PERSONAL.   Classrooms that are *personal* require that teachers know the children as well as they know the literature. Because each child brings unique life and literature experiences to the reading of a text, she or he can be expected to have unique responses to literature. Only teachers who know their children well are able to facilitate personal, high-level responses to the literature. Several strategies for getting to know children well include:

- Writing to children and their parents and asking them to share special things about the children, including their favorite books.
- Taking time to talk with individual children by inviting a small group to have lunch in the classroom one day a week.
- Corresponding with parents once a week and inviting parents to write back.
- Dialoguing with children in journals, or corresponding with them in notes exchanged through mailboxes.
- Providing time to individually conference with children about their life experiences, their reading, and their writing.

Dianne Walsh, a first grade teacher in Gainesville, Florida, designs her class so that she gets to know all of her students well. Her classroom is set up in four "centers." After an hour of large-group sharing, discussion on a theme, reading aloud, and preparation for the centers, her children leave for a half-hour visit to each center. The listening center contains books on tape with suggestions for responses. A parent volunteer remains at one center for activities related to the theme, and another center contains an activity that children can complete independently. The fourth center is the writing center, well stocked with a variety of types of paper and blank books. Children write their own fairy and folk tales, information books, personal narratives, riddle books, song books, ABC books, list books, and books on topics being studied. On a couch in the center of the room, Dianne sits with individual children for about 15 minutes each for a conference. She asks each child to share what he or she is writing and reading and to read aloud a short passage from the book. Using this format, Dianne has two hours in which to confer with individual children. Between conferences, she checks in at each center to be sure everything is going all right. Each day, Dianne visits with up to eight students, and she views the one-on-one time as her primary teaching time.

EMPOWERING.   Classrooms that are *empowering* allow children to take charge of their own learning. Children set goals, are offered choices, and are taught strategies for selecting books to read. They decide where to read, with whom to read, how to read, and how to respond to the literature. In order to allow students to make so many decisions, the teacher has to establish patterns and create an environment in which children will behave responsibly. The children in one first grade, for example, enter their classroom in the morning leaving their belongings in their cubbies and assisting the teacher to take visual attendance so as not to disrupt the learning that is likely to be going on early in the day. The children find partners to read with, select books from the many that are displayed face-front on low shelves under the chalkboard and in the book corner, and then read with one another for half an hour. After their reading time, the children meet in small groups to share their books.

AUTHENTIC.   Classrooms with *authentic* literature programs use authentic materials and provide authentic encounters with literature. Children's books, magazines, newspapers, and environmental print are authentic materials; textbooks are not. Even "literature-based" or "whole language" textbooks are unauthentic because the stories in them often do not match the original form of the literature. Stories in textbooks do not have covers, title pages, dedication pages, or copyright information. There is no way to read in a textbook version of a story something about the author and illustrator on the back flap of the book, nor are there extra comments about why the book was written, or acknowledgments of help in creating the book. Often illustrations are missing or they are not works by the original illustrator. In order to fit a 32-page picture book into a textbook, with stories that are typically 12–18 pages long, quite a bit has been omitted. Examining stories in a basal reader, children have been heard to comment: "That's not the way it s'poze to be. It's not that way in the real book!" While there is no doubt that textbooks containing real literature are more interesting to read than are older textbooks without it (those written with a controlled vocabulary) and yet the literature textbooks are still a far cry from the original book. Another important factor is that there is no comparison between the feeling a child gets when he or she finishes reading a whole, original book and when, instead, the story has been only one included in a thick basal.

It is also very hard for children to give a genuine, honest, personal, rich, deep response to a superficial or poorly written piece of literature. Quality literature is vital for a response-oriented program. Books that have vivid settings, characters with depth, honest themes, intriguing and interesting plots, and rich language provide the best stories for children's responses. Although it is tempting to let children read anything they choose, at times it is important to restrict their reading to certain authors, topics, or genre. Several guides are available for selecting quality literature that is appropriate for different subjects. A list of outstanding trade books in science, for example, is published each March in *Science and Children,* a journal of the National Science Teachers Association. A similar list of notable trade books in social studies appears in the April/May issue of the journal, *Social Education.* "Notable Books in Language Arts" appears in November in *Language Arts;* and *The Reading Teacher* publishes "Teachers' Choices" and "Children's Choices." Relying on these lists of books that are especially good for different areas in the curriculum assures that students will be exposed to books most likely to promote personal and informed responses to literature. Some teachers ask children to keep a reading log with the title, author, date, and a rating for each book they read. The children rate the book using a five-star system, and then tell why they rated the book the way they did. Gradually students formulate theories about what makes a good book and begin to be more discriminating in their selections.

Authentic responses are hard to generate. We are so accustomed to directing our students that it is very challenging for teachers to let children accept responsibility for responding to the books they read. Responding to literature is very different from answering comprehension questions. Comprehending a text does not ensure that children will want to read more. When we read a good book, we typically tell our friends about it or write to someone about it. We don't do a book project or an activity. Activities, like completing workbook pages, can make reading a drudgery. There are many ways in which children can authentically share the books they are reading with their peers in their own class and with children in other classrooms, or even, through computer networking, with children from around the world. It is always fascinating, for adults and children alike, to read about other people's perspectives on a book.

WAYS CHILDREN RESPOND TO LITERATURE

According to Peterson and Eeds (1990), a literature-based program that aims toward literacy is made up of four components:

1. *Story in the home:* Recognizing that children bring with them the language and experiences of their home community, you build on the diverse base that exists in the classroom and thereby open literacy to all children.
2. *Sharing stories:* Teachers should read aloud daily from books by many authors on many different subjects and in many genres.
3. *Extensive reading:* Children must read independently in many genres and on many subjects and share what they have read with others.
4. *Intensive reading* ("Giving deliberate thought to the literary experience by contemplating meaning"): In small literature study groups, children can share insights and connections made; the varied backgrounds and attitudes of children expand the meaning of a work for everyone.

Responses to literature reflect the comprehensive nature of the literature program and the quality of the literature that children read. There are many different responses to literature. We respond before we even get a book, when we hear others talking about it. We respond as we preview and read, immediately after we have finished reading, and often several days later. Sometimes we respond to rereadings of the book. "Our interpretations vary with our experiences, our attitudes, our personal literary histories, and our purposes. When interpretations are shared with a community of readers, different people's interpretations enhance the potential for making meaning for all" (Peterson & Eeds, 1990, p. 16).

Kiefer (1993) analyzed the oral responses of children to picture books and came up with four categories of response:

1. *Informative:* Children described or narrated pictured events.
2. *Heuristic (problem solving):* Children wondered about and offered solutions. The teacher asked questions about cause and effect, and possible story outcomes.
3. *Imaginative:* Students recalled, created, and participated in an imaginary world.
4. *Personal:* Children related personally to the events, expressed feelings and opinions, and evaluated the illustrations.

Written Responses to Literature

Children who write every day bring their experience as writers to their reading of literature. These children notice the author's writing techniques and point of view. They see how the author got them to laugh, smile, or cry. They predict why the author makes characters act in a specific way or why the author places the story in a particular setting. They read like writers. These readers are having transactional experiences, almost talking with the authors of the stories they read. This kind of empowered reading results in wonderful literary discussion when the book is finished. There are three ways that writing affects the literature program. In addition to reading as a writer, children can write responses in: literature response journals, letters to authors, book reviews for others to use for book selection, or dialogues with others who have read the same book. Thirdly, they can write literature themselves. The more children read, the easier it will be for them to write good stories of their own.

According to Routman (1991), teachers can encourage more student participation and ownership by using *literature response logs.* She explains that response logs are excellent for connecting reading to writing, for extending the meaning of text, and for giving readers ownership of their literary experience. Entries can be responses to open-ended questions or "free writing" that can be shared with a teacher or other students. Response logs, also called *literature response journals,* can be effective evaluation tools because the teacher, student, and parents have ongoing evidence of the student's reactions, interpretations, and thinking regarding books. In the primary grades it is important that we respond to the content of what children write in response journals and not to the mechanics. Children should feel free to share their ideas using the best writing they can, but revising and editing are not a part of responding to literature unless children decide to share them with audiences other than their peers, parents, and teachers.

In the primary grades, written responses to literature need to be kept light, short, and interesting. Urge children to express their opinions, relate their experiences, and refer back to the book they have read for response ideas and support for their comments. Teachers can model these kinds of responses to literature. Children are happier about writing responses when they see a practical use for them, so it is important to help children use their written responses as a basis for group discussion, and for them to track their progress over time. The point of responding to literature is to share different viewpoints and interpretations. The teacher's viewpoint should also be shared, but not considered more important than the students' opinions. The teacher should guide the discussion, but not dominate it (Routman, 1991).

Keenan (1993) describes the responses of primary grade children to the book, *The Jolly Postman* (Ahlberg & Ahlberg, 1986). Intertwining the study of fairy tales and a social studies unit on the postal system, the teacher equipped the classroom with mailboxes for class members as well as ones for fairy tale characters. The children were invited to respond in letter form through the Jolly Postman. In the children's letters, fairy tale characters came alive. Students addressed incidents in their own lives that were similar to those of the story characters. Several wrote extensions to stories. The written responses reflected the kind of talk taking place in class meetings; the letters complemented and advised story characters. These fictional written responses matched the fictional writing in the book, while at the same time generating enthusiasm even from reluctant readers. The letters allowed emergent readers to engage with a familiar piece of literature on their own terms in a way that reflected their knowledge of written language. Their simple messages were the first sign that the children were developing the habit and the capacity for aesthetic reading. Children took ownership of the letters, mailboxes, and jobs surrounding each.

We need to stop asking students questions, especially questions to which we already know the answers. Routman (1991) states that "If students are to become actively literate adults, they need to ask their own questions as they are reading, writing, thinking, and discussing" (p. 122). One kind of question that generates thinking and discussion is the *wondering* type of question. Teachers can model wondering questions as they share books with children. For example, one class group was having difficulty reading *At the Crossroads* (Isadora, 1991). Most of these children called their fathers "Dad," or "Daddy." Their confusion led the teacher to say, "I wonder if the children in *At the Crossroads* used the words, 'Our fathers are coming home,' or if those are words translated from another language." In regard to another story, the teacher asked, "I wonder why Ira decided not to take his teddy bear when he spent the night at Reggie's house?" (*Ira Sleeps Over*, Waber, 1972). There are no easy answers to questions, but questions can stimulate discussion and research to find the answers.

Sometimes teachers overstructure students' responses to literature in a way that can make response journals seem like worksheets. It is important to solicit students' views for responses rather than ask questions to which there are correct answers. Similarly, if students have to respond in writing to everything they read, they are probably going to cut back on the amount of reading they do, and they may spend more time responding—through writing and discussion—than reading. Instead, children should be allowed to select their favorite book, or a book about which they have strong feelings, at the rate of one book a week for written responses. Children also enjoy responding *while* they read, as well as after they read. In fact, primary age children are likely to forget what they might have wanted to respond to if they are encouraged to respond only at the end of the story.

Activities or Projects as Responses to Literature

Many teachers require children to complete activities or to do projects after reading a book. Some activities and projects are very helpful in gaining insight into literary elements, or in helping children develop strategies for sharing what they read; others are not. As with written responses, activities such as creating dioramas, constructing maps, making a timeline, dressing in period clothing, and doing "creative" book reports must occur sparingly if they are to have some impact on the children other than promoting the "getting it done" mentality. Typically, primary students are more enthusiastic about responding to literature if the responses are to books they have chosen to read, if they have chosen to respond to them, and if they have also chosen the format of the response. There are two driving motives for responding to literature: thinking more deeply about what we read and sharing what we read with others. Responses should never be used to determine if children comprehend what they read. Comprehension responses are assessments, or tests, and children are quick to place them in the same category as worksheets. They turn children off to reading every bit as much as do the workbooks that accompany basals.

Literature Discussion Groups

Literature discussion groups are formed according to the books children select to read or by the way they choose to respond to literature. The more diverse the group, the richer the discussion will be. Children construct meaning through dialogue. While students are discussing literature, the teacher can act as a guide, giving students practice and feedback. It is better for a teacher to participate by making statements and sharing thoughts as a member of the group than by asking questions, which is a more traditional teacher role (Smith, 1990). A positive, supportive, cooperative classroom climate promotes literature discussion groups. "In order for honest responses to literature to occur, there must be a trusting and supportive community for readers to respond within" (Danielson, 1992, p. 373).

For teachers who are making the transition from basal programs to literature-based instruction, literature groups can provide a comfortable format for instruction. Additionally, literature groups provide models for children to use when they read and respond to literature on their own (Tiballi & Drake, 1993). Literature groups can operate in many different ways. Typically, children choose any book they want to read, or one from a selection based on a theme, a genre, or an author. You can focus discussions by basing them on literary elements. Asking children to look for common elements among their books, to identify themes, to contemplate why the author wrote the book, and to notice how the author influenced the reading of the book prepares children for interesting discussions.

Sometimes teachers provide multiple copies of books, and children select which group to join for a common reading. The children form a group based on the book they chose to read. In this case, there is less to discuss within the group, since everyone read the same book. However, because other groups have not read the book, activities and projects related to sharing the book with others in the class become appropriate. In either of these two models it is the collaboration with others that supports children's efforts to transcend the text and to respond in thoughtful, personal, and literary ways.

LITERARY ELEMENTS

When children are aware of the literary elements, they will respond more imaginatively to a text (Peterson & Eeds, 1990). We should name the literary elements in the context of children's responses rather than directly teaching them. As children talk, perform, and write, the elements of literature will emerge. The trick is to recognize and label them at the appropriate moment, so that the insight deepens everyone's understanding of the work. Pointing out to the children when someone has noticed what contributes to the mood of a story, for example, not only teaches the other children what the mood of a story is, but also provides an example of that element. While it is important to garner children's opinions about the books they read, the sharing of feelings and thoughts will run dry if the program does not require children to dig deeper into the literature. At some point it is important to raise the question, "What is this book about?" (Peterson & Eeds, 1990).

PLOT.   Most primary age children respond predominately to the *plot* of a story. They like "what happened" in the story or they retell the plot in sharing the book with others. Retelling the plot of a story requires a degree of memory, but it does not require the higher level analytical thinking skills that lead to personal and literary responses to a story. "Readers do not give their imaginations a workout when they attend exclusively to the plot line of a story" (Peterson & Eeds, 1990, p. 27).

CHARACTERS. Typically, children then begin to notice *characters*. They can relate to characters and identify qualities in story characters that do or do not appeal to them. They are able to compare story characters to people they know, to describe story characters, and to take on a character's role in story retellings. They begin to see story events from a character's perspective instead of their own, which requires analytical thought. It can also be useful to examine how an author makes a character believable by keeping behavior true to that character (Peterson & Eeds, 1990).

Sandra Henney's second graders from Green Cove Springs, Florida, were very verbal during the reading of *Amazing Grace* (Hoffman, 1991). Because of their own past experiences with prejudice, they could relate to Grace's hurt and determination when her classmates claim that because she is black and a girl, she cannot be Peter Pan in a class play. They began to see issues in this book and in others from an African American girl's perspective.

SETTING. Although the setting impacts the characters and plot of a story, it often goes unnoticed by readers. In some stories the setting is a focus of the plot. *When Africa Was Home* (Williams, 1993) describes how an American child raised in Africa resists coming home to America, and *The Day of Ahmed's Secret* (Heide & Gilliland, 1990) shares the story of a young boy who delivers fuel, a responsible job for a youngster on the streets of Cairo. Setting involves time as well as place. A city street scene is the locale of a touching story about a poor immigrant family in *Peppe, the Lamplighter* (Bartone, 1993). The entire story of *Uncle Jed's Barbershop* (Mitchell, 1993) is immersed in the life led by African Americans in the South during the Depression. Children can't fail to respond to books like these without noticing how different the setting is from that of their own homes and, further, the impact the setting has on the lives of the story characters. Some teachers note on a world map or a timeline where and when each story they read takes place. Soon students recognize the impact of the setting on a story's events and characters.

MOOD. Setting is often related to the *mood* of a story. It is the mood that makes us react with emotion to the stories we read. Illustrations as well as words create a mood. Bill Martin Jr.'s *Knots on a Counting Rope* (1987) and Jane Yolen's *Owl Moon* (1987) are two examples of books that magically integrate text and illustration to create awesome moods. Determining how well illustrations match the text requires thoughtful consideration. Providing differently illustrated versions of the same story, such as "The Pied Piper of Hamelin," graphically displays the impact of illustration on responses to the literature (Cianciolo, 1993).

THEME AND AUTHOR'S PURPOSE.   Probably the most important literary element is *theme*. It is by theme that stories are linked to one another and to our common bond of experience. Lehr (1991) found that even four-year-olds are able to identify common themes among books. The theme, or underlying message of the book, relates to the *author's purpose* for writing it. Collins (1990) asks her students what they think the author is trying to tell us. Common themes in children's picture books are "growing up" and the increasing independence and self-reliance that greater maturity brings. Recent books on topics like war (*The Wall*, Bunting, 1990) and homelessness (*Fly Away Home*, Bunting, 1991), when told from the point of view of a child, broaden the themes that are present in children's picture books. Many books contain themes—like responsibility, helpfulness, altruism, truthfulness, and respecting diversity—that can be useful for framing a classroom management program (Lamme, 1992). Helping children see that most good stories are written with a purpose provides them with real reasons to write. It is the theme that drives a story, that makes it memorable.

LANGUAGE.   *Language* is a story element that is often overlooked; yet language is what children in the primary grades respond to immediately. They chime right in with the chants, rhymes, and rhythm of the language of predictable texts. Children move from enacting and chanting wonderful rhymes, like *Possum Come-a-Knockin'* (Van Laan, 1990) and *Old Black Fly* (Aylesworth, 1992b), to creating their own versions of chants. Jim Aylesworth creates his own verse variations of Mother Goose rhymes in *The Cat & the Fiddle & More* (1992a) and *My Son John* (1994). His books are wonderful models for children's innovations from rhymes. A poetry anthology, *And the Green Grass Grew All Around* (Schwartz, 1992), contains children's chants that have traveled around the world through play. Children might begin their own collections of jump rope rhymes and street chants.

Children acquire storybook language when listening to stories that are rich with vocabulary. They pick up figures of speech, images, and metaphors, even if they can't analyze them. "The sharing of literature aloud anchors the sounds of the language of literature in the minds of the students" (Peterson & Eeds, 1990, p. 9). When a teacher makes the language element conscious, children acquire a language for book discussion and realize that the author of the story uses words to create the mood, pacing, setting, and character of the story.

ILLUSTRATIONS AND FORM. Since many of the books that primary grade children read and respond to are picture books, illustrations and the form of these books generate responses. Help children notice the media with which books are illustrated. Art teachers are helpful in building children's awareness of the processes that illustrators use. Jeannie Baker's collages look so real you want to touch them. Children can mold with clay, fabric, and twigs to create similar effects. Tana Hoban and Bruce McMillan use color photographs for their book illustrations. Children can replicate the scratchboard techniques of Brian Pinkney (*Where Does the Trail Lead?* Albert, 1991). Many artists paint pictures for storybook illustrations. Using these media, as well as some art techniques like the use of color, line, and form, leads children to make informed interpretations of the pictures in the books they read. Children enjoy noticing how different illustrators depict trees, people, and scenes. They are fascinated with border illustrations, like those used by Jan Brett and Trina Schart Hyman. Since illustrations are as important as the text in communicating a book's meaning to children, taking time to observe and comment on the illustrations is an important aspect of children's responses to literature.

Two children in Linda McKinley's second grade class in Cocoa, Florida, so enjoyed Chris Van Allsburg's *The Z Was Zapped* (1987) that they adapted the format of the book to their own version, told with a black light show, complete with sounds to depict their letters' adventures.

ELICITING ENTHUSIASTIC RESPONSES TO LITERATURE

When asked why she shares literature in her first grade classroom, Leanne Baker (Gainesville, Florida) responds, "Why do I breathe? It's the most important thing in the world. If you can't read, you're out of touch with the world."

Surrounding Children with Good Books

You can tell by entering Leanne's classroom that literature plays a prominent role. Leanne surrounds her children with literature. There are several book shelves and a comfortable reading area attractively placed in the center of the room where all students see and walk by it constantly. Often books and book shelves are put in places out of the way so that students have to make a concerted effort to visit the reading center. In this classroom, books are everywhere in sight. Leanne uses current literature as well. The books on her classroom shelves are new, colorful, attractive, and appealing. Evidence of children's responses to literature line the walls. In a classroom environment like Leanne's, children can feel her enthusiasm for books by just walking in the door.

Children's responses to literature are interpreted by their past and present experiences and by their culture. When forming a collection for the classroom library it is important to gather authentic literature representing many different cultures. Typically, African American children, for example, are surrounded by literature depicting white people. Their responses are by necessity distanced from the experiences of the children in these books. Give them a book like *Dinner at Aunt Connie's House* (Ringgold, 1993), however, and their interest is piqued; their responses become far more enthusiastic. Books written in dialect, like those of Patricia McKissack, have immediate appeal. The problem is that many books in which African Americans are depicted, at least in illustrations, are written by white authors and are not authentic. Look for good stories written by persons who come from the culture they are writing about when selecting books for the classroom library.

Teachers need to balance the children's reading diets by providing them with literature from a variety of genres: fiction, nonfiction, poetry, folk literature, and fantasy. Make sure that many of the books have won awards. Every classroom needs several poetry anthologies, collections, and picture-book poems. Build your classroom collection around quality books reflecting the children's interests, your curriculum, and entertaining books to read aloud.

Reading Aloud

Melissa Isaacson overheard a child say, "You guys need to be quiet. We haven't had the chance to read a book today!" Reading aloud helps a group of diverse students become a community. It is the core of the reading program in the primary grades. Oral reading provides models for thoughtful reading and introduces children to literature that they can't yet read independently. How a teacher reads aloud has a profound impact upon what children take from listening to the story. The events surrounding the story reading are as important as the reading itself. The key to a successful book reading episode is the ability to extract from the book those ideas and concepts that will have a powerful impact on the children.

It is important to activate prior knowledge and experience before we read a book. We give a clue about the content of the book and ask children to think about any experiences or prior knowledge they have about the topic. If, however, a teacher is going to help children become avid readers, it is important to access prior book experiences with the author, topic, or illustrator of the book. Good readers move from book to book via authors, illustrators, and content. Teaching book selection strategies as well as avenues for response comes with asking students if they have ever read other books by the author or illustrator, or have read any other books dealing with the same content of the book you are about to read. Mentioning the author's name is a start, but more powerful is asking the children if they know anything about the author. When we feel personally connected to a writer, we read more intensely and look for specific identifiers more than when we know nothing about the author.

There are a number of sources of information about book authors and illustrators. Publishers distribute fliers on their authors free of charge. Writing to children's book publishers is a good way to acquire author information. Your public library has reference books containing detailed biographies and pictures of many children's book authors. Some book authors have fan clubs. Jan Brett wrote a little booklet about how she writes each of her books. Explaining *Trouble with Trolls* (1993), she says that she drew on her experiences as a child skiing with her sister; her visit to Norway where she asked people about trolls; Abbie Sullivan, whom she met at a horse barn in the Berkshires, and who became the model for Treva; and Laika, a Siberian husky who became Tuffi. Jan recounts that she felt sorry for the trolls, who were left without a pet at the end of her story, so she gave them a perfect pet, a hedgehog. The Brett family had their own hedgehog for two years. They named her "Hedga," and let her roam in Jan's studio every night. All of this information about how she wrote and illustrated *Trouble with Trolls* gives readers insight into themes and characters in Jan Brett's books, as well as information about how a writer writes.[2]

All of these ideas involve discussion before the actual reading of the book! The oral reading needs to be done in a hushed voice that accommodates great contrasts, reflecting the mood of the book and the voices of the characters. Inviting children's participation in predictable parts is great, but it is important not to stop the flow of the story with unnecessary questions. Captivate the children by adjusting your speed, tone, and volume to match their attention. Speed up if they get a bit distracted, and slow down if they are very attentive. Smith (1990) describes her process for generating responses: "During read-aloud time, I also demonstrate ways of responding that are reflective and informed. I listen for such responses from students and I emphasize them, so that students realize that there are many teachers in the room" (p. 24).

After the story reading you set the stage for any thinking that may result from the book reading. Smith (1990) recalls that initial responses are often personal associations that relate to the personal life of the student but have little to do with the story. Over time, and with coaching, children learn how to use literary elements to construct meaningful and reflective discussions about books. "I try to demonstrate critique by responding in ways that are sensitive, yet reflective and informed; and that recognize value but also discriminate among values," explains Smith (p. 24).

I have noticed that children's responses to literature change with subsequent story readings, so it is a good idea to read at least some of the class's favorite books more than once. As a rule, it is good to tape-record story readings, and to place the tape recording and the book in a listening center where children can treat themselves to as many repeated readings as they want. Be sure not to disrupt the mood of the story by asking questions after it is over. And while it is appropriate for teachers to share our responses to the book, it might be a good idea to let some of the children share their responses first, so that they don't copy ours. Genuine book discussion only occurs in nonthreatening classrooms where diversity of opinion is not only tolerated but valued.

Many responses to literature appear much later, in the course of conversations about books. It is then that we notice the details children remember from books. It is important to read aloud from only the very best, current literature, and from a variety of literature. We tend to rely too much on fiction literature for our read-aloud programs in the primary grades. Children should also hear, read, chant, and write poetry at least once a day. Poetry gives children an appreciation for language. When sharing children's writings from her school in Manhattan and talking about her students, Shelley Harwayne (1994) attributes their concise writing and precise language use to their immersion in poetry. When teachers select poetry with child-like language on topics sure to appeal to children, the children sing, chant, and read poetry daily. It is no wonder then that their writing contains many of the same poetic elements they hear in literature.

It is also important to read aloud nonfiction literature. Sharing information is a legitimate response to literature that is sometimes undervalued in classrooms. Nonfiction literature can arouse children's curiosity and lead them to wonder about science and social studies topics and issues. Wondering is a great enticement into the further reading of literature.

Many teachers conduct what I term a "dead end" curriculum. They read a book aloud without telling children why they are reading it, without accessing the children's prior experience, without allowing for responses to the reading, and most important, without linking the book to other books that children might like to read. As children respond, urge them to think about how the book they have just read is similar to others. Share strategies for finding more books by the same author, in the same genre, on the same topic, or with the same theme as the one you are reading aloud. The way to create avid readers is to teach strategies for weaving a path from one book to another.

Reading with a Partner

Children whose parents read to them on a regular basis have an easier time learning to read than do children who have not been read to at home. One-on-one reading is not only effective at home, it needs to be an integral part of the school program as well. When children look at books while sitting on an adult's lap or when sitting close by a more experienced reader, they interact with the book in a more personal way than they do when they listen to a story read aloud to a group. The children's responses to one-on-one book reading are more likely to tap their prior experiences and to include mention of the illustrations, text, and format of the book because they are closer to the book and can manipulate it. For children who are beginning to read, handling the book and noticing the words is obviously very important.

There are many ways in which primary teachers make provisions for lap reading. Some invite adults into the room at a certain time each day. Senior citizens often enjoy curling up in a comfortable chair with a child and a book. Some teachers provide for "buddy reading" with a class at a higher grade level. Buddy readers need training in methods to encourage emergent readers in ways that are empowering, so they do not just read aloud to them. Reading buddies can become good friends, with close relationships like those between parents and children. The closer relationships help children select more appropriate books and read in more encouraging ways.

One-on-one tutoring is an integral part of several remedial reading programs, such as Reading Recovery. Children who are slower at learning how to read are identified in first grade and given an extra boost from trained adults in daily tutoring sessions. Results from intensive tutoring while children are learning how to read are remarkable when compared with remedial programs for groups of children.

Linda Vandenberg, a kindergarten/first grade teacher in Gainesville, Florida, holds monthly or bi-monthly read-alongs where children's parents and caregivers are invited into the classroom. These sessions meet at noon, or in the evening, to give more parents opportunities to come. The children practice reading their favorite books and then share them with the adults who are present.

Teaching Book Selection Strategies

In order for children to become avid readers, they must learn how to move from one book to another. Most children begin looking at books long before the primary grades and the first strategy they use is to randomly select a book from the shelves. As any reader of picture books can attest, recently published picture books are as likely to be for upper elementary age children as they are for primary grade children, so random selection is no guarantee of an appropriate book. Henry (1992) studied how elementary school children select books. At the beginning of the year, the teacher greatly influenced the children's choices of books to read. The teacher read books aloud, gave book talks and author talks, and made book recommendations to individual children. The children read from self-selected books for at least an hour a day. By the end of the year the children were relying more on themselves and on one another for book recommendations. They learned to study the book cover, read book summaries and author information on jacket flaps, skim the book, and look at the illustrations for clues as to whether a book would appeal to them or not. They shared books through book projects, author talks, book talks, and book discussions. Since the quality of responses children give to literature is dependent on the quality of the book and its appropriateness for each child, book selection strategies are vital for sustaining a quality response-oriented literature program.

Amy Zele studied book selection strategies by interviewing primary grade children as they checked out books from their school library. These children had not been trained in book selection strategies except informally, as they asked the librarian for help. The most frequent responses were:

1. My teacher/librarian read it to me.
2. I read it before and want to read it again.
3. I do not know why I chose it.
4. It looked like I would like it.
5. I asked for help and you (or another person) found it for me.

Amy concluded that younger children feel more comfortable with texts they are familiar with, but that this preference is largely due to their lack of training on book selection.

Storytelling and Drama

Storytelling invites children to become deeply involved in stories. With no illustrations or book, the audience and the storyteller create a unique meaning from a story together (Blatt, 1993). Children respond more to stories related by a storyteller than they do to stories told with props or to stories that teachers read from books. In storytelling, and especially in retelling a story, considerable interaction and discussion occur, with the potential for generating high levels of response to literature. According to Soundy (1993), "The entire storybook experience is an active, meaning-gathering experience. Comprehension occurs and the reader constructs relationships between the text and his/her own knowledge and experience" (p. 147). The inclusion of story elements is one positive benefit of retelling activities. When they enact specific play roles, children see stories from the perspectives of characters in them.

Story theater is a form of sharing literature that is gaining popularity in primary classrooms. Children organize themselves to perform stories with one narrator reading from the book and other children taking the roles of characters in the story and either reading, reciting, or retelling what the characters say. Formal plays are not a good idea because memorizing lines can be too challenging for some primary school children, and plays typically highlight the academically talented children and invite envy on the part of the children who do not appear in starring roles. Story theater, also called *readers' theater*, a more informal dramatic activity, takes little preparation time and can be repeated with many different children in the storybook roles.

Bosma (1992) offers simple guidelines for conducting reader's theater:

1. The narrator and readers are on stools or stand in front of the class.
2. Simple props may be used, but nothing that might take away from the oral interpretation.
3. The reader uses voice to evoke mental images of characters and scenes.
4. The narrator speaks directly to the audience and does not interact with the other readers.
5. Each reader carries a script because the emphasis is on reading and not on acting or memorizing lines.
6. The relationship between the audience and the reader is made personal through emphasis on sounds. (Bosma, 1992, p. 89)

Providing simple props encourages small groups of children to perform stories as they retell them. Props serve as a "catalyst to awaken questions and thinking" (Soundy, 1993, p. 148). Once you start providing props, children can form groups and decide which props they might collect to share their story. Dramatic responses to stories tend to focus on plot. It is the teacher's responsibility to intervene in children's dramatic play and to structure it to produce deeper responses. Stories that are good for retelling include predictable books, chants, songs, picture story books with simple lines, and folk or fairy tales. Books should elicit enthusiastic responses from children and lend themselves to props.

Puppets and flannel board characters similarly stimulate storytelling and engage children in thinking about story elements. Performances ought not to be formal ones requiring rehearsals, but rather impromptu retellings shared with an audience of peers or merely performed for the fun of enacting the story. Sometimes groups from one class enjoy visiting another to share their story performance, but it is important to remember that time spent preparing for a performance is time not spent actually reading.

Dramatic play based on literature capitalizes on the natural inclination of children to pretend to be characters in the world of a story. Rather than using drama to help students act out a story, Edmiston (1993) suggests that teachers isolate moments from a story in which all students may take up the perspective of different characters. This type of dramatic play leads children to new insights into characters, themes, issues, dilemmas, and themselves. When children respond to stories through drama, we create "a shared world of the text in which we can walk around and interact with other people in a role" (Edmiston, 1993, p. 256), and everything that is said or done extends the meaning of the text, rather than focusing on the plot.

Genre Studies

Each genre of literature generates certain kinds of responses that are unique to that genre. When students acquire knowledge through the reading of nonfiction literature, they want to share what they have learned. Writing reports and books, setting up displays, creating posters and exhibits, and conducting demonstrations are all ways to share information.

Children who read a lot of poetry often chant, sing, and write poetry. They create innovations on catchy poems and then branch out to do their own original work. Since many poems are about science topics, poetry offers a natural link to the science curriculum and a unique way in which to gather information.

When reading biographical and autobiographical literature, children become curious about the lives of people who are important to them. A logical followup is to employ the tools of the biographer to interview and scour written sources of information about people, then to share what you found out. Children enjoy writing their own autobiographies. A third grade teacher gave her children note cards and told them to use the cards to interview their parents, and to ask questions about themselves when they were younger. One suggestion was to have their parents tell them stories about how they were born or joined the family. In class they wrote about what they had learned. The process was then repeated so the children could get information about when they were one, two, three, four, and five years old. The children compiled autobiographies from their parents' stories, some of which were illustrated by photos they brought in from home. Understanding the process of writing an autobiography helps children learn how to read and interpret the genre.

Several books share ideas for helping children respond to folk literature (Blatt, 1993; Bosma, 1992). Marva Collins (1990) comments that "fairy tales and fables whet a child's appetite for more reading . . . an excellent means for teaching the rudiments of literary analysis" (p. 66). Haase (1993) points out, however, that we must help children become awakened from the powerless enchantment of fairy tales to discover their individual ownership of the tales. We claim fairy tales as our own with every individual act of telling and reading. When we share versions of fairy tales from all over the world and a wide range of fairy tales, we encourage diverse responses, questions, and significant comparisons that empower children to realize that these tales can be theirs.

Again, it is the way in which we involve children in folk literature that determines the quality of thinking and responding. Some teachers share parallel fairy tales, for example, but few emphasize the important ties between cultures and stories. Cianciolo (1993) reports:

> One teacher working in a school attended by children from various regions in the United States and foreign countries began the school year with an oral reading of folktales from each country or region represented in the class. . . . Within a few short weeks, she had honored every child with a reading of a folktale from his or her homeland or region. (p. 97)

Any teacher could do the same thing, since every child has cultural or ethnic roots. What a nice way to get to know children and their families and to make a strong statement about valuing diversity!

Young children need concrete support for understanding abstract ideas. Creating a *Comparison Chart* helps children understand the similarities and differences among stories by highlighting story elements, or motifs, that are repeated in story after story. Cianciolo (1993) reports that the chart is useful as a springboard for discussion and as a guide for reading, comparing, and categorizing the tales by motif and country. Primary grade children can collect folklore if they begin with their own jump rope rhymes, comparing different versions they know with ones their parents remember. They can collect family stories as well. Collecting literature makes children notice the details in a story and gives them a sense of ownership of the literature. Other "concrete" and creative activities intricately linked to folk literature include mask making, music and dance, and reader's theater (Bosma, 1992).

According to Roney (1993), "If folklore is the oldest form of literature, then storytelling may be the oldest medium of education" (p. 9). Primary grade children love to hear stories and can learn to tell them. Storytelling is a wonderful companion to story writing; children who can tell good stories can write them. In one school, all of the teachers learned one story to tell. For the month of October, the last twenty minutes of the day in that school were devoted to telling stories, with teachers traveling to a different classroom each day. The teachers' models led to lots of storytelling and story writing among the children in the school.

Folklore is richly illustrated and beautifully written in current children's literature. An emerging genre is the parody, or spinoff, of traditional folk literature. In order for children to respond in more than superficial ways to folktale spinoffs, the child has to first know the original tale. *The Cowboy and the Black-eyed Pea* (Johnston, 1992) may be a slightly humorous tale in its own right, but it is downright hilarious when readers recognize that its origin lies in the story of "The Princess and the Pea."

Predictable books are the bread and butter of a whole language reading program in the primary grades. Unfortunately, by the very nature of their simplicity, many are poorly written and not especially good models of children's literature. Recently published books, though, offer meaty content in clever formats to entertain and inform, as well as provide easy reading material. In *The Broody Hen* (Dunrea, 1993), the hen lays an egg on the rafters of a windmill, on the trough of the pig sty, on the roof of a dovecote, and on a hayrack in the barn, providing children with a host of new vocabulary in a rhyming, rhythmical, and humorous text. A cumulative rhyme, *The Heart of the Wood* (Davol, 1992), explains how a woodcarver creates a fiddle. *The Old Man and the Fiddle* (McCurdy, 1992) uses a rhyming refrain to tell the absurd story of a man who cares for fiddling over all else:

> Sunshine, moonshine, rainbow, and cloud
> Everything's right when the music is loud.

By memorizing easy-to-read texts, children can move naturally into matching their memorized speech to the print in texts. It is important that the books we present as predictable books share authentic language and experiences, and provide a model of good children's literature.

Author/Illustrator Studies

Carlene Harmon, a first grade teacher at Glen Springs Elementary School in Gainesville, Florida, credits author studies for generating high levels of response to literature in her classroom. When her children arrive in the morning, they write in dialogue journals. Some of them write stories, even though there is no requirement to do so. Then they read quietly for thirty minutes by themselves. Carlene reads with several children, taking notes on their progress. For the next fifteen minutes they read with a buddy, and for the final fifteen minutes Carlene reads aloud to the class. The children's writing is usually a spinoff of the literature. Carlene explains that the class studies different authors, such as Mercer Mayer, Eric Carle, and Steven Kellogg. The children use these authors' themes in their own writing. After they write a rough draft of a story, the class edits a few together, using the overhead projector. In the writing center, the children revise and edit the rough drafts. Student peer editors double check each other's stories. Since the books in Carlene's classroom are organized by author and placed in cardboard magazine holders labeled with the author's name, the students' writing is on the shelves and labeled the same way. The children love to read their classmates' books. The concept of being an author, therefore, transfers from the reading program to the writing program and back again.

Carlene explains that for each author they study, the children talk about the author's style and how the author wrote the story. Later, when the children write, they ask each other questions about the strategies they used. They ask themselves: How did the author do it? What else do I want to know about the story? This reflection process carries over into their future reading. Carlene comments:

> I believe that writing helps kids learn to read, because it forces them to listen to the sounds in words and put to use what they hear for a real purpose. The daily journal writing helps a lot because they think that it is important and they take a lot of time on it. I see them learn to read during quiet reading time. Practice is important. You can guide them, but they have to pick up on reading their own way as they actually read.

Samples of the children's writing shows that they have captured some classic story forms in the writing of their own stories. Sean begins his stories: "Once there was a dog named Dodger," "One day Funny Bear went out to be funnier than ever," "Once there was a boy named Sean who wished to be . . . ," and "One day a little penguin named Pip wobbled to the sea." In four stories, Sean uses two different conventions for starting a story and introducing the characters.

Katie, in the same class, sets the scene and uses dialogue in her story: "It was a rainy day. Bear and little bird was in the house and the rain stopped and there was a rainbow. 'Look,' said bear, 'There's a fire.' 'No nonsense, it's a rainbow.'

'No, it's a fire,' as he grabbed a pot." The story continues until the conflict is resolved and her characters live "happily ever after." Children who read stories learn story conventions and employ them when they write. Having a daily writing program for primary grade children can be one of the best opportunities for children to respond, even in unconscious ways, to literature.

Just as children feel empowered when they can identify the writing of an author, they are equally excited about recognizing the artwork of an illustrator. On the way to lunch, one second grader in Sharon Sanders' class (Pinellas County, Florida) yelled out, "Look, Miss Sanders, a Ruth Heller book that we haven't read yet!" Then he turned the book around and said, "False alarm. We've read it. Oh well, maybe she'll write a new one soon."

On another occasion, Sharon showed a videotape about Faith Ringgold, author of *Dinner at Aunt Connie's House* (1994), to her class and to two other second grade classes. As the video started up her students yelled out, "Look, it's Faith Ringgold!" One of the other teachers stopped the film to ask who Faith Ringgold was. Sharon reports, "Of course my kids were all too willing to educate her and offer to read our books to their classes." Children are vitally interested in people. Teachers capitalize on this interest when they make authors and illustrators come alive in the classroom.

A Cautionary Tale

The following account may provide some insight into the choices facing teachers for appropriate activities in the realm of a whole language literature response program.

Four first grade teachers decide to collaborate on author studies. Right after winter break, they launch forth on a project in which each class reads many of one author's books and writes to the authors about them, hoping to elicit a response. The teachers determine which authors will be studied by asking a local librarian for the names of authors who have published a large enough number of books and who might be inclined to respond to student-dictated letters. At the end of February, the parents are invited to a "literary tea." Hordes of parents arrive in the "centrium" of the kindergarten wing and beam as their children "perform" for them. Each teacher explains how the students became excited about the author under study, and has her class chant a class-written story modeled on the writing style of the author. Charts display which children have read each of the authors' books. Framed letters from the authors are attractively displayed.

As you read the above account, perhaps you felt as I did, that it was wonderful that these children were gaining an appreciation for a particular author's work, and that the literary tea and surrounding activities might be a school event long remembered by the children. Did you also wonder if spending a full two months studying one author might have limited the children's exposure to a wider variety of good literature? Did you wonder who the authors were who gained the attention of these students for such a long time? Not one of the authors was African American or

Latino, I noted. In the context of the characteristics, described in this chapter, of a whole language literature response program for the primary grades, how does this activity meet those criteria? Is the unit personally involving? To a degree. The children did cooperate to make a book; yet for some children the book making and stories might not have related to their life experiences. There was clearly a lot of teacher direction involved in the process. And each page of the children's books, though created by different children, had to fit into the whole; thus, all the pages looked remarkably similar. The activities did not empower the children, with the exception of the one in which they chanted the words to the story they had written. Being able to "read" a text made the children feel successful and empowered. The project also lacked authenticity, although avid readers sometimes do confine themselves to reading one author for a long period of time.

ESTABLISHING THE BOOK READING AND RESPONSE HABIT

If children are going to become avid readers and literate individuals, they need to develop the reading habit at home as well as at school.

Home Reading Programs

In the long run, it is not what happens in school that is important but what children do at home. In many homes, children do not have access to the number and kinds of books that real literacy development requires. In one survey I conducted, most of the books children had access to were the grocery store variety of literature, not exactly the best models of language, story, and illustration. It is important for teachers to provide children with good books to read at home until the children are able to fuel their own reading habits with books from the public library.

A technique used by Virginia Berry, a primary teacher in Gainesville, Florida, is to copy the words to predictable books onto blank "big books," and then invite the children to illustrate the pages. She attaches a class roster to the back of the book with a place for parents' comments. Students are eager to sign up to take the book home to read to their parents.

Teresa Carter, a first grade teacher in Gainesville, Florida, requires students to check out books daily for the WEB—Wonderfully Exciting Books—program. They bring home an index card with each book, on which they or their parents record the book title, author, what they liked about the book, and a picture. These cards are glued into students' WEB journals.

Blackburn Elementary School in Manatee County, Florida, initiated a

Read with Me program in which senior citizens and a local sorority made canvas book bags for each child in the school with the words "Read with Me" stenciled on them. The librarian gathered a box of books for each teacher, specifically for the home reading program. Children took books home every night and returned them in their special book bags the next day. In class, they shared their thoughts about the books they had read and exchanged books. One box of books lasted a month and then teachers switched boxes. Some of the teachers provided forms for the parents and children to use for responding to the books.

Libraries

Children usually have access to three libraries: the classroom library, the school media center, and the public library. They can apply strategies they learn in their classroom to other library settings. Teresa Carter notes that her first graders check out nonfiction books most often; primary grade children have an intense curiosity about real things, events, and places. Yet most classroom libraries contain exclusively fiction books. Inviting children to organize, monitor, and straighten up the classroom library teaches them, in a limited way, to value the library collection and the process of how a library system works.

Children also need access to a school media center when, for example, they are working on projects or reports, or when they are trying to find good books to read. Instruction in how to use the available resources should be given on the occasions when the class is engaged in activities requiring those resources.

Experiences in class and school libraries pave the way for use of the public library. Children rely on public libraries for books not only during the summer school break but also in the evening, when the school library is closed. They also need public libraries to find resources not available in the school media center. If librarians from public libraries are able to visit the classroom and help children obtain library cards, children will become more enthusiastic users of this public resource. A class field trip to the local public library or bookmobile, especially when there is a need for materials located there, is also an effective strategy.

Libraries offer many opportunities for responses to literature in a setting that is somewhat more formal than that of the classroom. Children's book reviews can be posted on a bulletin board for other children to consider as they are selecting books. Librarians can coordinate videotaped reviews of books in the Reading Rainbow model for transmission into other classrooms in the school. Librarians provide an informed audience for book discussions.

Extensive Reading Programs

In many primary grade classrooms, children spend some time each day reading silently or, in the case of young readers, reading quietly, since it is difficult for children who are beginning to learn how to read to be silent readers. Programs like Sustained Silent Reading (SSR) and Drop Everything and Read (DEAR) provide children with practice that sustains their independent reading. Typically, these programs require that teachers model silent reading and that children share, but not be tested on, what they read. During the children's sharing, teachers gain insight into children's responses to books they read independently. These responses may be very different from their responses to books read aloud, with book buddies, or in small groups, because the interaction with others can influence children's thinking about books.

ASSESSING CHILDREN'S RESPONSES TO LITERATURE

In a whole language program, assessment serves two purposes. It helps children (and their parents, teachers, and school) to see and interpret growth, and it helps teachers to learn what materials and activities are useful and how to work with them to sustain children's learning. Assessment, in the context of a literature response program, is an ongoing part of instruction rather than a competition for grades. If teachers are operating their whole language program in a school district that requires grades on report cards, holistic measures can be transferred into grades.

Assessments need to include both process and products. Children can take responsibility for recording the books that they read and note how well they liked the books. Periodically, they can analyze their list to learn how much and what kind of reading they are doing. Are the books all of the same type? Are some more challenging than others? Are they all on the same topic? Are they all by the same author? Children can then plan to broaden their reading selections or to focus on an author, theme, or genre. When children set goals for their personal reading, for example, assessment can include explanations of how they met their goals.

In a similar manner, children can examine their responses to literature. If responses are written (in a journal or a reading log), children can determine if the responses are repetitive or if they change according to the various book selections. Children can reread their responses to assess whether or not they include honest and frank opinions, mention of literary elements and linkages with other literature, or personal experiences expressed as a basis for opinions. Storytelling is an excellent way to assess children's responses to literature because teachers can note which elements of literature from the original appear in the child's version. They can note how children apply story structure in an authentic situation. Another valued assessment tool (and much-appreciated gift for parents) is a collection of the stories their children have read and told throughout the school year, recorded on cassette tape.

Children can collect artifacts like literature logs, projects that are responses to literature, and storytelling tapes in portfolios that demonstrate their growth, but it is important to make the portfolios more than simply a random collection. Children can review the materials they have worked on and select examples of their best work for their portfolios. They can use portfolio material to set new goals and to analyze effective strategies for promoting their own learning. By reflecting on their work, children add a new dimension to the learning process.

Observation is another key element in assessment. Teachers can take notes about their students' behavior, keeping these notes in their own portfolios and using them to interpret the students' progress. Sometimes, however, teachers overwhelm themselves with note-taking. It helps to think of this kind of portfolio as if it were a "baby book" in which significant observations can be recorded, not every little event that occurs in the classroom. Teachers can observe whether or not their students are enthusiastic about writing and about sharing their responses. They can record interesting and surprising comments that appear in students' journals. One of the best assessment tools for a literature program is an analysis of the children's writing of their own stories and poems.

Evaluate literature discussion groups by observing them. Are the students equally participating or are some dominating the discussion? Are the students looking at each other or at the teacher? If the teacher is the focus of the attention, then his or her voice is still the dominant one in the group. To what degree are literary elements emerging in the discussions? Do children share honest and frank views about issues? Do children accept one another's opinions? Are the attitudes expressed enthusiastic and positive? At the end of each discussion, teachers can ask the students to rate the discussion on a scale of 1–5, and to explain the reasons for their score. When children share their opinions and critical judgments they will learn pointers for making future discussions even better than the previous ones.

Observation is also the best way to note the strategies children use when selecting books and reading. A checklist of strategies can simplify the process of recording this information. Sometimes it helps to interview children, or to poll their parents to learn about their responses to literature outside school. Children give us amazing insights when we ask them about how they learn and how they feel about school activities.

SUSTAINING THE PROGRAM

In relation to how teachers can improve their effectiveness in literature programs, Smith (1990) explains that:

> Teachers must know literature from the inside out. . . . Therefore, I believe the most critical thing that teachers of literature need to do is to read and then read some more. Additionally, we need to form discussion groups in order to share in the lived-through experiences of others. Furthermore, we need to reflect on our own response processes so that we can understand what it means to respond reflectively and critically. We need to refresh our understandings of the structure of story and the elements that make up a story. (p. 26)

Teresa Carter, a first grade teacher in Gainesville, Florida, suggests that one of the most important things to do is to find a support system. Reader's groups, Teachers Applying Whole Language (TAWL) groups, local reading associations, and informal school teams can provide the networking that keeps any program innovation fresh and inspiring.

Teresa lists the obstacles teachers must overcome to operate a successful literature response program. She comments that teachers have to learn to trust themselves and to realize that they know what is best for their students. Teachers need to be reflective, always analyzing what is going on in their classroom and why. She says that, in the long run, teachers are the ones best informed to make judgments about how their class of children learns best. Teresa says you need to realize that you are always growing; you're never *there*. "If you're there, you need to get out, because that means you're not reflecting."

Finally, Teresa says that whole language is a belief about the way kids learn and that this belief takes time to grow. We need to be patient with ourselves and not expect perfection the first time we try something new. Most of us have been educated under teacher dissemination models of teaching, and we are naturally inclined to teach the way we have been taught. It takes a lot of reading, thinking, networking, and reflecting to gradually accommodate a radically different theoretical base for our instruction. Allowing children to socially construct knowledge by responding to literature shows that you value individuality and diversity instead of rewarding conformity.

The good news is that the children will lead the way if we listen to them and ask their advice about how they learn best. One of the joys of teaching is watching in awe as children respond in enthusiastic and fascinating ways to children's literature.

NOTES

1. The following master's degree students at the University of Florida assisted with the preparation of this chapter: Christy Davis, Jennifer Fannin, Melissa Isaacson, Robin Jones, Jonda McNair, Lorrie Wren, and Amy Zele.

2. Jan Brett also welcomes mail from her readers. Her address is: 132 Pleasant Street, Norwell, MA 02061.

REFERENCES

Barone, D. (1990). The written responses of young children: Beyond comprehension to story understanding. *The New Advocate, 3* (1), 49–55.

Blatt, G. T. (1993). Introduction: Children and folklore. In G. T. Blatt (Ed.), *Once upon a folktale* (pp. 1–6). New York: Teachers College Press.

Bosma, B. (1992). *Fairy tales, fables, legends, and myths: Using folk literature in your classroom.* New York: Teachers College Press.

Cianciolo, P. (1993). Folktale variants: Links to the never-ending chain. In G. T. Blatt (Ed.), *Once upon a folktale* (pp. 97–108). New York: Teachers College Press.

Collins, M., & Tamarkin, C. (1990). *Marva Collins' way.* Jeremy P. Tarcher.

Danielson, K. E. (1992). Literature groups and literature logs: Responding to literature in a community of readers. *Reading Horizons, 32* (5), 372–382.

Edmiston, B. (1993). Going up the beanstalk: Discovering giant possibilities for responding to literature through drama. In K. Holland, R. Hungerford, & S. Ernst (Eds.), *Journeying: Children responding to literature* (pp. 250–266). Portsmouth, NH: Heinemann.

Haase, D. (1993). Motifs: Making fairy tales our own. In G. T. Blatt (Ed.), *Once upon a folktale* (pp. 63–77). New York: Teachers College Press.

Harwayne, S. (February, 1994). The impact of literature on writing. Keynote Address at the Alachua County TAWL (Teachers Applying Whole Language) meeting, Gainesville, Florida.

Henry, A. (1992). Book selection strategies of fourth grade students. Unpublished doctoral (Ed.D.) dissertation, University of Florida.

Keenan, J. W. (1993). The Jolly Postman comes to call: Primary writers' response to literature. In K. Holland, R. Hungerford, & S. Ernst (Eds.), *Journeying: Children responding to literature* (pp. 72–88). Portsmouth, NH: Heinemann.

Keifer, B. (1993). Children's responses to picture books: A developmental perspective. In K. Holland, R. Hungerford, & S. Ernst (Eds.), *Journeying: Children responding to literature* (pp. 267–283). Portsmouth, NH: Heinemann.

Lamme, L. (1992). *Literature-based moral education.* Phoenix, AZ: Oryx.

Lehr, S. (1991). *The child's developing sense of theme: Responses to literature.* New York: Teachers College Press.

Peterson, R., & Eeds, M. (1990). *Grand conversations: Literature groups in action.* New York: Scholastic.

Roney, R. (1993). Telling stories: A key to reading and writing. In G. T. Blatt (Ed.), *Once upon a folktale* (pp. 9–23). New York: Teachers College Press.

Rosenblatt, L. M. (1978). *The reader, the text, the poem: The transactional theory of the literary work.* Carbondale, IL: Southern Illinois University Press.

Routman, R. (1991). *Invitations.* Portsmouth, NH: Heinemann.

Smith, K. (1990). Entertaining a text: A reciprocal process. In K. G. Short & K. M. Pierce (Eds.), *Talking about books* (pp. 17–31). Portsmouth, NH: Heinemann.

Soundy, C. S. (1993). Let the story begin: Open the box and set out the props. *Childhood Education, 69* (3), 146–149.

Tiballi, B., & Drake, L. (1993). Literature groups: A model of the transactional process. *Childhood Education, 69* (4), 221–224.

Children's Book References

Ahlberg, J., & Ahlberg, A. (1986). *The jolly postman.* Boston: Little Brown.

Albert, B. (1991). *Where does the trail lead?* Illus. by Brian Pinkney. New York: Simon & Schuster.

Aylesworth, J. (1992a). *The cat & the fiddle & more.* Illus. by Richard Hull. New York: Atheneum.

Aylesworth, J. (1992b). *Old black fly.* Illus. by Stephen Gammell. New York: Holt.

Aylesworth, J. (1994). *My son John.* Illus. by David Frampton. New York: Holt.

Bartone, E. (1993). *Peppe the lamplighter.* Illus. by Ted Lewin. New York: Lothrop.

Brett, J. (1993). *Trouble with trolls.* New York: Putnam.

Bunting, E. (1990). *The wall.* Illus. by Ronald Himler. New York: Clarion.

Bunting, E. (1991). *Fly away home.* Illus. by Ronald Himler. New York: Clarion.

Davol, M. (1992). *The heart of the wood.* Illus. by Sheila Hamanaka. New York: Simon & Schuster.

Dunrea, O. (1992). *The broody hen.* New York: Doubleday.

Heide, F. P., & Gilliland, J. H. (1990). *The day of Ahmed's secret.* Illus. by Ted Lewin. New York: Lothrop, Lee, & Shepard.

Hoffman, M. (1991). *Amazing grace.* Illus. by Carol Binch. New York: Dial.

Isadora, R. (1991). *At the crossroads.* New York: Greenwillow.

Johnston, T. (1992). *The cowboy and the black-eyed pea.* Illus. by Warren Ludwig. New York: Putnam.

Joyce, W. (1992). *Bentley & egg.* New York: HarperCollins.

Martin, B., Jr., & Archaumbault, J. (1987). *Knots on a counting rope.* Illus. by Ted Rand. New York: Holt.

McCurdy, M. (1992). *The old man and the fiddle.* New York: Putnam.

Mitchelll, M. K. (1993). *Uncle Jed's barbershop.* New York: Simon and Schuster.

Ringgold, F. (1994). *Dinner at Aunt Connie's house.* New York: Hyperion.

Schwartz, A. (1992). *And the green grass grew all around: Folk poetry from everyone.* Illus. by Sue Truesdell. New York: HarperCollins.

Van Allsburg, C. (1987). *The Z was zapped: A play in 26 acts.* Boston: Houghton Mifflin.

Van Laan, N. (1990). *Possum come-a-knockin'.* Illus. G. Booth. New York: Alfred A. Knopf.

Waber, B. (1972). *Ira sleeps over.* Boston: Houghton Mifflin.

Williams, K. L. (1993). *When Africa was home.* New York: Lothrop.

Yolen, J. (1987). *Owl moon.* Illus. by John Schoenherr. New York: Philomel.

6

Whole Language in Play and the Expressive Arts

JOAN P. ISENBERG

A major premise of whole language is that literacy develops through purposeful communication in specific social and cultural situations. Using play and the expressive arts as significant contexts for communication acknowledges the many ways children come to know about their world. These ways of knowing are central to good early childhood practice and to whole language philosophy because they are "rooted in child-centered, integrated, and whole-child experiences" (Whitmore & Goodman, 1992, p. 21).

Yet, mere exposure to these forms of communication is not enough. Only through systematic design can whole language teachers help children express their ideas through different avenues. A literacy classroom that utilizes play, art, and music as serious forms of communication opens the way for children to reach their full potential as whole human beings. To be conversant with these forms of communication is essential to becoming a more literate person.

In the agenda for school reform, the national legislation *Goals 2000: Educate America Act* (U.S. Dept. of Education, 1994) acknowledges the need for alternative forms of communication. Educational experiences involving play, art, and music have the power to transcend barriers of language, culture, race, and ethnicity, making communication accessible to as many people as possible.

This chapter affirms the role of play and the expressive arts in a whole language primary classroom as fundamental to the way teachers teach and to how children learn. It begins with an examination of play in relation to literacy learning; it then examines art and music as central forms of communication within a whole language primary classroom.

CONFRONTING MISUNDERSTANDINGS ABOUT PLAY

Play is one of the most misleading and misunderstood terms in our language. Many teachers associate it with frivolous, non-productive behavior that has no place in school-based learning. However, current literature on the role of play in human development contradicts this perception (Bredekamp, 1986; Garvey, 1977; Isenberg & Jalongo, 1993; Isenberg & Quisenberry, 1988; Piaget, 1985; Vygotsky, 1978; Wassermann, 1990). These researchers affirm that play:

- Is children's way of thinking about their world
- Encourages risk-taking behavior and active learning
- Challenges flexible and open thinking
- Develops language and literacy abilities
- Increases children's social and cultural understandings through encountering the perspectives of others
- Encourages children to negotiate and work cooperatively
- Enables children to express their ideas and feelings
- Provides opportunities for authentic problem solving
- Builds self-confidence and respect for others

Despite the fact that play empowers children as learners, it is still seriously misunderstood. Two of the most typical misunderstandings concerning play in the primary curriculum are that it lacks content and that it lacks structure (Daiute, 1991).

Content

When children use play to challenge themselves, design their own lessons, and test themselves, they are using what they know to develop important concepts of the curriculum rather than focusing on remembering minor facts and details. After reading *Little House on the Prairie* (Wilder, 1941) as part of a project on pioneers, a group of third graders decided to build a model of a house of the 1800s. Using Legos and art materials that the teacher made available, the third graders built a house following the nine steps described in their book. They designed and labeled each step, beginning with collecting the wagon logs and ending with "moving in." The students' three-dimensional, illustrated model revealed their detailed understanding, gained from their reading, of how pioneers built their houses (e.g., making skids to roll logs). In essence, they tested and evaluated themselves, through a play setting, on how to build a house in the 1800s. Encouraging children to "play out" their understandings invites children to communicate them in a different way while at the same time respecting the children as learners.

Structure

A second misunderstanding about play concerns structure. The literature on play shows that there is indeed structure to play-based learning for primary grade children. While the structure of activity looks different from the traditional classroom—where children work alone and are seated in rows of desks—there is, nevertheless, structure. In a classroom that fosters literacy through play, teachers encourage children to work in small groups and engage in playful exploration of the subject matter. A glimpse into one first grade teacher's classroom illustrates this notion. In a unit on communication, Jennifer Poulin, a first grade teacher, set up a facsimile of a television news station in her classroom to help the children become familiar with current events while developing and using literacy behaviors. After a field trip to the local television station, she introduced a learning station in which children could enact what they had learned at the television news studio. She provided a prop box containing authentic materials (e.g., camera, tripod, old video camera, scripts, clipboards, desk microphones, pens, charts, badges). In the learning station, some children assumed the roles of reporters and wrote lengthy news reports of sports events, weather, and a parade that had occurred in their community. Others read news releases that they or another reporter had written. Still others discovered dressing rooms and enacted roles associated with preparing to be filmed.

The holistic structure in this whole language first grade was provided by the materials, the time allotted for playful activity, the common goals of communication, and the children's knowledge about themselves and the community. When children wrote news reports with classmates, for example, they used their own language, lingered over aspects that interested them, and experienced rich personal and public writing opportunities (Ruddell, 1992). Thus, the children themselves were designing the curriculum and adapting it to what they knew. Far from being chaotic, children's play in school is remarkably structured, on-task, absorbing, and elaborated (Daiute, 1989).

Clarifying the misunderstandings about play is a central issue for whole language teachers. Teachers who are conversant with the reasons for incorporating play into whole language classrooms articulate its value and advocate it for children's literacy learning. Teachers who are not conversant with this knowledge easily capitulate to pressure from administrators and parents and, unfortunately, deprive primary grade children of the opportunity to learn through a most powerful tool—play in the classroom.

WHY PLAY IS CENTRAL TO THE CURRICULUM

Teachers need to know which strategies and experiences further literacy for primary children. It is equally essential for them to know how, why, and when to use play to develop literacy skills and concepts (Bredekamp & Rosegrant, 1992). Play contributes to children's growth across areas of development; it increases children's imagery; and it serves as an effective learning strategy.

Growth Across Areas of Development

The theories of Erikson (1950), Piaget (1985), and Vygotsky (1978) form the basic understandings of how children develop and learn through play. In school-based play, primary children have occasions to construct knowledge and to develop and practice newly acquired skills and concepts. Through active exploration, participation, and investigation with people and materials, children enhance their cognitive development. By working together in cooperative groups, they increase their social competence and engage in divergent and innovative thinking. They also learn how to express and cope with feelings and emotions. Through active use of their bodies, children learn to "feel physically confident, secure, and self-assured" (Isenberg & Quisenberry, 1988, p. 139). Concept development, meaning making, and risk taking in play are also required as the children learn to be readers and writers.

Colette Daiute (1991) illustrates these three principles in the following description of a playful conversation between two third grade boys exploring the sounds of Christopher Columbus' name.

RUSS: Put, Mr. Columbus.
ANDY: Mr. Columbus.
RUSS: Columulumbus.
ANDY: Column, Columbumps (Laughter).
RUSS: Colum.
ANDY: Columnus? Column, Cloum, Come, Columbus?
RUSS: Lumberjack (Laughter).
ANDY: Colombos, Columbus, Columbus.
RUSS: Colummmmbababababbb. Ohew. B U S I think that's how you spell it . . .
ANDY: Col-um-bus. Ya, you're right.
RUSS: Christopher Columbus. Collumm. (Daiute, 1991, p. 31)

In this interaction, both boys demonstrated their conceptual knowledge of spelling rules by playing with the sounds of Columbus' name, an unfamiliar spelling word. They revealed their spontaneous understandings

(Vygotsky, 1978) of these rules by playing with the sounds and word parts, testing different sound combinations, and arriving at an orthographically correct spelling. Spontaneous understandings are those concepts that children figure out mentally by themselves by direct experience without assistance from adults; they parallel Piaget's (1985) notion of construction of knowledge. Being able to play with the material enabled Andy and Russ to take risks in their own learning in a setting other than a teacher-directed, formal spelling lesson. In their writing, they made meaning from the rules underlying our written language system. This self-directed, playful activity is necessary for conceptual development and construction of knowledge. Whole language teachers view this kind of experience as essential to literacy learning because "these systems reflect children's current theories of how language works" (Ruddell, 1992, p. 613).

Whole language teachers—who focus on broad opportunities for communication—help children make sense of their own knowledge. They accept children for what they "can do" and what they "already know," rather than for what they "should know" (Fulwiler, 1992, p. 31).

Play as Imagery

In play situations, children use symbols to represent objects, actions, and ideas that are not directly present. This symbolic ability has a direct relationship to reading and writing. Children who have experienced a variety of play contexts easily ascribe meaning from their own world to the world of print and literacy (Genishi, 1985; Isenberg & Jacob, 1983).

Imagery, the ability to create mental pictures, is essential to reading for comprehension (May, 1994). Reading for meaning requires that readers picture in their minds what authors are writing. Those images not only depend on the text but also on what the reader brings to the text (i.e., past experiences and present understandings).

The ability to create images to aid meaning is particularly critical for content-area reading (May, 1994). A good example comes from a second grade classroom where the children had been studying outer space. The teacher had created a large play area with blocks and other building and writing materials in which the children could enact their growing understandings of the world of space. The second graders created and used space suits, a mission control center, space food, and navigational maps as part of their inquiry groups. Their teacher reported that the stories they wrote about their imaginary visits to another planet were richer in detail, deeper in characterization, more descriptive in setting, and more logically oriented than she had ever experienced while teaching this unit to other second graders. As she said:

The only thing I changed was the inclusion of a space play area. It contributed greatly to their deep understandings of the concepts involved in space travel. I saw the children take risks, negotiate roles, and solve problems as they used what they were reading about in their inquiry groups as part of their play to consolidate their learnings. The traditionally complex tasks of reading and writing became more natural for them once the occasions for play were introduced.

The teacher's observations affirm that the very components needed to be successful players (e.g., negotiating roles, taking risks, solving problems) are the same components that contribute to strong readers and writers.

Play as an Effective Learning Strategy

One of the most important tasks for whole language teachers is to foster children's meaning making. Consider this scenario from Shawneen Petersen's third grade class. The children were exploring different island communities to increase their global awareness. Throughout her unit, they read books, such as *The Little Island* (MacDonald, 1946); *My Little Island* (Lessac, 1984); *As the Crow Flies* (Hartman, 1991); and *Island of the Blue Dolphins* (O'Dell, 1990). They also kept travel logs containing interesting facts and discoveries, made story maps in cooperative groups detailing characters' travels in *My Little Island,* and constructed a K-W-L chart on islands as a basis for finding out what they knew and what they needed to know to compile a data-retrieval chart. (See Chapter 2 for a discussion of K-W-L charts.) They compared and contrasted experiences about life in their school/community with life in other island schools/communities, such as Taiwan and Montserrat.

As part of their math/science program they played cooperative problem-solving games, such as "Island Hop," and conducted disappearing island experiments as they observed water breaking up rocks. In art/music they critically discussed the jungle paintings of Henri Rousseau and created their own tropical island collages using construction paper; danced the "Tinkling" dance from the Philippine Islands; and created a song parody of "Tingalayo." In social studies, they created a travel agency with travel posters and vacation tours. As a culmination to this captivating thematic unit, the children invented, constructed, and played original "island" board games in small groups. Having had previous experience playing board games and working in cooperative groups, these third graders were already familiar with shared experiences. To create their games, each three-member group needed to negotiate ideas for their particular game, create a draft, and work together to form a board game that they could play with their peers. One group created "Island Monopoly" and included fact cards on clothing, weather, foods, and transportation for seven different islands.

The experiences and activities in Shawneen's classroom illustrate the following three factors that make play an effective learning strategy for literacy learning: ownership, sense making, and risk taking.

TAKING OWNERSHIP OF CONTENT. These third graders used the information about different island communities in a meaningful game. Their teacher easily determined what they had learned by viewing the game board and question cards. Some of their cards asked questions about special foods (e.g., guavas, mangoes, and soursops); climate zones and sources for determining the climate (e.g., globe, atlas, island books); population; clothing; and tourist attractions. Through self-selection of topics and personal accountability to the group, these third graders moved toward "independence, self-direction, and the development of metacognition" (Ruddell, 1992, p. 613). These conditions are necessary for children's continuing language growth.

MAKING SENSE OF INFORMATION. A second reason that play is an effective learning strategy is that it helps children make sense of new information. Working together in cooperative groups to make their island games and story maps helped these third graders "make sense" of life in different island communities. Making sense of print is the primary force behind reading growth. As the third graders illustrated story maps about *My Little Island*, for example, they used information from this story, told through the eyes of a child, to take a cultural visit to the island of Montserrat. Their fascination with the names of available fruits, animals, and transportation was clear as they incorporated these unique cultural artifacts into their invented games. The opportunity to play with knowledge—to try out and test new concepts and facts—contributed to deeper understandings of island cultures.

TAKING RISKS. There is a strong relationship between risk taking and literate behavior. In their travel agency, these third graders designed travel posters, wrote travel information for prospective travelers about their island, created travel brochures, and made models of interesting tourist attractions. In this dramatic play opportunity, the children reenacted what they knew about the islands (e.g., climate, food, tourist attractions, special vocabulary) and explored different roles (e.g., travel agent, tour operator, traveler) in low-risk settings. This context differs significantly from formal contexts in which children are less likely to take such risks. In dramatic play contexts, all children can take up the challenge of playing with new knowledge, new roles, and new ideas (Daiute, 1991).

We have seen in this third grade class how play can be an effective strategy in whole language classrooms. It supports children's use of their own knowledge as a springboard for learning because it makes sense to them; it encourages risk taking, an essential component of the reading process; and it provides a social context for learning in the company of peers while supporting intellectual development. To accomplish this goal, the climate of the whole language classroom must be conducive to play.

INVITATIONS TO PLAY

Teachers who provide children with purposeful experiences in whole language primary grades invite children's expression and communication. Whether and how teachers invite children to play determines how enriched it will be. Invitations can be extended through the daily schedule, the classroom environment, and the amount of encouragement teachers provide.

Arranging a Schedule to Include Play

A schedule for play includes play experiences as central to, rather than in addition to, the core curriculum. Selma Wassermann (1990) suggests that the school day for the primary grade child should begin with a 45–60-minute free choice time block during which children engage in productive learning experiences. She calls this time period *Breathing Out*. "No matter what the shape of the day, breathing out is the preferred starting point" (Wassermann, 1990, p. 67). This critical transition time from home to school enables children to "unpack" their ideas and thoughts. Once children are comfortable in a Breathing Out routine, the teacher can then use the time for other literacy activities (e.g., buddy reading, individual reading, mini-lessons) that need attention.

Visiting Gail Ritchie's first grade classroom, where Breathing Out is institutionalized, you might see the schedule shown in Table 6.1.

As the children arrive, they place their homework and notes from home in the "homework" basket and are greeted warmly by their teacher. They put their coats away and then choose a destination from among the many investigative centers and materials in the classroom. On this day, four children were working together on the computer and using *Kid Pix* (Hickman, 1991), a computer program that enables them to plan a variety of designs, to guess what animal is hidden in a picture, and print out their creations. Children described their creations as "awesome" and helped one another with the printing functions. In the Library Area, two girls were reading books to stuffed animals, taken from a basket of stuffed animals in

Table 6.1. *First Grade Schedule*

8:18–9:15	Breathing Out
9:15	Groups and Language Arts
10:00	Bathroom
10:15	Lang. Arts/ Music/ Playground
11:30	Lunch
12:15	Breathing In, Story, and Lang. Arts
1:15	Math
2:15	Reading Rainbow
2:45	Wrap Up
3:00	Dismissal

Note: Adapted from Wassermann, 1990.

the corner. Jill said to Rashida, "I'll help you find the book about the little house that you were looking for yesterday."

On the Discovery Table, in the center of the room, there were jars containing teeth immersed in a cola drink, a magnifier, and teeth molds. Near the jars, the teacher had written some notes asking the children to predict what would happen to the teeth in the cola. In the construction area, several children were building with manipulatives—making shelters for their animals—while two other children were "playing school" and pointing to the words and phrases on a poetry chart of Jack Prelutsky's poem, "Loose Tooth."

In the Writing Center, one first grader chose to copy a poem from the poetry book to hang on the Poet Tree. Others could choose from easel painting, chalk board writing, or forms of writing. During this time, Mrs. Ritchie heard five children read and took running records of their oral reading.

After making the transition from the Breathing Out period to a *Breathing In* period with a song to take them through clean-up, the children gathered on the rug. This is the time for traditional morning activities (e.g., calendar, weather, daily schedule, morning news) as well as for other group activities that support their morning investigations. On this particular day, the children and the teacher enacted "Loose Tooth," recorded their predictions of the tooth, engaged in shared reading of original stories, played a word game, and read a story aloud to the class.

The Breathing In period is the instructional time in whole language activities (Wassermann, 1990). Here, children engage in individual, small group, and flexible group language activity. An alternative schedule for a second or third grade that would begin with a Breathing Out block might look like the one in Table 6.2.

Using this approach enables children to learn together, to interact with the teacher, and to self-select projects. It provides the teacher with time to observe and assess children and to work with individuals and small

Table 6.2. *Second Grade Schedule*

8:15	Free Choice
8:30	Breathing Out: Investigative Centers
10:00	Cleanup
10:15	Group Time
10:30	Outdoors
10:45	Science
12:00	Lunch
1:00	Language Arts
2:00	Math
2:45	Cleanup/Music/Dismissal

Note: Adapted from Wassermann, 1990.

groups. Studies of classrooms using Breathing Out indicate that children actually increased their levels of achievement. According to Wassermann (1990), "breathing out is an emotionally, socially, and intellectually responsible way of beginning the school day" (p. 67) because it empowers children through choices.

Several primary grade teachers in my area are trying the Breathing Out technique. They have shared comments like, "In all my years of teaching, this has been my easiest," or "I can't believe how much more the children are learning and I am teaching since I changed my schedule to include Breathing Out. I'll never go back to my old schedule." Another teacher talked about how the tone of the classroom had changed.

> With Breathing Out, I see the children beginning their long day happily. They are sharing and playing with lots of different children rather than building cliques. Something that really stands out is the development of the children's writing and spelling skills. Previously, I had a daily writer's workshop and I continue to do this. But now many of the children are writing in the morning and in the afternoon writer's workshop. The practice they are getting from free choice time has improved their written expression.

Encouraging Players

Teachers in whole language classrooms also invite children's play by supporting their construction and co-construction knowledge. These teachers believe that learning is a social process (Vygotsky, 1978); they urge children to converse and to listen to others in order to communicate with everybody in the classroom. In Gail Ritchie's first grade classroom, described earlier, she encouraged children's conversations and interactions by providing large blocks of time that children could share with one another. Children in that room knew that their teacher valued their choices and their ideas.

Whole language teachers also respond to individuals' ideas and use the children's ideas to press their thinking. Sometimes teachers record children's responses and encourage new questions and insights; sometimes they listen and clarify children's conversations; and other times they help children generate future questions or hypotheses from their investigations to continue on with deeper activity (Edwards, Gandini, & Forman, 1993). In this same class, during the group meeting, Mrs. Ritchie recorded children's predictions about the teeth in the cola and used that data to motivate further group questions, investigations, and activity.

Teachers also encourage children's play through their observations. Good teacher observers can determine: (1) whether or not children need help with a problem; (2) if the materials are adequately stimulating and inviting; and (3) how play situations are contributing to children's developing social, motor, and cognitive skills. Knowing how to use the information from observations is more important than knowing that teachers must be good observers of children.

The following interchange between two first graders during free choice time illustrates how Liz Klein, another first grade teacher, assumed the role of observer and listener, enabling children to support one another.

> THEA: Let's make books. I'll help you spell the words.
> JAMIE: I don't know what to write about.
> THEA: I'll help you spell the words. We is W E. Like is L I K E. To is T O. Play is P L A Y.
> JAMIE: I don't know what to draw.
> THEA: I'll help you. You know this summer I couldn't read or spell. I don't know what happened. Just like that (throwing up her hands) it happened. It will happen to you, too, Jamie.

When Jamie does not proceed on her own, Thea starts to help her. Their play continues on until finally Jamie and Thea work together on one page of a book.

In this class, Liz observed this lengthy interaction but chose not to intervene. She did, however, ask the girls to share their book with the class when the group came together at the end of the day. Being able to watch children helps teachers grow in their understanding of who the children are, what point they have reached in their learning, and where they need to go next. When whole language teachers use their observations of children's learning to frame curriculum, they see "their students as sense makers and mediators of their own knowledge . . . [and] approach curriculum as an evocative and open-ended phenomenon" (Fulwiler, 1992, p. 32). Thus, whole language teachers "serve as the children's partners, sustaining the children, and offering assistance, resources, and strategies to get unstuck when encountering difficulties" (Edwards et al., 1993, p. 157).

Classroom Environment

In addition to arranging the schedule and encouraging players, the third way to issue invitations to play is through the environment. The message conveyed to children as teachers move from behind what Nancie Atwell (1987) calls "the big desk" to a different kind of environment that creates a classroom community is a powerful one. Three basic features of classroom environments that support children's play and self-expression are climate, space, and time (Garreau & Kennedy, 1991; Isenberg & Jalongo, 1993; Jones, 1977; Phye-Perkins, 1980).

1. *Climate* refers to the feeling one gets from the environment and dictates to what extent children can be productive learners. It includes design features that evoke a warm, homelike atmosphere, like carpeted areas; materials that challenge children's thinking and conversation and support their projects; teachers who care and support children's efforts; and children who are "absorbed in learning, have choices, and make decisions about work to be done" (Isenberg & Jalongo, 1993, pp. 174–175).
2. *Space* includes how the physical environment is developed to provoke creative thinkers so that children take hold of their own learning. Whole language teachers foster children's independence by arranging materials and supplies in regular storage places; instituting favorite and private reading corners; and defining enough space for group times (Isenberg & Jalongo, 1993).
3. *Time* sends the message of how important activities are. When children have long blocks of time, their play "is more constructive, cooperative, and expressive than with short, interrupted time periods" (Isenberg & Jalongo, 1993, p. 176). In addition, children must experience regular daily routines (e.g., arrival time rituals, class meetings, Breathing Out, read-alouds). The regularity and predictability of such rituals enhances children's independence and opens the door for children's energy in more creative endeavors.

Clearly, the elements of climate, space, and time are powerful invitations to children's self-expression. The physical features, the organization of the group, and the roles of the teacher affect children's ability to concentrate and reflect on their work. To better understand the dynamic nature of play in a whole language primary classroom, it is necessary to understand the types of play typically attributed to the school-aged child.

TYPES OF PLAY IN PRIMARY CLASSROOMS

Some typical play activities that are universal, cross cultural, and developmental for school-age children are language play, constructive play, and games with rules.

LANGUAGE PLAY.   In language play, elementary children play symbolically with age appropriate, socially acceptable mental games, such as riddles, number games, and secret codes (Bergen, 1988; Sutton-Smith, 1980). Children's spontaneous play with materials, including language, paves the way for their development. Given the freedom to work on challenging tasks with their peers, school-age children invent useful lessons as part of their classroom play. A good example is the humor children enjoy in riddles and jokes. First graders are intrigued by the absurdity of the sound ambiguity in "knock knock" jokes. They also enjoy manipulating language in ways previously impossible, as in the lyrics of Raffi songs like "I like to eat, eat, eat apples and bananas; I like to oat, oat, oat oaples and banonos." Second graders, on the other hand, like ambiguous jokes, such as "knock knock" jokes, idioms, and homonyms. A popular book among 7-year-olds is Fred Gwynne's *The King Who Rained* (1970), in which a king is seen floating like a cloud with rain pouring from his royal robes. Third graders particularly enjoy enacting humorous scripts involving multiple meanings and rhymes.

CONSTRUCTIVE PLAY.   In constructive play, children create something according to a preconceived plan, such as a mural or a mobile. They know how to make murals and mobiles and choose to make them as a way of playing. In order to qualify as play, however, children must freely *choose* to do the activity, and find it pleasurable. A good example is the pioneer house built by the third graders described earlier in this chapter.

GAMES WITH RULES.   In games with rules, children focus on prearranged rules that guide acceptable play behavior. These are the most popular games for school-age children. Their more logical ways of thinking and advancing social skills make it possible for them to follow a set of rules and negotiate with peers. Games with rules take priority in the life of school-age children.
     Connie Kamii (1985, 1989) has written extensively about the value of games—as compared to worksheets—for enhancing children's mathematical understandings. Games are also a natural learning vehicle in the whole language classroom because they provide immediate and specific feedback in a cooperative learning context. They are intrinsically motivating, offer opportunities to develop socially and morally, and provide the teacher with a new lens on assessment (Dickerson, 1982; Kamii & Lewis, 1992). One second grade teacher used store coupons to develop a card game called

"Coupon Concentration," which the children used in a variety of ways to match sight words.

Games encourage the development of children's autonomy, increase children's social skills, and improve their ways of communicating their newly acquired concepts and skills (Dickerson, 1982; Kamii & Lewis, 1992). They also enhance children's physical coordination, refine their social and language skills, and build concepts of cooperation and competition (Elkind, 1981).

CHANGES NEEDED FOR A WHOLE LANGUAGE PLAY ENVIRONMENT

Understanding a whole language play environment requires a new mind-set and an ability to see learning through a new lens (Whitmore & Goodman, 1992). There are four conditions needed for this change. First, an environment conducive to play provides enough *time* to develop and carry out a play theme. A good place to increase the amount of time is during center time or Breathing Out. Cooperative learning groups, where children make collaborative decisions and engage in buddy, or partner reading, also require time and encourage more opportunity for playful development with language and speech. Second, whole language classrooms need enough *space* in which children can enact a theme or construct something. The inclusion of learning areas (e.g., writing center, flannel board, blocks) enables children to explore and reenact familiar books and experiences. Third, classrooms need a variety of *materials* that encourage all forms of play (e.g., literacy materials in all the centers, choice boards, message boards) to communicate in all settings. Finally, children need *common and familiar experience* so that they can enact roles they understand (Johnson, Christie, & Yawkey, 1987).

Teachers, therefore, must establish a "supportive community of learners in which everyone (including the teacher) is free to take risks and make decisions without fear of negative consequences and in which everyone is supported by others" (Weaver, 1992, p. 12). They should maintain a playful attitude, encourage children's ability to solve problems, and facilitate their connection making (Fromberg, 1990).

WHOLE LANGUAGE, ART, AND MUSIC

The arts as a means of communication are vital to the education of all children. They not only increase children's aesthetic ways of knowing but also enhance the development of their language, creativity, and problem-solving ability. More importantly, they nurture children's imagination and representational ability—necessary elements for the formation of concepts that transcend all subject areas (Eisner, 1992; Gardner, 1983). Such evidence is convincing more and more educators and policymakers that arts education is essential to the curriculum of primary children.

Connecting Play to Art and Music

Play, art, and music can all be considered types of "language" that children use to express their ideas and understandings. They are active ways of communicating and they make learning across all subject areas come alive for children. In play, children express their understandings through oral language as well as through symbolic representations and gestures. In art and music, children explain their ideas and understandings of subject matter through different media. They also use the specialized "language" of art and music to describe the unique elements and techniques of those disciplines (Galda et al., 1993).

By engaging their minds through these alternative ways of representing their experiences, ideas, and feelings, play, art, and music connect children's own lived experiences with new and unfamiliar ones. Whole language teachers who use these "languages" as integral forms of communication in their classrooms assist children in their attempts to construct meaning. Opportunities to communicate through art and music provide a counterbalance for those children who have difficulty communicating through traditional forms.

Katz (1993) has said that the portrayal of ideas through the arts can be

> The basis for hypotheses, discussions and arguments, often leading to further observations and fresh representations. Using [the arts as a legitimate way of knowing] . . . we can see how children's minds can be engaged in a variety of ways in the quest for deeper understanding of the familiar world around them. (p. 25)

In this way, teachers capitalize on children's keen sensory awareness and create dispositions toward aesthetic appreciation (Isenberg & Jalongo, 1993; Katz, 1993).

Guidance from National Associations

Whole language primary teachers can look to the position statements of four national associations to inform their practice in the arts. The Association for Childhood Education International (ACEI) endorses the following precepts:

- Every child has a right to opportunities for imaginative expression.
- Educating the child's imagination is education for the future.
- The educated imagination is the key to equity and intercultural understanding.
- Children's creative productivity is qualitatively different from adults.
- Creative expression should permeate the entire curriculum.
- Imagination is the key to artistry in teaching and excellence in our schools. (Jalongo, 1990, pp. 198–200)

The Getty Center for Education in the Arts (1985) also believes that arts education should be integrated across the curriculum and that it should include experiences in four related aspects: art production, art history, art criticism, and aesthetics. Similarly, the National Association for the Education of Young Children (NAEYC) supports the importance of "daily opportunities for aesthetic expression and appreciation through art and music" (Bredekamp, 1987, p. 52).

And the International Reading Association (IRA) position statement asserts that teachers should "provide reading experiences as an integrated part of the broader communication process, which includes speaking, listening, and writing, as well as other communication systems such as art . . . and music" (Early Childhood and Literacy Development Committee, 1988, p. 8).

Each of these positions, taken by national professional organizations, provides teachers with a framework to use in encouraging their students to explore their world through a variety of paths, to unlock their creative potential, and to promote their powers of communication. They can guide teachers as they seek to create appropriate classroom environments; to understand the artistic characteristics of primary grade children; to utilize time, materials, and lived experiences; and to transform the classroom for whole language.

CREATING A CLASSROOM ENVIRONMENT FOR ART AND MUSIC

Creating a classroom environment where children are free to take risks requires teaching for understanding rather than teaching isolated facts and skills. This kind of climate manifests itself through teachers' understanding of children's characteristics as artists, and the provision of adequate time, materials, and background experiences to develop children's appreciative dispositions (Garreau & Kennedy, 1991; Katz, 1993; Lowenfeld & Brittain, 1987).

Characteristics of Children as Artists and Musicians

In artistic development, children in the primary grades are most likely to be in the stage of either "emerging representation or representation" (Kellogg, 1979; Lowenfeld & Brittain, 1987). In emerging representation, children's artwork may include two or more shapes, such as "suns" or "tadpole" persons floating on a page. In the representational stage, their art looks realistic, has a baseline, gives evidence of a plan and details, and has a sense of proportion and arrangement.

In musical development, school-age children parallel Bruner's (1968) stages of cognitive development. In the *iconic stage,* children represent their ideas through objects and pictures, perhaps representing those games on a flannel board (Isenberg & Jalongo, 1993). They also operate at the *symbolic stage,* using language to represent their ideas. At this stage they can learn to use symbolic systems, such as musical notation and special words. Illustrated song charts and song picture books help children move from the iconic to the symbolic stage in their musical development (Jalongo & Bromley, 1984).

Providing Time, Materials, and Background Experiences

Primary grade children need *time* to explore and experiment with art and music, independent of the pressure to produce something "artistic." Only then will they become confident in the ability to communicate their ideas through more than one medium.

Children also need *access* to art and music materials. Teachers can locate appropriate resources for classroom use by asking the school librarian to identify the most popular children's musicians (e.g., Pete Seeger or Raffi); taping quality children's programs, like *Reading Rainbow;* or developing a collection of recyclable materials for artistic creations (Isenberg & Jalongo, 1993). Providing easy access to materials frees children from their dependence on the teacher to express their ideas, while respecting the child's ability to select appropriate materials with which to share ideas.

Extending children's experience with creative materials means that children need to have a vocabulary of art and music. Talking like an artist or a musician means they need exposure to and use of both design elements and musical terminology.

Enabling children to learn in environments that promote children's safe expression of ideas and feelings recognizes the importance of building these abilities. Integrating the arts across the curriculum is a natural transition to holistic teaching. As whole language teachers, the arts must be viewed as "additional languages" available to all children (Katz, 1993).

They are particularly important forms of communication for those children whose native language is not English, and who have limited means of communication through language.

TRANSFORMING THE ART AND MUSIC CLASSROOM INTO A WHOLE LANGUAGE CLASSROOM

Art and music integrate across subject areas and meet the stated goals of each school division. Knowing how and when to integrate these disciplines is the epitome of a whole language classroom. Art and music enhance each curriculum area in the following ways.

Integrating Art and Music Across the Curriculum

In Social Studies, art and music celebrate the special qualities of different cultures. Songs like "Yankee Doodle" and "Johnny Comes Marching Home Again" enhance children's understanding of history, and music like Aaron Copeland's "Appalachian Suite" can be used to study geographical locations and characteristics.

In Language Arts, teachers can use songs in different languages as well as in English. Children can also enjoy the poetry in songs (e.g., limericks, quatrains) and create sounds with haiku or other sound stories. Song picture books (Jalongo & Bromley, 1984) enhance all of the language arts while increasing children's musical growth as well. Detailed discussions of how to source-integrate literature with music into units of study have been published by Linda Lamme (1990) and Mary Jalongo and Karen Bromley (1984).

When children have the opportunity to talk about their art, their oral language improves along with their reflections on their work. When a first grade child used *Linnea in Monet's Garden* (Bjork, 1987) to draw a spring garden, she said: "I like to paint pretty flowers in pastels just like Monet. It makes me feel good. I love flowers." The infusion of oral language with thinking about art is a necessary part of every subject area.

In the arts, children can draw to music, create sounds to express a drawing, draw like an artist, or create like a songwriter. In Shawneen Petersen's third grade class (described earlier), the children examined Henri Rousseau's jungle paintings (e.g., "exotic landscape"). They discussed the colors, the story, the mood, the lines, and the space, and learned that Rousseau liked to tell people about the "fantasy trips" in his mind. Using this as a background, the third graders also took "imagined trips" to an island, using Rousseau's techniques with color (going from light to dark), size (large to small), and overlapping (tucking cut-out animals and people among the foliage). The resultant conversations about Rousseau, and the children's own artwork, invited critical and individual interpretations utilizing a rich "vocabulary" of art.

Transforming the Curriculum

An example of how a primary grade teacher might begin to transform a classroom into a whole language classroom is depicted in the following description of a unit on "families." The unit might include readings, such as *The Pain and the Great One* (Blume, 1974), *The Little Red Hen* (Galdone, 1974), and *The Relatives Came* (Rylant, 1985). In art, the children could use their own lived experience and observation of detail to illustrate scenes from *The Relatives Came*. They might use colored pencils, the medium utilized by the book's illustrator, Stephen Gammelli, or make handprints on construction paper using tempera paint. On each finger they could write five different adjectives, describing their grandparent or some other older person they know well. In addition, they could create a class mural of their own families using tempera paints, colored chalk, or colored pencils; or utilizing the paper collage techniques employed so effectively by Eric Carle in his books. As part of the unit, the teacher might want to create an "Art Learning Area" containing displays of various artists' works in different media to create an inviting atmosphere for all emerging artists.

In addition to art experiences, teachers might want to incorporate quality listening and singing experiences. They might want to connect joyful singing experiences with literacy lessons through the use of song charts that children can illustrate. Or they may invite the children to create special music booklets containing children's original songs. Some possibilities in the music arena might include creating song parodies from familiar songs (like changing "The Bear Went Over the Mountain" to "The Family Went Over the Mountain"). Another possibility might be to clap out the rhythm of the old and new versions of the song using the word syllables to guide the rhythm. Each of these variations provides children with opportunities to communicate through music.

IMPLICATIONS FOR PRACTICE

The literature on play and the expressive arts clearly states the centrality of these forms of communication to a whole language classroom. Whole language teachers, therefore, would be well advised to consider this literature as they develop their own best practice for primary children. The following suggestions closely align primary grade classrooms with the precepts and beliefs that inform the whole language philosophy.

1. *Provide opportunities for alternative ways of communication.* In the past, schools have emphasized linguistic and logico-mathematical knowledge as the primary ways of knowing. Research by Gardner (1983) suggests that individuals have multiple ways of knowing, or "multiple intelligences." Having a music or art learning station offers children rich opportunities to communicate their ideas through these media. Representing their knowledge in this way increases the likelihood that they will reach their full potential.

2. *Create learning experiences that support children's imagery.* Active learning experiences, like literature responses, book talks, and journal writing, can all be expanded to incorporate play, art, and musical ideas. Writing responses to a painting or a piece of music or articulating what they liked or did not like about it "can help children become aware of what they hear and see, as well as help them begin to develop some critical ability" (Galda et al., 1993, p. 308). Writing and talking about the images they create in their minds helps to heighten sensory awareness, sharpen children's representational abilities, and nurture meaning making.

3. *Prepare environments that support children's divergent thinking and problem-solving.* Play, art, and music cultivate children's ability to reflect on and think through their world. Because they capture children's enthusiasm easily, children spend time thinking about and revisiting details, ideas, and feelings. Playing with and illustrating different syntactical structures, for example, enables children to focus on style and meaningful usage of grammar by "manipulating . . . the effect of stylistic choices" (Galda et al., 1993, p. 226). When children use play, art, or music to articulate their understandings, they are exploring opportunities to think about subject matter in exciting new ways.

4. *Support a community of learners.* Whole language classrooms that respect the power of the expressive arts create and sustain meaningful relationships. Time is invested in helping children create projects together that convey information, provoke oral communication and listening abilities, and challenge children's thinking. Displays of group work (such as murals, original, illustrated song charts, or a musical score with musical notations) validate the cooperative nature of learning and instill a sense of pride in the final group project.

5. *Create environments that invite aesthetic appreciation.* In whole language classrooms, attention must be paid to the organization and utilization of space, time, and materials. These environmental dimensions send a message to visitors, colleagues, and learners. Classrooms that nurture literacy development are pleasant and welcoming. They celebrate an atmosphere of discovery and inquiry. Walls are designed with both temporary and permanent children's exhibits. Space and time are used flexibly. But most important, there is a sense of security and appreciation within the children themselves (Gandini, 1993).

SUMMARY

Recognizing the essential role of play, art, and music in the primary grades is critical to becoming a teacher of whole language. Through the arts, children learn that "learning to learn" is worthwhile. Encouraging children to respond to their world through play, art, and music in the same way that they respond to literature helps them see the world with new understanding. It also helps them recognize the different ways of communicating. In all cases, a curriculum that encourages children's self-expression regards "the child as a meaning-maker and constructor, a discoverer and an embodiment of knowledge rather than a passive recipient of someone else's ready-made answers" (Jalongo, 1990, p. 196).

REFERENCES

Atwell, N. (1987). *In the middle: Writing, reading, learning with adolescents.* Portsmouth, NH: Heinemann.

Bergen, D. (1988). Using a schema for play and learning. In D. Bergen (Ed.), *Play as a medium for learning and development: A handbook of theory and practice* (pp. 169–180). Portsmouth, NH: Heinemann.

Bredekamp, S. (Ed.). (1987). *Developmentally appropriate practices.* Washington, DC: National Association for the Education of Young Children (NAEYC).

Bredekamp, S., & Rosegrant, T. (1992). *Reaching potentials: Appropriate curriculum and assessment for young children. Volume I.* Washington, DC: NAEYC.

Bruner, J. (1968). *Toward a theory of instruction.* New York: W.W. Norton.

Daiute, C. (1989). Play as thought: Thinking strategies of young writers. *Harvard Educational Review. 59* (1), 1–232.

Daiute, C. (1991). Play is part of the learning process, too. *Education Week,* (Oct, 31), 31–32.

Dickerson, D. P. (1982). A study of the use of games to reinforce sight vocabulary. *The Reading Teacher, 36* (1), 46–49.

Early Childhood and Literacy Development Committee. (1990) *Literacy Development and Early Childhood (Preschool through Grade 3).* Newark: DL: International Reading Association.

Edwards, C., Gandini, L., & Forman, G. (1993). *The hundred languages of children: The Reggio Emilia Approach to early childhood education.* Norwood, NJ: Ablex.

Eisner, E. (1992). The misunderstood role of the arts in human development. *Phi Delta Kappan, 73* (8), 591–595.

Elkind, D. (1987). *Miseducation: Preschoolers at risk.* New York: Alfred A. Knopf.

Erikson, E. (1950). *Childhood and society.* New York: W. W. Norton.

Fromberg, D. P. (1990). Play issues in early childhood education. In C. Seefeldt (Ed.), *Continuing issues in early childhood education* (pp. 223–243). Columbus, OH: Merrill/Macmillan.

Fulwiler, L. (1992). The constructivist culture of language-centered classrooms. In

C. Weaver & L. Henke (Eds.), *Supporting whole language: Stories of teacher and institutional change* (pp. 27–42). Portsmouth, NH: Heinemann.

Galda, L., Cullinan, B., & Strickland, D. (1993). *Language, literacy, and the child.* New York: Harcourt Brace Jovanovich.

Gandini, L. (1993). Educational and caring spaces. In C. Edwards, L. Gandini, & G. Forman (Eds.), *The hundred languages of children: The Reggio Emilia Approach to early childhood education* (pp. 135–151). Norwood, NJ: Ablex.

Gardner, H. (1983). *Frames of mind: The theory of multiple intelligences.* New York: Basic.

Garvey, C. (1977). *Play.* Cambridge, MA: Harvard University Press.

Garreau, M., & Kennedy, C. (1991). Structure time and space to promote pursuit of learning in the primary grades. *Young Children, 64* (4), 46–51.

Genishi, C. (1985). Talking to learn: The child takes charge of literacy. *Dimensions, 13* (3), 9–11.

Genishi, C., & Dyson, A. H. (1984). Learning through argument in preschool. In L. C. Wilkonson (Ed.), *Communicating in the classroom* (pp.49–68). New York: Academic.

Getty Center for Education in the Arts. (1985). *Beyond creating: The place for art in America's schools.* Los Angeles: John Paul Getty Trust.

Isenberg, J., & Jacob, E. (1983, June). Playful literacy activities and learning: Preliminary observations. Paper presented at the International Conference on Play and Play Environments, Austin, TX.

Isenberg, J., & Jalongo, M. (1993). *Creative expression and play in the early childhood curriculum.* New York: Macmillan.

Isenberg, J., & Quisenberry, N. (1988). Play: A necessity for all children. *Childhood Education, 64* (3), 138–145.

Jalongo, M. R., & Bromley, K. D. (1984). Developing linguistic competence through song picture books. *The Reading Teacher, 37* (9), 840–845.

Jalongo, M. R. (1990). The child's right to the expressive arts. *Childhood Education, 66* (4), 195–201.

Johnson, J. E., Christie, J. F., & Yawkey, T. D. (1987). *Play and early childhood development.* Glenview, IL: Scott Foresman.

Jones, E. (1977). *Dimensions of teaching—learning environments.* Pasadena, CA: Pacific Oaks.

Kamii, C. (1985). *Young children reinvent arithmetic.* New York: Teachers College Press.

Kamii, C. (1989). *Young children continue to reinvent arithmetic, Second Grade.* New York: Teachers College Press.

Kamii, C., & Lewis, B. (1992). Primary arithmetic: The superiority of games over worksheets. In V. Dimidjian (Ed.), *Play's place in public education for young children* (pp.85–94). Washington, DC: National Education Association.

Katz, L. (1993). What can we learn from Reggio Emilia? In C. Edwards, L. Gandini, & G. Forman (Eds.), *The hundred languages of children: The Reggio Emilia approach to early childhood education* (pp. 19–37). Norwood, NJ: Ablex.

Kellogg, R. (1979). *Children's drawings/children's minds.* New York: Avon Books.

Lamme, L. L. (1990). Exploring the world of music through picture books. *The Reading Teacher, 44* (4), 294–300.

Lowenfeld, V., & Brittain, W. L. (1987). *Creative and mental growth.* (5th ed.). New York: Macmillan.

May, F. B. (1994). *Reading as communication.* (4th ed.). New York: Macmillan.

Moninghan-Nourot, P., & Van Hoorn, J. L. (1991). Symbolic play in preschool and primary settings. *Young Children, 46* (6), 40–50.

Phye-Perkins, E. (1980). Children's behavior in preschool settings: The influence of the physical environment. In L. G. Katz (Ed.), *Current topics in early childhood education,* Vol. 3 (pp. 91–125). Norwood, NJ: Ablex.

Piaget, J. (1985). *The equilibration of cognitive structures: The central problem of intellectual development.* Chicago: University of Chicago Press.

Ruddell, R. B. (1992). A whole language and literature perspective: Creating a meaning-making instructional environment. *Language Arts, 69* (8), 612–620.

Smith, R. A. (1992). Toward percipience: A humanities curriculum for art education. In B. Reimer & R. A. Smith (Eds.), *The arts, education, and aesthetic knowing,* Ninety-first yearbook of the National Society for the Study of Education (pp. 51–69). Chicago: University of Chicago Press.

Sutton-Smith, B. (1980). Children's play: Some sources of play theorizing. In K. A. Rubin (Ed.), *New directions for child development: Children's play No. 9* (pp. 1–16). San Francisco: Jossey-Bass.

U. S. Department of Education. (March 31, 1994). *Goals 2000: Educate America Act.* Washington DC: U. S. Department of Education.

Vygotsky, L. S. (1978). *Mind in society.* Cambridge: Harvard University Press.

Weaver, C. (1992). A whole language belief system and its implications for teacher and institutional change. In C. Weaver & L. Henke (Eds.), *Supporting whole language: Stories of teachers and institutional change* (pp. 3–23). Portsmouth, NH: Heinemann.

Wassermann, S. (1990). *Serious players in the primary classroom.* New York: Teachers College Press.

Whitmore, K. F., & Goodman, Y. M. (1992). Students delight in taking charge of their learning. *The School Administrator, 49* (5), 20–26.

Children's Book and Software References

Bjork, C. (1987). *Linnea in Monet's garden.* Illus. by Lena Anerson. Stockholm, Sweden: R & S Books.

Blume, J. (1974). *The pain and the great one.* New York: Bradbury.

Galdone, P. (1973). *Little red hen.* New York: Seabury.

Gwynne, F. (1970). *The king who rained.* New York: Simon and Schuster.

Hartman, G. (1991). *As the crow flies: A first book of maps.* New York: Bradbury Press.

Hickman, C. (1991). *Kid Pix [computer program].* Novato, CA: Broderbund.

Lessac, F. (1984). *My little island.* Great Britain: Macmillan.

MacDonald, G. (1946). *The little island.* New York: Doubleday.

O'Dell, S. (1990). *Island of the blue dolphins.* Boston: Houghton Mifflin.

Rylant, C. (1985). *The relatives came.* Illus. by Stephen Gammell. New York: Bradbury.

Wilder, L. I. (1941). *Little house on the prairie.* New York: Harper & Row.

7

A Complete Whole:
Social Studies and the Language Arts

CAROL SEEFELDT

"Count them again," suggests Alberto, as the children try to figure out how many packages of carrots are needed to make enough "stone soup" to feed everyone in the class.

"My favorite thing about this year was the trip to see the robot at the university," reported 8-year-old Vanessa during a group discussion at the end of the school year. "Well, that was a pretty good trip," agreed Rachel, "but my favorite thing this year was when we measured a big dinosaur on the playground."

"This is the state flower of Wyoming, and this is our state flower, the Brown-Eyed-Susan," Shawna said, explaining a chart of flowers to a visitor. "We read Tomie de Paola's *The Legend of the Indian Paintbrush* (de Paola, 1988) and then we researched the legend of our state flower."

Working together to solve the problem of purchasing carrots, recalling their own immediate history, or exploring legends: all of these classroom experiences involve content from social studies. Of high interest to children, experiences in social studies are integral to the total curriculum. Experiences from the fields of economics, history, geography, anthropology, or any of the other social studies disciplines serve to unite the entire curriculum. These experiences bring meaning to the students' other academic pursuits. They also serve to inform the attitudes and sharpen the skills required of citizens in a democratic society.

The following definition, by the National Council for the Social Studies (NCSS), reflects the integrative and critical role of this discipline:

The study of political, economic, cultural, and environmental aspects of societies of the past, present, and future, the social studies are designed to equip children with the knowledge and understanding of the past necessary for coping with the present and planning for the future, enabling children to understand and participate effectively in their world and explain their relationships to other people and to social, economic, and political institutions. (NCSS, 1989, p. 15)

Broad and all-encompassing, this definition suggests that the content of the diverse disciplines comprising social studies are totally integrated.

Because social studies and language arts are integrated into every aspect of the primary grade curriculum, it is not surprising that they form a complete whole. Because social studies revolve around the social lives of humans, children experience them naturally and on a daily basis.

Social studies holds deep personal meaning. An activity like visiting the post office, and then categorizing stamps from around the world before creating a personalized class stamp, gives children reasons to communicate with one another. It is important for them to talk, listen, and find out more. Vygotsky (1986) put it this way: "Children not only speak about what they are doing, their speech and action are part of one and the same complex psychological function" (p. 43).

When given the freedom to talk informally, children converse fully and completely about their experiences. This talk takes place naturally as children make "stone soup" or research a legend. Informal talk makes a significant contribution to "intellectual development in general, and literacy growth in particular" (Dyson, 1987, p. 535).

Formal speaking and listening are also meaningful within the context of social studies experiences. Teachers encourage children to express their ideas, experiences, and feelings more formally in groups. Talking and listening together, whether informally or formally, children gain insight into each other's perceptions of shared experiences.

By thinking about an experience—perhaps a trip to the store to purchase carrots, or observing the way mail is handled in their school—children develop images, feelings, and ideas. Langer (1942) believed humans have an innate physiological need to express the meaning of their experiences in a symbolic way—a need no other living creature has.

The expression of ideas that stem from an experience with social studies can take many forms. Children may draw or paint a picture about it, describe it through dance, tell about it, or write about it. When expressing ideas or feelings, children have the opportunity to clarify and organize their ideas. They reflect on the past as they give form to their thoughts.

Social studies experiences make functional language real as well. As the need arises, children use spoken and written language to communicate with others. They may send "stone soup" party invitations to parents, or thank-you notes to the university physicist who demonstrated the robot.

As they participate in learning experiences, the written language of others becomes important. Books are located and read as children search for information about the legend of their state flower. The children keep journals and diaries of daily events.

Literature—from uplifting poetry, stories, or folk-tales to reference and textbooks—is used to extend and expand children's firsthand social studies experiences. The thoughts, ideas, and knowledge of others, recorded in books, gives children a rich mental model of their world and the language that can be used to describe it (Snow, 1983).

This chapter presents the wholeness of the language arts and social studies. It states the goals of social studies and describes two organizations' frameworks for this discipline. By describing the beginning of a day in two different classrooms, it illustrates how teachers can bring children and social studies together. Because history is believed to be the core of social studies (National Commission on Social Studies in the Schools [NCSSS], 1989) and one of the great integrative disciplines (California State Board of Education, 1987), it has been selected to illustrate the oneness of social studies and the language arts.

THE SCOPE OF SOCIAL STUDIES

In the past, social studies in the primary grades was often an incoherent and disorganized subject. At one time, its primary goal was the development of social skills and habits. In 1923, Patty Smith Hill, attempting to apply principles of democracy to school organization, developed an inventory of habits and skills children were to learn. *A Conduct Curriculum for the Kindergarten and First Grade* (Burke, 1923) states, in measurable form, a similar inventory of desirable habits. If current kindergarten and primary grade report cards are any indication, the development of social skills and habits as a goal of social studies continues. An analysis of report cards showed that over 80% of school systems include a report of children's social skills development or work habits (Freeman & Hatch, 1989).

Another common approach to social studies in the primary grades also stems from the past. In the 1920s, Lucy Sprague Mitchell (1934), concerned with the practice of teaching social studies as an unchanging body of facts to be learned through rote drill, developed a curriculum based on the "here and now" expanding world of the child. Mitchell's basic idea was that social studies should be planned around children's firsthand experiences in their homes, neighborhoods, schools, and communities.

Even today, social studies instruction continues to be based on an "expanding communities" model (Brophy, 1990). This approach has been criticized as simplistic, sterile, and void of intellectual content (California State Board of Education [CSBE], 1987; NCSSS, 1989). According to the critics, primary grade children are familiar with their families, homes, and neighborhoods, and are bored with this content in a school setting.

Mitchell (1934), however, viewed the basing of social studies on the child's environment—the child's here and now world—as highly complex. She wanted teachers to recognize that children's firsthand experiences with their social world are the foundation for their thinking. Teachers were to carefully select play experiences so that children could begin to see and understand relationships between and among them, and to develop concepts and generalizations from their experiences. Her idea that experiences should be recreated or expressed through symbolic or dramatic play, art, music, story, or journal are consistent with the popular Vygotskian and Piagetian theories guiding teaching and learning today.

A number of commissions and associations have proposed goals and directions intended to bring order and coherence to social studies. The national bodies mentioned above (NCSS and NCSSS) and the California State Board of Education (CSBE) have developed outlines with the purpose of organizing and synthesizing social studies into a coherent body of knowledge. Both the NCSSS and the CSBE curriculum guides are based on the study of history. Long recognized as the central core of the social studies, history has been called the "jewel in the crown of the social studies curriculum" (Jarolimek & Parker, 1993, p. 12).

National Commission on Social Studies in the Schools Guidelines

With its proposal for a history-centered social studies curriculum, the NCSSS believes it has created a "model that will challenge and encourage social studies educators to look to the future and to undertake a school program that will help all of America's children and adolescents to meet the challenges that lie ahead of us now, and in the century to come" (1989, p. xi).

According to the guide, organizing social studies in early childhood around the discipline of history allows children to gain an "understanding of their own history, appreciate political and cultural diversity, and understand the economic and sociological realities of a rapidly changing world" (p. xi). Social studies education in kindergarten and the primary grades will set the tone and lay the foundation for social studies education to come. The guide states that "In these formative years it is imperative that the social studies curriculum avoid superficiality and be well defined and relevant to the needs and interests of young learners" (p. 7). This curriculum can include:

- Examination of children's immediate environment, through walks in the neighborhood, pictures, videos, and films
- Understanding the concept of community: Through a study of different environments, students can begin to understand that laws regulate larger communities the same way rules keep order in the classroom
- Stories about and descriptions of different types of people, living in various situations, conditions, and locales
- Development of mental models of the physical world: While young children may not fully comprehend the concept of time, they do know the difference between long ago and the present, and can understand the potential for future possibilities
- An emphasis on the study of heroes and heroines, to provide models for emulation and admiration
- Celebration of holidays to serve as occasions for projects that will acquaint pupils with social studies concepts and information

California State Board of Education Guidelines

With the goal of setting forth, in an organized way, the knowledge and understanding that students need, the CSBE (1987) prepared a social studies framework based on the study of history. This framework:

- Centers social studies on the chronological study of history
- Proposes an integrated and correlated approach to teaching history–social science
- Emphasizes history as a story well told
- Emphasizes the importance of enriching the study of history with the use of literature of the period and literature about the period
- Emphasizes the study of major historical events and periods
- Proposes a sequential curriculum
- Incorporates a multicultural perspective
- Emphasizes the importance of ethical understanding and civic virtue to public affairs
- Encourages the development of civic and democratic values
- Supports the frequent study of the principles embodied in the United States Constitution and the Bill of Rights
- Encourages teachers to present controversial issues fairly
- Acknowledges the importance of religion in human history
- Proposes that critical thinking skills be taught at every grade level
- Supports using a variety of content-appropriate teaching methods
- Provides opportunities for student participation in school and community service activities

HISTORY AS THE CORE

With history as the foundation of the social studies, the NCSS and NCSSS propose the integration of the curriculum to prepare children to assume adult civic responsibilities. "Each generation faces new challenges for which lessons from the past have relevance. Individuals do not think well if they do not understand their own history" (NCSSS, 1989, p. xi). "By studying the human past, students will see the connection between ideas and behavior, between the values and ideas that people hold and the ethical consequences of those beliefs" (CSBE, 1987, p. 3).

Nevertheless, history is time-oriented: It revolves around what we know of the past. How can this subject serve as the organizer of social studies for primary grade children? Children are believed to have little concept of conventional time before the age of 8 or 9 (Vukelich & Thornton, 1990) and, due to limited memory skills, have even less knowledge of the past. It may seem absurd, and potentially overwhelming, to teach primary grade children a subject as enormous and as complex as history.

It is, however, because of the complexity and enormity of the study of history that it must be included in the primary grade curriculum. Children's early experiences with history lay the foundation for later social studies learning. "Unless children acquire the foundations of knowledge, attitudes, and skills in social studies in the opportune elementary years, it is unlikely that teachers in the junior and senior high schools will be successful in preparing effective citizens for the 21st century" (NCSS, 1989, p. 14).

Teaching social studies through history seems less overwhelming when teachers realize that primary grade children need only develop anticipatory, intuitive ideas and interests. Vygotsky (1986) termed these first ideas and concepts "embryonic." Children's early concepts "stand in the same relationship to true concepts as the embryo to the fully formed organism" (p. 58).

Children, like humans of any age, learn through firsthand experiences. In the small democracy of the primary grade classroom, children spontaneously experience many of the concepts considered key to the study of history. Selecting from these naturally occurring experiences, teachers carefully turn them into learning experiences.

Each of the key concepts of history can be introduced to children, including:

1. *Time.* The time-oriented study of history, when taught through children's everyday experiences with the time of day and school routines, is meaningful for primary students.
2. *Change.* Change is inevitable: It is an intimate part of children's lives. The changes that occur in children's lives, classrooms, schools, and neighborhoods give meaning to the study of history.

3. *Continuity of Life*. Regardless of how things may change, there is continuity in children's lives. Through interactions with others older and younger than themselves, children can comprehend the uninterrupted flow of life.

4. *The Past*. Children are aware of, and interested in, the past. Examination of objects and records from their immediate past, as well as from the distant past, can increase primary children's understanding of history.

5. *Methods of the Historian*. The processes involved in recognizing problems, making observations, collecting and analyzing data, and inferring conclusions are an integral part of the primary grade curriculum. By studying history, children can apply these processes as an historian would, thinking and reflecting on their own experiences and on the experiences of others.

BRINGING HISTORY AND CHILDREN TOGETHER

The concepts considered key to the study of history are complex, and nearly as broad as the field of social studies itself. Nevertheless, each of these concepts can be introduced to children when they are based on meaningful, firsthand experiences.

The following opening exercises led by two first grade teachers illustrate ways children and concepts of history are brought together. Both teachers are following curricula mandated by their school system. The first teacher follows a mandated lesson plan, while the second integrates the mandated learnings with meaningful activities that require language, thought, reflection, and interaction and involvement with others.

Classroom 1. It is February 1, the start of another school day. Twenty-eight children sit on a rug in front of the room looking at a calendar. "What month is it?" the teacher begins, holding up a small cutout of a heart with the word February printed on it.

"It's February," the children shout in unison.

"And what special day comes in February?"

"It's Valentine's Day!"

"That's right, how many days until Valentine's Day? Count them."

The children count, shouting out in unison.

"Good," the teacher continues. "What was the name of the last month?"

"January," the children reply.

"And next month is . . ." the teacher asks, and the children answer "March."

"Good!" the teacher says as she holds up another cutout heart, this time with the word Tuesday printed on it. The process of teacher querying children and children responding with shouts continues with the names of the days of the week.

Restless, the children begin to squirm and wiggle. Two engage each other in a small game of hiding and finding a piece of candy.

Sighing, the teacher reprimands the group, "Pay attention! You must learn to tell time. It's very important."

The lesson goes on. For the next 20 minutes the teacher directs the children through another exercise involving bundles of straws. The number of days until Valentine's Day are counted out with straws the teacher holds up as the children mechanically call out the numbers. The two children with the candy are sent to time-out, where they continue their game.

Then the number of days the children have been in school are counted, again with bundles of straws. More restlessness breaks out. Children poke and pinch one another. Three more children are sent to time-out, and the number of days in school are counted with straws by fives and by tens.

Classroom 2. In another primary classroom in the same school, 27 children are also gathered in the front of the room. Their teacher begins singing "Zippity-Do-Dah" and the children join in. When they finish, Shawna says, "Let's sing the song from Oklahoma, you know the one, about a beautiful day." The group joins in singing "Oh what a beautiful morning, oh what a beautiful day."

The teacher asks Shawna why she thought of singing "Oh What a Beautiful Day." Shawna replies that after all the rain yesterday, the sun is shining and "everything looks beautiful today." The children take turns telling why they think the day is beautiful and write their reasons on a chart. The teacher asks if there are other words that say the same thing as "beautiful." Brainstorming, the children list a number of words, including awesome, pretty, nice, and supercalifragilisticexpialidocious.

"You know," says the teacher, "this is the first day of a beautiful month. It's the first day of February. There are several beautiful special days during the month of February."

"We know, we know," the children giggle together, "it's Valentine's Day." The children count the days until Valentine's Day. Amanda notices February 14 falls on a Saturday and a discussion about whether to hold the class celebration on Friday or Monday ensues. Committees are formed to plan the celebration.

"And it's my birthday, February 19—I'll be 8 years old," chimes in Rona. "Rona, come and mark the 19th as your birthday." Together the children count the days until Rona's birthday.

After a discussion of the other events and special days that will take place during the month, the teacher says, "Time to plan for this beautiful day." The teacher helps the group negotiate their plans for the day, which are then listed on the board.

Each child will read with the teacher; take part in a math lesson; and go to music, lunch, and recess. Some activities revolve around last week's visit to the local post office. Group A, the Post Office Group, will finish construction of a post office. Group B will continue planning the class stamp, and Group C will visit the office and interview the secretaries about how the school's mail is handled.

The two ways of starting a school day illustrated above contrast sharply, even though they are both designed around concepts of history, mandated by the school system, that involve counting the days, naming the days of the week, learning the names of the month, and identifying holidays.

In the first group, children responded only to the teacher. Their rote answers left little room for thought or reflection. The only interaction with the teacher was calling out the answers to direct questions. There was no continuity between past and present learning. But most importantly, the lesson was not meaningful to the children. Without personal meaning, children have no way to reflect on past experiences or to consider the future. Language isn't necessary: There is nothing to discuss. Children who attempted to interact with one another were ostracized and expelled from the group.

In the second classroom, no child became restless and not one was sent to time-out; each was involved and active. Using the same mandated lesson plan, the teacher tied the activities to firsthand experiences and to things that held meaning to the children. There was continuity to the discussions—a thread of meaning among past, present, and future events and activities.

The children reflected on and solved problems. They interacted, responding not only to the teacher, but also to each other. The vocabulary of time—names of the days of the week and months—was used throughout. Number concepts were practiced. Oral discussion was transformed into writing. Perhaps most importantly, each child made a contribution. Each child left feeling confident, competent, self-directing, and independent. No child lost self-esteem by being cut off from the group.

The second teacher, explaining how she worked with the mandated goal of teaching history, stated:

Children can't gain a sense of history by routinely responding to direct questions, or just through an opening exercise. Concepts of history, whether of time, change, or the past, are taught throughout the day, in connection with children's needs and actual experiences. Children can develop concepts of history only through an integrated curriculum. I internalize the goals and mandates of the school, and then find ways to make these meaningful as children are involved or experiencing them.

The concepts of history—time, change, continuity of life, the past, and methods of the historian—were taught exactly as the teacher claimed, through children's own meaningful interactions with one another, their environment, and the content.

Concepts of Time

> Undoubtedly most children would learn how to tell time, would learn the days of the week and months of the year, and would become familiar with terms ordinarily used in referring to units of time, such as noon, midnight, afternoon, and morning, even if these were not taught in school. (Jarolimek & Parker, 1993, p. 181).

But in the primary grades, the routines of the day, months, and school year help children develop a sense of time.

DAILY ROUTINES.   These habits and schedules clarify, extend, and expand children's concepts of time. The technical language of time and chronology is introduced (Jarolimek & Parker, 1993). Instead of using vague phrases such as "in a while it will be time to clean up," a teacher might say: "In about 10 minutes it will be time for lunch," or "This afternoon at 3 p.m." instead of "later on." Words such as fortnight, yesterday, and season are used.

Children make books about their daily routines. One first grade teacher had children create three booklets. In the first volume, "Before School," the children drew and wrote about what they did before leaving for school in the morning. The second booklet, "At School," contained a printed copy of the school schedule. Children drew and wrote about their perceptions of these school routines. In the final volume, "After School," children recorded their after-school activities.

The books were read to the class. Charts were created, categorizing routines all children participated in, such as brushing teeth; those that took place in some homes, such as feeding pets; and those that were specific to individual children, such as going to Grandma's or to the community center after school.

Having children reflect on their daily routines was continued during the year. Children documented their own activities involving special events with booklets such as "Before Halloween," "On Halloween Night," and "After Halloween."

Reference, text, and trade books are often used to expand children's sense of time. *Good Morning, Good Night* (Martin, 1969), *The Snowy Day* (Keats, 1962), and *One Morning in Maine* (McCloskey, 1952) and *Ten, Nine, Eight* (Bang, 1983) are good examples.

TIME MEASUREMENT. Children are not usually able to measure conventional time until after the age of 8 or 9; nevertheless, in the primary grade classroom, time is measured as the need arises. Rather than measuring time with a clock or in some other conventional manner, primary grade children's first experiences involve the use of arbitrary measures. These experiences with the concepts of duration, sequence, and temporal order will prepare them to tell time in the traditional way later on.

The following are some timing devices children can use:

- A stopwatch, either independently or in connection with structured activities: Children enjoy seeing how long it will take to put blocks away, hang up coats, or complete a puzzle. One primary group, as part of a project on birds, used a stopwatch to record how long different species spent at the feeder outside their window.
- Kitchen timers that buzz: Children might use one to determine when bread should be taken from the oven, when vegetables for "stone soup" have simmered for five minutes, or when it is time to end or begin an activity.
- Sand and hour glasses: Children are intrigued by these and love to play with them. The sand glass can be used in connection with children's games.

Time is measured in the primary grade classroom as well. A teacher had children record special events on large monthly calendars, which were hung in the coat area at the end of the month. As children dressed they frequently referred to the calendars, recalling events and discussing the days and months that had passed. In the process, these children realized that history is the story of people, recorded by people like them, and that they were "right now making the future" (NCSS, 1989, p. xi).

Older primary grade children may look to records of the past to find other ways time was measured. The story *Knots on a Counting Rope* (Martin & Archaumbault, 1987) inspired one class to research how people throughout the world, and in different ages, measured time. They found that people had once measured time by looking at and recording changes in the sky, the sun, the stars, and the moon. One group of children made a sundial for the play yard, another charted the changes in the moon over several weeks, and a third made a water clock for the classroom.

Change

If children are to gain a sense of history, they must have some understanding of the concept of change. For young children whose thought is dominated by perception, change is a difficult concept to master. Since children have little ability to understand logically until after age 7 or 8, changes that occur with the passage of time must appear magical.

It is unlikely that direct instruction or planned experiences can affect children's understanding of the concept of change. Nevertheless, children's spontaneous experiences help them grasp that changes continuously affect their lives and can be recorded, and that this documentation helps others understand what has changed.

The changes that take place in the classroom, school, and neighborhood are observed and studied. In our transient society, the arrival and departure of children is a common occurrence. Recognizing children's need to deal with these changes, teachers have helped children find out about the place they will be moving to. Maps and books are consulted and letters are written to the new school. After the child has moved away, class letters are mailed to keep the child up-to-date. New children are made to feel welcome when the class researches the city or neighborhood they have come from.

Changes occur in the school building itself. Bulletin boards change, rooms are painted, and schools are renovated. One third grade class, in the process of recording changes in the school over the course of the year, came across old photographs of their school building. They made a timeline of the history of the school. They began with the date the school was built; explained why, how, and when the school was named; recorded the dates and nature of renovations; and ended with the present date (Tiene, 1986). As with time measurement, children do not have the cognitive maturity to fully understand a timeline. However, the timeline did expose the children to the idea of recording changes in an organized way.

An apple tree in the school yard stimulated a year-long study of change. In the fall, children collected and counted apples and sorted them according to size, color, and shape. Apple sauce was made with a second harvest. One father dipped some apple slices in honey to show how his family celebrated the Jewish new year. Throughout the year, charts recorded children's findings and ideas; stories and journals were written and read to one another and the group.

As the leaves began to turn, the children gathered them and charted their sizes, shapes, and colors. Estimates were made of when the last leaf would fall. The children listed questions about what would happen to the tree during the winter. "Is the apple tree dead?" "Will it have leaves and apples again?" Again, hypotheses were recorded on charts and in journals.

For a unit in the spring, new observations and discussions began. When would the first leaves appear? What color would the blossoms be? How will the blossoms turn into fruit? The tree was examined daily and texts and reference books were consulted as children sought answers to their questions.

As the semester progressed, changes in the apple tree, while continuous, were not noted every day or even every week or month. Sometimes the children mentioned changes they had noticed, or a book about apples or trees they had read. At other times the teacher initiated discussion by asking questions or focusing children's attention on the tree.

Perhaps it is most meaningful when children study changes that occur in themselves. "If you want to do some beginning historical work in the early grades, set children to uncovering their own personal histories" (Elkind, 1981, p. 436).

Children change; they grow, learn new skills, lose teeth, and get hair cuts. Stories and books give children the opportunity to contemplate these changes. *You'll Soon Grow into Them* (Hutchins, 1983) is a story of a boy who grows out of his clothes and receives hand-me-downs that are too large. *One Morning in Maine* (McCloskey, 1952) tells about losing a baby tooth. *The Purple Coat* (Hest, 1986) is the story of Gabrielle, who wants a different coat each year. These and other books can stimulate thinking and discussion about growth and change.

One primary grade teacher initiated a unit about the changes that occur in the children themselves by introducing the A. A. Milne poem, "The End" (1927), which begins, "When I was one I was just begun." A discussion ensued about how the children had changed, including what they could do now that they couldn't when they were 1, 2, 5, or 6 years old. Each child made a book called "Growing," illustrating each line of the poem. A mural for the door was made, with numerals alongside children's illustrations of themselves at each age. Others in the school stopped to look at the mural and joined in the study of growth and change.

The principal initiated another bulletin board in the hallway. She put up a baby picture of herself and added the question, "Do you know this baby now? Write your guess on the chart at the bottom." Other adults in the school—teachers, custodians, cooks, and secretaries—added their own photographs. A covered folder was posted which, when opened, revealed the babies' identities.

Children as young as the Head Start 3-year-olds and as mature as the sixth graders gravitated to the board. Children wondered who the babies were and discussed their own histories. Adults found the board interesting as well, and were frequently seen laughing with the children over the changes that had occurred in themselves.

These informal meetings and discussions led children to think about changes that might occur in the future. A group of second graders wrote and illustrated stories about what they would do when they were 10-year-olds, how they would look and dress as teenagers, and finally, what they would be like when they were grown up.

As the school year drew to a close, a yearbook was created. Each child was asked to think about what they could do now, at the end of the school year, that they could not do when the school year had begun. Each child wrote and illustrated a story about the things they had learned. The stories were edited and published in a class booklet. Copies were given to each child as a memento.

Continuity of Life

Just as the study of history is the study of change, so is it a study of the continuity of life. Regardless of how much children or apple trees change, there is continuity to the human experience. With each change, children are reminded that life goes on.

Children can best gain a sense of the continuity of life through contact with older people. Unfortunately, in today's society, children sometimes have limited contact with elders and report limited knowledge of old age or of older persons. They can name an older person in their family, but not outside the family. They often have limited knowledge of alternative terms for "old people" (Seefeldt, Jantz, Galper, & Serock, 1977).

Recognizing that interaction between the young and the old is less common in today's society, teachers have structured contact by enlisting elders as classroom volunteers and by encouraging children to explore their own family histories. Elders invited to class have discussed traditional games such as "Cootie," and the children and elders have exchanged information about how games are played now and how they were played decades ago.

Other teachers have invited elders to share their hobbies, interests, and crafts with children. Teachers can survey the class interests and then seek out older volunteers to bring their insect collections, model trains, rocks, shells, or whatever else the class would like to see. The children can be involved as much as possible in planning for the day. They can plan for and bring refreshments, send out invitations if parents or others are invited, and help set up the room for the speaker or presentation. After the event, thank-you notes are written. If the visitor was from a hobby club, another meeting could be arranged so the children could see more of the club's collections and meet other older people. *I Know a Lady* (Zolotow, 1984) is an interesting book to read as a follow-up to these activities (Seefeldt, Warman, Jantz, & Galper, 1990).

In one class, an amateur spelunker fascinated the third graders with slides of cave exploring, a display of the tools and gear used, and a sample of a stalactite. An elderly philatelist shared her stamp collection portraying African Americans. Other elders have taught children how to weave, quilt, make pottery, and work with wood.

Interaction with elders leads naturally to a variety of language arts activities designed to extend and expand children's understanding of age, the elderly, and the continuity of life. Some third graders, while too young to complete a thorough oral history, may be ready to interview a grandparent or older person in their family. *Golden Days: An Oral History Guide* (Blaustein, 1985) can be helpful. Selecting some questions from the guide, children can question elders about friendships they have had, what they did when they were in the third grade, and what interests they share. *Me and My Family Tree* (Showers, 1978) gives children information on genealogy by introducing the relationships between generations through one child's family tree.

Vocabulary is strengthened through contact with elders. After working with elders for several months, one class made an illustrated dictionary called "Words for Growing." Words such as infant, toddler, preschooler, adolescent, teenager, juvenile, retiree, adult, and senior citizen were included.

Whatever the experience, children will also begin to sense the continuity of their own lives through contact with elders. By coming into contact with elders, they will create an image of how they will change and grow in the future, as well as of how they were in the past. They will internalize the fact that they will still be the same person, no matter how much they change with age.

The Past

To understand the past, children must comprehend that the present is but a single moment in a continuous process, and they must be able to store and retrieve memories. The primary age child has yet to fully develop these two skills. A chronological understanding of the past will not be present until the period of formal operational thought begins.

Yet, primary children are intensely interested in both the immediate and distant past. Children have an urge to understand what has gone before.

Adults must shuttle back and forth with children from the present to the past. This dipping into the past without concern for a logical development of chronology from the past to the present does not violate basic principles of learning. To wait until children can handle true chronology is to deprive them of one of the most important learnings of early childhood. (Wann, Dorn, & Liddle, 1962, p. 58)

Yet another reason, added to those above, to involve elders in the primary classroom is to introduce children to concepts of the past. As older people tell stories of their past, share photos, or teach a craft, children not only develop a sense of the continuity of individual lives but also of a shared history.

Oral as well as physical records of the past are of interest to children. They can compare old-fashioned egg beaters, wooden cookie cutters, rolling pins, and other tools with newer versions; or antique toys with new models of antique cars, planes, or boats. This gives children the opportunity to compare the things they know and use today with things from the past. Children might engage in an activity like classifying model cars, planes, or boats according to use and/or age, and make charts sequencing the models, from oldest to newest.

With any object from the past, teachers should initiate discussions to extend and clarify children's concepts. "Why do you think the train was made like this?" "How do you know it was used a long time ago?" "How is it just like the one we use today?" (Seefeldt, 1993).

Almost every community has a museum that preserves traces of the past. The local library and fire station, or local churches, may also house relics children can examine. Where larger museums are the only ones available, children can still benefit from a visit, which will be made more profitable for young children if the focus is on only one room or exhibit.

The past is also recorded in writing and, according to some experts, stories and myths are ideal vehicles for learning (Egan, 1988). Through reading myths and fictionalized stories of the past, children's inability to comprehend concepts of time or change can be transcended (Finn & Ravitch, 1988). Egan suggests that, even though primary grade children have only embryonic concepts of time, change, and the past, they do experience, know, and understand concepts of power, ambition, and revenge—the universal themes of many myths, folk tales, and stories.

Brophy (1990) believes, however, that stories used to teach children concepts of the past should be factual and accurate. If teachers use myths or fictionalized accounts of the past to teach history, children might learn to distrust them. Well-chosen biographies and engaging accounts of the past—such as *When I was Young in the Mountains* (Rylant, 1982), *Children of Long Ago* (Little, 1988), *If You Grew Up with George Washington* (Gross, 1982), and many others—can, however, bring a meaningful awareness of the past to children.

Methods of the Historian

Primary grade children are not historians, yet with each social studies experience they use the methods of an historian. When working with social studies concepts, children will sense problems; collect, observe, and analyze information; and reach conclusions.

SENSING A PROBLEM. From deciding how many carrots to buy to make soup, to thinking about what they will be like when they are old, social studies offers children real problems to solve. Throughout the curriculum, children should be presented with experiences that give them the opportunity to ask questions, identify problems, and puzzle over solutions.

GATHERING INFORMATION. To find out what games their grandparents played when they were in school, or how to record the passage of time, children must collect information. The methods of the historian are used as children observe traces of the past, interview people, or examine texts and reference materials.

OBSERVING DATA. Having gathered the necessary information, children observe. Observation skills can be fostered by directing children to look for specific things and to feel, listen, and think about what they have observed.

ANALYZING THE INFORMATION. Historians who collect and analyze data from the past make inferences about life in the past: what it was like, how people lived, what they did, and what they believed. Children make the same analyses and inferences from their data and observations.

REACHING CONCLUSIONS. Just as historians do, children reach conclusions about the past based on available data. The data collected may not be complete, and their conclusions may not be thorough or accurate, yet children should be asked to reach conclusions and summarize their findings and ideas.

SUMMARY

Even when organized around concepts central to the study of history, social studies still constitutes a broad and all-encompassing subject matter. Integrated into every part of the curriculum and school day in a primary grade classroom, social studies cannot be separated out.

Social studies truly is one with the language arts. Children must talk and listen to one another as they experience social studies content. Finding meaning in their experiences, written expression follows. Social studies is also integrated with other areas of the curriculum—science, art, music, or mathematics.

To bring social studies and primary grade children together, an astute teacher internalizes key concepts and then presents them to children in meaningful ways. Skilled teachers—knowing that children learn through activity—structure learning to include mental, physical, and social experiences. One experience should lead to another, which in turn leads to yet another. Thus, children can see relationships between and among their experiences, and develop generalizations about the world. Through well-planned lessons in language arts and social studies, the overall goals of education will be fulfilled. By learning and living in the primary grade classroom, children will develop the knowledge and skills required of citizens of a democracy.

REFERENCES

Blaustein, R. (1985). *Golden days: An oral history guide.* (Available from Center for Appalachian Studies and Services, East Tennessee State University, P. O. Box 70556, Johnson City, TN, 37614.)

Brophy, J. (1990). Teaching social studies for understanding and higher-order applications. *The Elementary School Journal, 90,* (4), 352–417.

Burke, A. (1923). *A conduct curriculum for the kindergarten and first-grade.* New York: Scribner's.

California State Board of Education (CSBE) (1987). *History–social science framework.* Sacramento: Author.

Dyson, A. H. (1987). The value of time off tasks: Young children's spontaneous talk and deliberate text. *Harvard Educational Review, 57* (4), 534–564.

Egan, K. (1988). *Primary understanding: Education in early childhood.* London: Routledge.

Elkind, D. (1981). Child development and the social science curriculum of the elementary school. *Social Education, 45* (6), 435–437.

Finn, C. E., & Ravitch, D. (1988). No trivial pursuit. *Phi Delta Kappan, 69* (8), 559–564.

Freeman, E. B., & Hatch, J. A. (1989). What schools expect young children to know and do: An analysis of kindergarten report cards. *The Elementary School Journal, 89* (5), 595–607.

Jarolimek, J., & Parker, W. C. (1993). *Social studies in elementary education* (9th ed.). New York: Macmillan.

Langer, S. (1942). *Philosophy in a new key.* Cambridge: Harvard University Press.

Mitchell, L. S. (1934). *Young geographers.* New York: Bank Street College.

National Council for the Social Studies (NCSS). (1989). *Social studies for early childhood and elementary school children: Preparing children for the 21st century.* Washington, DC: Author.

National Commission on Social Studies in the Schools (NCSSS). (1989). *Charting a course: Social studies for the 21st century.* New York: Author.

Seefeldt, C. (1993). *Social studies for the preschool/primary child.* Columbus, OH: Macmillan.

Seefeldt, C., Jantz, R., Galper, A., & Serock, K. (1977). As children see old folks. *Today's Education, 66* (2), 70–74.

Seefeldt, C., Warman, B., Jantz, R., & Galper, A. (1990). *Young and old together.* Washington, DC: National Association for the education of young children.

Snow, C. (1983). Literacy and language: Relationships during the preschool years. *Harvard Educational Review, 53* (2), 165–189.

Tiene, D. (1986). Making history come alive. *The Social Studies, 77* (5), 205–206.

Vukelich, R., & Thornton, S. J. (1990). Children's understanding of historical time: Implications for instruction. *Childhood Education, 67* (1), 22–25.

Vygotsky, L. (1986). *Thought and language.* (Revised ed.). Cambridge, MA: MIT Press.

Wann, K., Dorn, M., & Liddle, E. (1962). *Fostering intellectual development in young children.* New York: Teachers College Press.

Children's Book References

Bang, M. (1983). *Ten, nine, eight.* New York: Greenwillow Books.

de Paola, T. (1988). *The legend of the Indian paintbrush.* New York: Putnam.

Gross, Ruth Belov. (1982). *If you grew up with George Washington.* New York: Scholastic.

Hest, A. (1986). *The purple coat.* Illus. by Amy Schwartz. New York: The Four Winds.

Hutchins, P. (1983). *You'll soon grow into them.* New York: Macmillan.

Keats, E. J. (1962). *The snowy day.* New York: Viking.

Little, L. J. (1988). *Children of long ago.* Illus. by Jan S. Gilchrist. New York: Philomel.

Martin, B., & Archaumbault, J. (1987). *Knots on a counting rope.* Illus. by Ted Rand. New York: Henry Holt.

Martin, B. (1969). *Good morning, good night.* New York: Holt, Rinehart & Winston.

McCloskey, R. (1952). *One morning in Maine.* New York: Viking.

Milne, A. A. (1927). *Now we are six.* New York: Dutton.

Rylant, C. (1982). *When I was young in the mountains.* Illus. by Diane Goode. New York: Dutton.

Showers, P. (1978). *Me and my family tree.* New York: Crowell.

Zolotow, C. (1984). *I know a lady.* New York: Greenwillow.

8

Whole Language and Primary Grades Mathematics and Science: Keeping in Step with National Standards

ROSALIND CHARLESWORTH AND KAREN K. LIND

Instructional practices in primary grade mathematics and science, in the wake of changing professional guidelines and standards, are moving away from the treatment of content areas as separate entities. An integrated approach to curriculum and instruction is being promoted by many major professional organizations, including the National Association for the Education of Young Children (NAEYC) (Bredekamp, 1989), the National Council of Teachers of Mathematics (NCTM) (1989, 1991), the American Association for the Advancement of Science (AAAS) (1989, 1994), the National Research Council (NRC) (1993), and the National Science Teachers Association (NSTA) (1994).

These organizations emphasize the critical place of spoken and written language in the integration of the content areas. The NCTM Board of Directors has endorsed the position statement from the National Council of Teachers of English (NCTE) (1993), which specifies that all classrooms should be language-intensive in instruction in all the disciplines ("NCTM endorses," 1994). The whole language philosophy and the whole language approach to communication are major elements in the integrated mathematics and science curriculum.

This chapter opens with a summary of the essential components of the national professional guidelines and standards relevant to mathematics and science, followed by a description of the aims and goals of the science and mathematics programs in the primary grades. The relationship of the whole language philosophy to mathematics and science is then delineated. The following section describes the movement toward whole language math and science, focusing particularly on literature and writing. Integration through themes and webbing is described, followed by descriptions of instruction guided by the learning cycle, and inclusion of cooperative learning groups. Finally a visit is made to a classroom where the integrated curriculum is seen in action in the unfolding of a lesson that integrates language arts with basic mathematics/science concepts.

PROFESSIONAL GUIDELINES AND STANDARDS

In 1993, the National Council of Teachers of English published a position statement, *Learning Through Language,* that focused on the integration of language-intensive classrooms. Students in a language-intensive classroom:

- Write in journals, make lists, and exchange ideas with peers as they learn new concepts and processes
- Work together through talking, collaborating, and sharing both oral and written communication
- Ask and respond to questions, along with the teachers
- Select topics for study, do independent research, and share what they learn with their peers
- Maintain learning logs and journals
- Develop portfolios of their work, which they frequently review and update.

The NCTE (1993) position is summed up in the following statement: "We reiterate, classrooms where language is used for learning are fundamentally different classrooms. They are places where students talk, read, and write frequently, places where they learn better and their learning lasts longer" (p. 5). This position is congruent with and supportive of the professional standards and guidelines for mathematics and science.

Communications; Reasoning; Connections

The NCTM Standards (1989) stress three language-related areas: *communications, reasoning,* and *connections.* Communications should afford children opportunities to express their ideas through physical materials and through drawing pictures and diagrams. Language can be used to clarify ideas and to "relate their everyday language to mathematical language and symbols" (p. 26). Opportunities for communications can help children "realize that representing, discussing, reading, writing, and listening to mathematics are a vital part of learning and using mathematics" (p. 26).

Reasoning requires the use of language and enables students to draw logical conclusions, explain their thinking, justify their answers and solution processes, apply patterns and relationships to arrive at solutions, and make sense out of mathematics. Connections involve applying mathematical concepts to other areas, such as science, and using mathematics in everyday life. Language in all its aspects, written and oral, is critical to communications, reasoning, and making connections.

The field of science has not as yet published a set of standards comparable to those for mathematics. However, there are two national reform efforts underway. Two different perspectives are being developed: one by the American Association for the Advancement of Science (AAAS) (1989, 1994) and the other by the National Research Council (NRC) (1993). The AAAS's Project 2061 (1989) initiative is developing a long-term plan to strengthen student literacy in science, mathematics, and technology. Activity-based science instruction that makes connections with other disciplines through real world experiences is stressed. In the second Project 2061 report (AAAS, 1994), the organization emphasizes the importance of connecting with the other disciplines. This emphasis is also supported by the National Research Council (NRC, 1993).

An Integrated Curriculum

The emphasis on communications, logical reasoning, and connections—with language serving as the glue that holds it all together—leads naturally into the concept of the *integrated curriculum,* a major component of the NAEYC guidelines (Bredekamp, 1989) for developmentally appropriate practice. In the section of the guidelines for the primary grades (ages 5–8) the importance of the integrated curriculum in mathematics is described as follows: "The goal of the math program is to enable children to use math through exploration, discovery, and solving meaningful problems. Math activities are integrated with other relevant projects, such as science and social studies" (p. 71). The goal for science is described as follows:

> Discovery science is a major part of the curriculum, building on children's natural interest in the world. . . . Through science projects and field trips, children learn to plan; to dictate and/or write their plans; to apply thinking skills such as hypothesizing, observing, experimenting, and verifying; and to learn many science facts related to their own experience. (p. 72)

The NCTM standards (1989) also contain components that demand integration with other content areas. For example:

A developmentally appropriate curriculum encourages the exploration of a wide variety of mathematical ideas in such a way that children retain their enjoyment of, and curiosity about, mathematics. It incorporates real-world contexts, children's experiences, and children's language in developing ideas. (p. 18)

The goals and objectives of these national organizations' standards and guidelines clearly state the essential position of language in the achievement of the goals of mathematics and science.

GOALS OF THE PRIMARY GRADE SCIENCE AND MATHEMATICS PROGRAMS

The goals of primary grade mathematics and science programs are overlapping and logically integrated. Both math and science focus on the development and application of fundamental concepts. As students proceed from prekindergarten through the primary grades, the major goal is to develop concepts through problem solving and the use of process skills rather than to have them memorize facts. The total amount of scientific information now available is so immense that it is impossible to learn it all. Further, the body of scientific knowledge is changing rapidly and may be outmoded by the time today's primary grade student finishes high school. Technology has moved mathematics into new frontiers; calculators and computers can do complex calculations and ordering of data while the problem solver/investigator looks at the overall picture (Charlesworth & Lind, in press).

Problem Solving

The problem-solving focus emphasizes children working independently and in cooperative groups. The teacher's role is that of a facilitator and a guide. The content of problems comes from students' real-life experiences and interests, and might be focused in science, social studies, art, and/or music. Children interact with materials and activities that promote logical thinking. "A problem is a question which engages someone in searching for a solution" (Skinner, 1990, p. 1). That is, a problem involves a question that is important to the student and therefore engages the student's enthusiastic attention to arrive at a solution. Science investigations are one type of problem that children usually find interesting. Mathematics is an essential part of science investigations, since the process skills applied in a science investigation are also fundamental concepts and skills in mathematics (Charlesworth & Lind, in press).

Process Skills

The content of science is discovered through the application of *process skills*. Students use process skills to process new information through concrete experiences. The vehicles for application may be hands-on activities accompanied by reading, listening, and discussing to promote thinking. As primary grade students investigate to find answers to questions of interest, they apply the skills of observing, comparing, measuring, classifying, and communicating: skills that are fundamental to mathematics problem solving as well. As they move through the primary grade level, students gradually master the intermediate process skills: gathering and organizing information, inferring, and predicting. With a strong base of primary- and intermediate-grade process skills, students in intermediate and secondary grades move on to the abstract skills of forming hypotheses and separating variables. As students work with primary- and intermediate-grade process skills they are applying higher level mathematics concepts and skills, such as using number symbols and standard units of measurement, doing higher order classifying, constructing graphs, and doing whole number operations. The development of these skills and concepts is gradual and overlapping. Simultaneously, children's whole language skills are emerging. The expanding ability to work with written and oral language can be applied to support problem-solving investigations as vehicles for recording and communicating students' thoughts and findings. Children's literature can serve as a major starting point for problem-solving investigations.

THE WHOLE LANGUAGE PHILOSOPHY AND MATHEMATICS AND SCIENCE

The emphasis on communications, reasoning, and making connections in mathematics and science relates naturally to the whole language philosophy in reading and language arts. Just as mathematics and science teachers have turned toward a conceptual emphasis for instruction lodged in real-world experiences (versus memorization and drill and learning basic facts and formulas) so too have reading and language arts teachers turned to the whole language philosophy, which integrates written and spoken language into meaningful contexts. Reading and writing are learned through active involvement in the context of meaningful experiences with literature, drama, movement and music, art, science, mathematics, and social studies. The critical elements in whole language (see Chapter 1) are: immersion in language and print; opportunities and resources, such as materials, time, space, and activities; meaningful communication; a teacher who is a communication role model; acceptance of children as readers and writers; and the expectation that children will become literate. In the whole language classroom, children listen to good literature, experiment with writing, and learn to read naturally. They explain and discuss, record data, and write about their explorations in science and mathematics. Through these activities, children develop integrated skills in listening, reading, writing, and spelling in a meaningful context.

WHOLE LANGUAGE INFLUENCES ON MATH AND SCIENCE

While some educators have supported the importance of language per se—using children's literature and students' own writing in the learning of mathematics in response to the NCTM emphasis on communication (NCTM, 1989)—others have proposed direct adaptations of whole language to mathematics and science instruction to develop a total instructional conceptualization. These latter efforts will be described first.

Direct Applications

Direct applications of the whole language philosophy to mathematics instruction are suggested by Brown (1991) and by Stead and Semple (1992). Brown outlines a plan for "whole concept mathematics" based on the whole language concept; its purpose is to avoid rote learning and ability grouping. Through whole concept mathematics, students see the whole picture rather than a group of individual, unrelated skills. The emphasis is on problem solving using situations that are real and significant to the students. Brown uses the term *whole concept* rather than *whole language* in order to place the emphasis on concepts, but follows, nevertheless, a whole language type of pattern. Brown proposes an emphasis on real-life problems, cooperative learning activities where students can exchange ideas, and the writing of daily logs and math journals as an opportunity to record knowledge and express ideas. Brown proposes that the curriculum be reformulated to emphasize learning universal concepts and the process of learning *how* to learn. Such a curriculum would focus on the in-depth study of a few concepts rather than on the currently prevalent approach that attempts surface coverage of many concepts. Brown suggests studying concepts in different ways that fit a variety of learning styles. Thus, whole concept mathematics is learner centered and holistic in its focus.

Stead and Stemple (1992) became concerned that their mathematics program was not nearly as interesting to students, and as successful, as their language program, which is based on a whole language philosophy. Therefore, they decided to try a *whole-to-parts* approach in mathematics, following the pattern that was so successful in language instruction. They began by letting the students explore problems that were interesting to them. Their new approach to math was based on the best features of their language instruction and was built on the following ideas:

- Math needs to be explored in meaningful contexts.
- Children need to develop a positive attitude toward math in order to effectively acquire math skills and understandings.
- Children benefit from the experiences of finding themselves being mathematicians when they look for math in their environment, form hypotheses, and then justify the results they have gained.
- The teacher's role is crucial not only in promoting positive attitudes towards math, but also in modeling effective ways for children to explore areas of interest.
- Math should be integrated with other curriculum areas. (Stead & Stemple, 1992, p. 43)

There should be a balance between, on the one hand, teacher-directed modeling activities and, on the other, child-directed activities that provide an opportunity for the students to use the strategies that have been modeled.

Malecki (1990) outlines a plan for teaching whole science. She defines *whole science* as science taught "with an interdisciplinary scope" (p. 232). This is achieved by teaching through thematic units. She believes that by emulating the whole language approach of thematic unit teaching, students can be involved in the scientific method through participation in several subject areas. Links can be developed with shared reading, process writing, art, and other areas of the curriculum. Whole science should include the following components:

- Topics and activities should have personal meaning and social relevance for the students.
- Science is integrated with other subjects, specifically language arts and mathematics.
- Instruction begins with students' current knowledge. (Malecki, 1990, p. 232)

In this way, a smaller number of topics is explored in more depth than is done conventionally.

It is evident from these examples that the whole language philosophy is easily adapted to mathematics and science to provide more conceptually based, student-centered, in-depth study.

Applications Using Literature

Recently there has been an explosion of ideas and materials designed to place literature at the center of the mathematics and science curriculums. A multitude of children's books that include mathematics and science concepts can be identified and used as a core for whole language and math and science integrated instruction. Charlesworth and Lind (in press) include a selected bibliography of children's books with math and science concepts; *Science and Children* publishes a yearly, annotated bibliography of books containing science concepts; Thiessen and Matthias (1993) provide an annotated bibliography of books containing mathematics concepts; and Schon (1992, 1994) provides annotated bibliographies of books in Spanish that contain science concepts. Whitin and Wilde (1992), Whitin (1994), and Whitin and Gary (1994) provide descriptions of books that contain math concepts, along with examples of children's written and drawn responses to the stories. Welchman-Tischler's (1992) book presents sample lessons and ideas and examples of children's drawn and written responses to selected pieces of literature.

Some books were written with math in mind while others, which were not originally created with math in mind, may offer opportunities for applying mathematical concepts and skills. For example, Lewis, Long, and Mackay (1993) describe how *So Many Cats* by Beatrice Schenk de Regniers (1985) stimulates a first grade group to count, and how *The Doorbell Rang* by Pat Hutchins (1986) stimulates some second graders to write and dictate division stories. Gailey (1993) provides guidelines for selecting concept books that will enhance mathematics instruction. She suggests that the books should have interesting formats and type that is of an appropriate size for young children. Books should also be mathematically correct, accurate, and depict current social and economic settings. Children's concept books should present concepts in a logical sequence, from simple to complex and from specific to general, with vocabulary at the appropriate level for the intended audience. Thrailkill (1994) describes some specific activities that she has introduced with her second graders. She found that by weaving literature into her math program, she could better tap the strengths of her students in reading and in math. They worked with classification attributes using "The Lost Button" from *Frog and Toad Are Friends* by Arnold Lobel (1985); using numbers from 1–105 with *The Philharmonic Gets Dressed* by Karla Kuskin (1986); using spatial relations with *Round Trip* by Ann Jonas (1983); and using beginning division skills with *The Doorbell Rang* by Pat Hutchins (1986). Midkiff and Cramer (1993) suggest still other concepts that can be stimulated through literature, such as money (*Caps for Sale*, Slobofkins, 1968); size and classification (*Sizes*, Pienkowski, 1983); time

(*Clean Your Room, Harvey Moon!* Cummings, 1991); and measurement (*The Popcorn Book,* de Paola, 1978). Kliman (1993) describes how students explore relative size after reading *Gulliver's Travels* (Swift, 1983).

Books can also enrich the study of science topics. McMath and King (1993) suggest that books with science concepts be read aloud, then followed up with related activities that explore the topic, and then placed where they are accessible for children to look at again. McMath and King suggest several themes that take off from books. Some examples are plant life activities, following a reading of *Planting a Rainbow* (Ehlert, 1988); *Guinea Pigs Don't Read Books* (Bare, 1985), which opens the way to a unit on pets; and *And Still the Turtle Watched* (MacGill-Callahan & Moser, 1991), which introduces the topic of environmental awareness. From another view, Stiffler (1992) suggests starting with a hands-on science activity and following it up with books that illustrate the concepts learned from the concrete activity. For example, she suggests that first graders play "marbles" with tennis balls and then observe and share what happens. The activity can then be related to the content of the book *Playgrounds* (Gibbons, 1985). Of course, children can also create their own books. Having their own creations on hand based on child-selected topics is a good motivation for reading. Reif and Rauch (1994) suggest that children might create alphabet books centering on a science topic, such as "animals" or "the ocean." Child-created books might be focused on describing a field trip, or on answering a question, such as "How do we use water?" or "What kinds of creatures live in the sea?" The children can dictate or write the narrative and create their own illustrations.

Math and science can also be integrated into more broad-based literature units. For example, Raines and Canady (1992) suggest a variety of activities to expand the existing concepts in primary grade children's books. A variety of books inspire science and nature, mathematics, and/or cooking (math and science) activities. For example, to expand on the book *Crow Boy* (Yashima, 1955), Raines and Canady suggest cooking Crow boy's rice balls (math and science) and going for Chibi's listening walk (science and nature). Follow-ups to *The Magic School Bus at the Waterworks* (Cole, 1986) include measuring water consumption (math), assembling plastic water pipes (science), and taking a trip to the waterworks (science).

Applications Using Writing

In the whole language philosophy, writing and reading are integrated for communicating and recording information. When children dictate information for the teacher to write and then write their own ideas—as they reach the point where they can—this supports communication of and reflection on mathematics problems and science investigations. Ideas for children writing in journals, developing problems, and writing their own problem books are bursting onto the mathematics and science scene.

Wadlington, Bitner, Partridge, and Austin (1992) suggest a three-phase process for connecting writing and cooperative problem solving. In the first phase, students brainstorm ways that writing can be used with mathematics—such as making a mathematics bulletin board, writing a letter about mathematics, creating a mathematics story or poem, etc. Next, students do a mathematics writing activity and then begin keeping a mathematics journal, where they record and reflect on their daily mathematics activities. In the second phase, students move into heterogeneous cooperative learning groups of three or four. Each group works together to complete a math task. Once they understand the rules of working in a cooperative group, they move on to phase three, problem solving. In phase three, children work in cooperative groups to solve everyday problems. They record in their journals the problem, the possible strategies, their solutions, and their reflections.

Scott, Williams, and Hyslip (1992) describe how journals are used as part of the mathematics curriculum in two second grade classrooms. First, the children participate in a math experience using unfamiliar materials, followed by class discussion to stimulate thinking. From oral communication, the students progress to written communication as the teacher writes students' ideas on the chalkboard or charts of numbers on chart paper. Then the teacher models writing sentences as the whole class develops a class journal. Finally, the students begin writing in their own journals. Some copy off the charts, others write their own ideas, and some draw pictures and/or diagrams. Students who wish may share their journal entries with other students. On a weekly basis the teachers write responses in the journals.

Mills (1993) describes how children in a K-1 classroom wrote math stories centered on losing and growing teeth—an important part of life for 6-year-olds. The children drew pictures of mouths and teeth and wrote word and number sentences describing what it's like to lose baby teeth and to have second teeth grow in.

Children can gain an understanding of time through acquaintance with predictable sequences that are contained in storybooks, in recipes for cooking, or in the daily classroom schedule (Van Scoy & Fairchild, 1993). Some of these daily experiences can be recorded on calendars and/or in journals. Children might also record the sequence of steps in a science investigation. Srulowitz (1992) describes a project, "Diary of a Tree," in which children recorded the attributes of the trees in their school yard as the buds and leaves emerged from March through May. At the end of the study period the students wrote about what they had observed (younger students could dictate their findings).

Skinner (1990) teaches mathematics through problems created and presented as books. Skinner presents the first problems to her students in book form, in order to integrate mathematics and reading/language arts. The tiny books are on sturdy cardboard with an illustration and one sentence on each page. They are held together with spiral binding. The students are encouraged to use manipulatives, such as Unifix cubes, to aid in solutions or to act out their solutions. Eventually Skinner moves the students into dictating and then writing their own problems. She begins with her students at age 5, and by age 7, they are creating their own problems.

PLANNING THE INTEGRATED CURRICULUM

As described earlier, a major component of the NAEYC guidelines (Brede-kamp, 1989) for developmentally appropriate practice is that the curriculum should be *integrated*. Curriculum integration has been developed at the national level in Great Britain (Association for Science Education, 1989) and is described in the works of an ever increasing number of authors (i.e., AIMS educational products; Beougher, 1994; Burke, Snider, & Symonds, 1992; Charlesworth & Lind, in press; Edwards, 1990; Harcourt, 1988; Katz & Chard, 1989; Krogh, 1990; Piazza, Scott, & Carver, 1994; Raines & Canady, 1992; and Workman & Anziano, 1993).

Integration is usually accomplished by focusing on a theme or a topic (i.e., air, water, space, classification, ecology, the zoo, number sense, a piece of literature, etc.), deciding on the important concepts associated with the topic, and developing a plan through brainstorming a web. The thematic web, like a spider web, has a central point from which ideas grow in many directions, like the spokes of a wheel. The spokes of the web might be the major curriculum areas: mathematics, science, language arts, social studies, art, and music and movement (as suggested by Krogh, 1990), with various activities attached to each spoke. The spokes could also be the areas in the mathematics standards (NCTM, 1989) as suggested by Piazza, Scott, and Carver (1994) and Workman and Anziano (1993); or they might be important concepts within the theme or topic. For example, if the topic was air, the major concepts or spokes might be:

- Air can be hot or cold
- Air can make noise
- Air is all around us
- Air takes up space (Charlesworth & Lind, in press)

Various activities would then grow from each concept (see Figure 8.1). The selection and number of activities done with each class would vary with the time available and the interests of the students. Language activities would be an integral part of the plan.

INSTRUCTION

Early childhood instruction as recommended by the NAEYC (Bredekamp & Rosegrant, 1992) should follow guidelines derived from the NAEYC's science *Learning Cycle*. Bredekamp and Rosegrant have adapted the science Learning Cycle to early childhood education, and it encompasses three repeating processes:

- *Awareness:* a broad recognition of objects, people, events, or concepts that develops from experience.

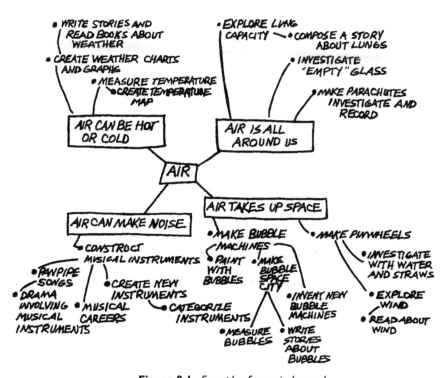

Figure 8.1. *Example of a curriculum web.*

- *Exploration:* the construction of personal meaning through sensory experiences with objects, people, events, or concepts.
- *Inquiry:* a comparison of the learner's constructions with those of the culture. Commonalities are recognized and generalizations are made that are more and more like those of adults.
- *Utilization:* the application and use of the learner's understandings in new settings and situations. (Bredekamp & Rosegrant, 1992, pp. 32–33)

Children at the primary grade level have just reached the point where they can move through all four stages of the cycle as they meet new concepts, themes, and topics of study. Each time a new situation for learning is encountered, the cycle begins with awareness, moves up to exploration, then inquiry, and finally utilization. Bredekamp and Rosegrant provide an example from mathematics in the measurement area:

- Three- and four-year-olds are aware of and explore comparative sizes.
- Fours, fives, and sixes explore with nonstandard units such as measuring the width of the rug using their own feet as units.
- Seven- and eight-year-olds begin to understand standard units of measurement and use a ruler or yardstick to measure the rug. (Bredekamp & Rosegrant, 1992, p. 35)

Bredekamp and Rosegrant caution that the cycle is not a hierarchical one. That is, utilization is not necessarily more valued than is awareness or exploration. Young children might be aware of concepts that they cannot yet utilize in the technical sense. For example, they might realize that the sun and moon take turns in appearing with day and night, but not understand the technicalities of the relationship of the earth, the moon, and the sun. It is important to provide experiences at the awareness and exploration levels before moving on to inquiry and utilization. If children come to school without these experiences at home—through having had opportunities to interact with and talk about these concepts, and to be read to at the awareness and exploratory levels—then it is especially important that these opportunities be provided at school.

Cooperative Learning Groups

Peer interaction, as well as adult interaction, is a critical component of learning. The whole language philosophy emphasizes this aspect of learning. While peer interaction usually comes about through informal groupings and self-selection during the preschool and kindergarten years, more formal grouping may be introduced in the primary grades. A popular approach in use today is the cooperative learning group (Cartwright, 1993;

Ellis & Whalen, 1992; "Warm up to," 1992; Wasserman, 1990). Groups may be child-selected or teacher-selected and are usually heterogeneous.

Wasserman suggests an instructional format for the primary grades that begins with an open-ended, exploratory play activity carried out in small, cooperative learning groups. The children contribute to one another's explorations and creative endeavors. An example of such an activity might be one for beginning a study of seeds and plants, designed to develop the concept that living things grow and change. In this activity, the children are provided with: a variety of seeds; fresh flowers and leaves; dried flowers and leaves; photographs of flowers, plants, and trees, either budding, in full bloom, or dormant; magnifying lenses; and scissors, measuring tools, and knives. The children observe the materials and record everything they learn about how plants, flowers, and trees grow and change. Younger children will dictate their findings; older children will write them down. Following the exploration there is a debriefing discussion and then the children are turned loose again in their groups to further explore the materials.

There are abundant resources available to guide the planning of the integrated curriculum. Now it's time to visit a primary classroom where mathematics and oral and written language are integrated.

A Visit to a Primary Classroom

North of Salt Lake City, at the foot of the Wasatch Mountains and adjacent to the Great Salt Lake, nestles the town of Kaysville, Utah. Not long ago it was a peaceful, small town isolated from the urban areas to the south. Today it is integrated into the thriving Salt Lake City suburban sprawl that has expanded north throughout Davis County. Kaysville Elementary School is in a relatively new building that the visitor finds to be bright and cheerful, with an atmosphere of constructive activity. School expansion has not caught up with the growing Davis County population; therefore, the county is going onto an all-year plan to have enough space for all the children. Claudia Wangsgaard and her 29 first graders have just returned from three weeks off track and have begun a new nine-week session.

Claudia explained that, as an elementary student, she found mathematics very stressful, so when she was introduced to *Mathematics Their Way* (Baratta-Lorton, 1976), she was very open to trying a hands-on approach that would make math exciting for her students. With time and experience she has integrated many other approaches into her program and developed a first grade sequence of developmentally appropriate activities that motivates her students' total involvement in and enjoyment of math. Although the school system has adopted a textbook series for mathematics, Wangsgaard has obtained permission not to use the text and to teach mathematics instead through the program she has developed. She is frequently asked to provide inservice workshops for other teachers who wish to make their mathematics instructional practices more developmentally appropriate.

MATH JOURNALS.   As the children enter the classroom, it is clear that they know the morning routine and settle right down to work. While Ms. Wangsgaard meets with small groups to go over the previous night's homework, the other students select something from an assortment of individual activities that support math, language arts, and perceptual motor development. During this time, Sara, a budding writer, brings over her math journal. The following two entries not only reveal Sara's thinking regarding mathematics but also show her progress in composing, spelling, and grammar. At the top of the first entry, dated *August 24, 1993* (the beginning of first grade), Sara has drawn an ABAB pattern, with alternating triangles and squares. Underneath she has written:

I did a Parent To Day	[I did a pattern today]
this is the Pratin	[This is the pattern]
I did iT with Letrs	[I did it with letters]
And with saps	[And with shapes]

The second entry, dated *January 25, 1994*, reads:

> there Were 4
> Boys playing
> Baskitball. And they
> Lost it. And a Girl
> Finded it. How Many
> is there Now?

5

CREATIVE COUNTING.   The day's math activities center on the book *One Gorilla* by Atsuko Morozumi (1990). This is a delightfully illustrated counting book. The narrative starts with one gorilla, who then wanders from page to page. Each illustration contains the gorilla and increasing numbers of different animals up to ten: two butterflies, three parakeets, four squirrels, and so on. Ms. Wangsgaard reads the book and promotes student discussion of each illustration. The group locates and counts the animals in each illustration and talks about where the gorilla is located.

Following the group book sharing, the children break up into small groups to work cooperatively on the following problem: *How many animals all together in this story?* The students gather their materials: large sheets of blank paper, tubs of Unifix cubes, pencils, and crayons. They are to figure out the number of animals using any method they wish. Ms. Wangsgaard suggests that they draw their solution and then write at least two sentences explaining the methods used to solve the problem. She reminds them that they need to decide who will write the words, who will draw, and who will manipulate the Unifix Cubes. There is a buzz of activity as the students organize themselves and go to work. Ms. Wangsgaard circulates from group to group, facilitating the problem-solving process. When everyone has finished, the class moves back into a whole group and one reporter-volunteer from each small group, in turn, reports the group results. The group holds up the large sheet of paper with their work and the reporter explains the method used to arrive at the number of animals in the story. Each of the resulting posters is pinned up on the wall at child level.

Examination of the group posters reveals a variety of approaches to the task, the students' methods of organizing, and their writing process. One group has counted out Unifix cubes and then, using one-to-one correspondence, written tally marks; another group has made one long row of cubes stuck together; a third group counted out the cubes and then drew each cube; and a fourth group created the subgroups and then counted the total. The written descriptions of the solution process reflect the children's thinking and provide examples of first grade invented spellings and of the children's concepts as they are first learning about punctuation:

> *Jason, Caitlin, Malorie, and Kady*
>
> We did unafick cubes
> and then we did tally
> Marcks and there were 56
> *Alyson, George, Chance, and Tim:*
> We counted them up
> and there was 56.
> It was fun!

> *Rafferty, Laura, Austin, and Morgan*

W huk't the Nomber of	[We hooked the number of
yunufixcud's We thot	Unifix Cubes we thought
that hawe meny animals	that how many animals
There were We huk't 56	there were We hooked 56
yunifixcud's together.	Unifix Cubes together.]

Michelle, Mary, and Eric

We + up the thing to 55.	[We plus up the thing to 55.
We + 1 + 10 Then we had 55.	We plus up one to ten then we had 55.]

David, Tina, and Jonathon

We figured it out by uoonqulds [Unifix Cubes]
We uoose [use] tale [tally] marx [marks].

Krysta, Sara, and Steve B.

We guessed 57 because we used
The Unifix Cubes.
Why? Because it helped us to count.

This portion of the activity provided for communication of thinking through concrete representations, drawings, and both written and oral language.

FINDING AND MAKING PATTERNS.   Following this whole class activity, the students are given another question to answer: *Was there a pattern in our story?* Ms. Wangsgaard reads the story again to refresh their memories. They work again in small groups with Unifix Cubes but have the choice of making the pattern individually or as a group. Again there is a buzz of activity as the students develop their versions of the pattern in the story. Some children make models of the basic pattern (gorilla, X cubes; gorilla, X + 1 cube; gorilla, X + . . . cubes). Others construct models that show the increasing number of different animals in each illustration, that is, 1 cube (gorilla), 2 cubes (butterflies), 3 cubes (parakeets), and so on. The patterns are constructed in a variety of configurations. When everyone is finished the children show their pattern constructions and explain their rationales, providing for communication using concrete materials and oral language.

Now it was time for recess. As the students leave the room, one is overheard to comment, "Math is fun!" Following recess the students make bead necklaces using the pattern "gorilla, X animal," but extending the pattern as far beyond ten as their length of yarn will hold. Ms. Wangsgaard explains that they can use the necklaces to tell the story at home. When the necklaces are finished Ms. Wangsgaard suggests that the children write gorilla stories. Two of the stories are shown in Figures 8.2 and 8.3. Note the pattern in Laura's story (the sun shining, then rain, then the sun shining again, etc.). Note that Alyson's older sister was in California at the time Alyson was writing her story, participating in a cheerleader contest, and that

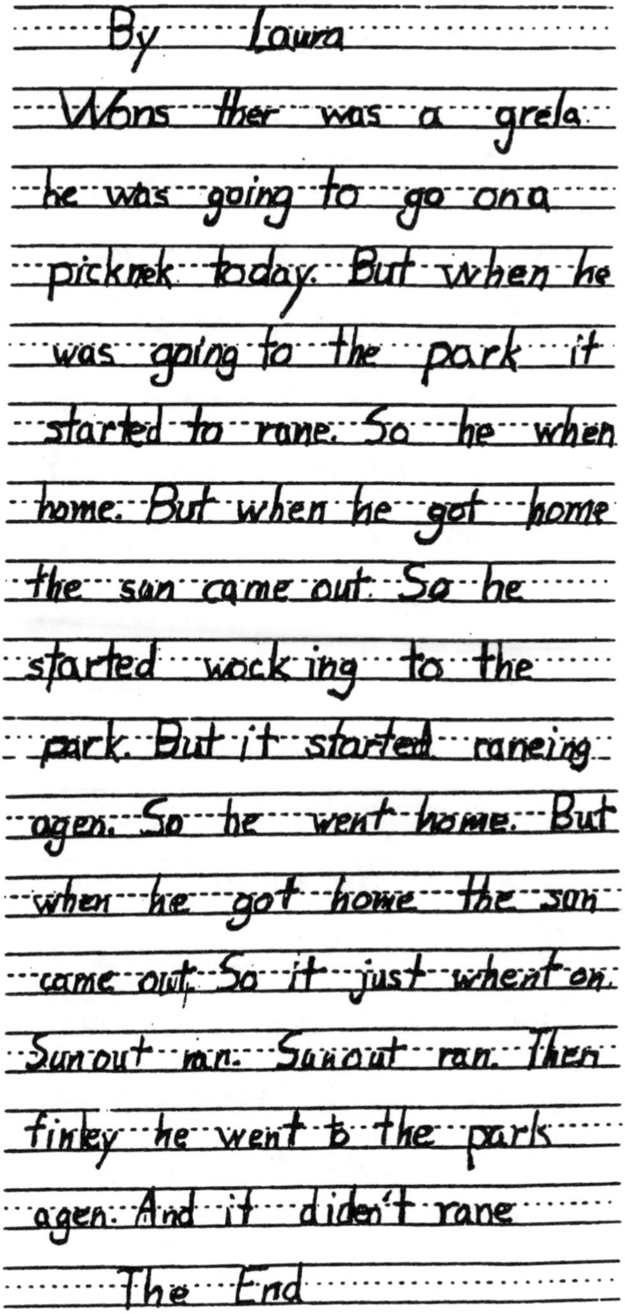

By Laura

Wons ther was a grela
he was going to go on a
picknek today. But when he
was going to the park it
started to rane. So he when
home. But when he got home
the sun came out. So he
started wocking to the
park. But it started raneing
agen. So he went home. But
when he got home the son
came out. So it just whent on.
Sun out man. Sun out ran. Then
finley he went to the park
agen. And it diden't rane
The End

Figure 8.2. *Laura's gorilla story.*

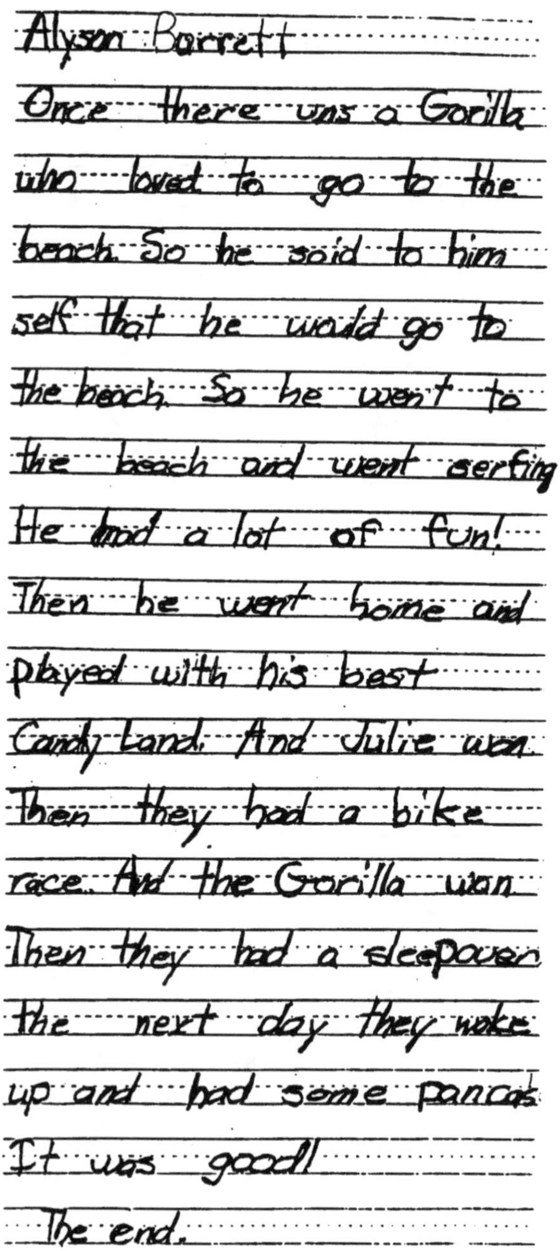

Alyson Barrett

Once there was a Gorilla who loved to go to the beach. So he said to himself that he would go to the beach. So he went to the beach and went serfing He had a lot of fun! Then he went home and played with his best Candy Land. And Julie won Then they had a bike race. And the Gorilla won Then they had a sleepover the next day they woke up and had some pancas It was good! The end.

Figure 8.3. *Alyson's gorilla story.*

the sister had gone surfing. Alyson uses the gorilla as a vehicle to describe her vision of what her sister is doing. In Ms. Wangsgaard's classroom, it's time to go to lunch. The children go off to the cafeteria proudly wearing their story necklaces.

This visit to Ms. Wangsgaard's first grade classroom provides a brief glimpse into the relationship between whole language and mathematics and science concept development. Counting, patterning, and problem solving are important concepts and skills that lay the foundation for competency in mathematics and science. Centering the lesson on information in a book builds on children's interest in books in general and provides them with an example of how basic information may be woven into the text and illustrations. The children learn how writing can serve their needs as they use their emerging competencies to describe a real life experience and to create fantasy experiences. Finally, working in groups provides opportunities to develop cooperative social interaction skills and to fine-tune oral language competencies in a non-threatening situation with peers.

SUMMARY

The current trend toward a whole language philosophy in the early childhood classroom fits well with the emphasis on communication, reasoning, and making connections in mathematics and science. The current and developing national standards for mathematics and science emphasize the need for an integrated curriculum that provides opportunities to read, write, talk, and draw about both content areas. The processes involved in reasoning and problem solving—rather than those involved in rote memorization—are the current and future emphases in mathematics and science instruction. The emphasis is on exploring and investigating through concrete activities, with real things and with real people. More and more, *whole* math and *whole* science will be in the forefront of these content areas.

REFERENCES

American Association for the Advancement of Science (AAAS) (1989). *Science for all Americans: A Project 2061 report on literacy goals in science, mathematics and technology.* Washington, DC: Author.

AAAS (1994). *Benchmarks in science literacy.* Washington, DC: Author.

AIMS Educational Products. AIMS Educational Foundation, P.O. Box 8120, Fresno, CA 93747-8120.

Association for Science Education (1989). *The national curriculum—making it work for the primary school.* College Lane, Hatfield, Herts AL109AA, England: Author.

Baratta-Lorton, M. (1976). *Mathematics their way.* Menlo Park, CA: Addison-Wesley.

Beougher, C. (1994). Making connections with teddy bears. *Arithmetic Teacher, 41* (7), 354–362.

Bredekamp, S. (Ed.) (1989). *Developmentally appropriate practice in early childhood programs serving children from birth through age eight.* Washington, DC: National Association for the Education of Young Children.

Bredekamp, S., & Rosegrant, T. (1992). *Reaching potentials: Appropriate curriculum and assessment for young children.* Washington, DC: National Association for the Education of Young Children.

Brown, C. L. (1991). Whole concept mathematics: A whole language application. *Educational Horizons, 69* (3), 159–163.

Burke, D., Snider, A., & Symonds, P. (1992). *Math excursions 1: Project-based mathematics.* Portsmouth, NH: Heinemann.

Burns, M. (1992). *Math and literature (K-3).* (Available from Math Solutions Publications, Cuisinaire Co. of America, White Plains, NY.)

Cartwright, S. (1993). Cooperative learning can occur in any kind of program. *Young Children, 48* (2), 12–14.

Charlesworth, R., & Lind, K. (in press). *Math and science for young children* (2nd ed.). Albany, NY: Delmar.

Edwards, D. (1990). *Maths in context: A thematic approach.* Portsmouth, NH: Heinemann.

Ellis, S. S., & Whalen, S. F. (1992). Keys to cooperative learning. *Instructor, 101* (6), 34–37.

Gailey, S. K. (1993). The mathematics-children's-literature connection. *Arithmetic Teacher, 40* (5), 258–261.

Harcourt, L. (1988). *Explorations for early childhood.* Menlo Park, CA: Addison-Wesley.

Katz, L. G, & Chard, S. C. (1989). *Engaging children's minds: The project approach.* Norwood, NJ: Ablex.

Kliman, M. (1993). Integrating mathematics and literature in the elementary classroom. *Arithmetic Teacher, 40* (6), 318–321.

Krogh, S. (1990). *The integrated early childhood curriculum.* New York: McGraw-Hill.

Lewis, B. A., Long, R., & Mackay, M. (1993). Fostering communication in mathematics using children's literature. *Arithmetic Teacher, 40* (8), 470–473.

Malecki, C. L. (1990). Teaching whole science: In a departmentalized elementary setting. *Childhood Education, 66* (4), 232–236.

McMath, J., & King, M. (1993). Open books, open minds. *Science and Children, 30* (5), 33–36.

Midkiff, R. B., & Cramer, M. M. (1993). Stepping stones to mathematical understanding. *Arithmetic Teacher, 40* (6), 303–305.

Mills, H. (1993). Teaching math concepts in a K-1 class doesn't have to be like pulling teeth—But maybe it should be! *Young Children, 48* (2), 17–20.

National Council of Teachers of English (NCTE) (1993). *Learning through language; A call for action in all disciplines.* Urbana, IL: Author.

National Council of Teachers of Mathematics (NCTM) (1989). *Curriculum and evaluation standards for school mathematics.* Reston, VA: Author.

NCTM (1991). *Professional standards for teaching mathematics.* Reston, VA: Author.

NCTM endorses NCTE position statement (1994, January). *NCTM News Bulletin,* pp. 1, 13.

National Research Council (NRC) (1993, July). *National science education standards: July 1993 progress report: A working paper of the National Committee on science education standards and assessment.* Washington, DC: Author.

National Science Teachers Association (NSTA) (1994). An NSTA position statement: Elementary school science. *NSTA handbook.* Washington, DC: Author.

Piazza, J. A., Scott, M. M., & Carver, E. C. (1994). Thematic webbing and the curriculum standards in the primary grades. *Arithmetic Teacher, 41* (6), 294–298.

Raines, S. C., & Canady, R. J. (1992). *Story S-T-R-E-T-C-H-E-R-S for the primary grades.* Mt. Rainier, MD: Gryphon House.

Reif, R. J., & Rauch, K. (1994). Science in their own words. *Science and Children, 31* (4), 31–33.

Schon, I. (1992). Ciencia en espanol. *Science and Children, 29* (6), 18–19, 46.

Schon, I. (1994). Libros de ciencia en espanol. *Science and Children, 31* (6), 38–40.

Scott, D., Williams, B., & Hyslip, K. (1992). Mathematics as communication: Journal writing in second grade. *Childhood Education, 69* (1), 15–18.

Skinner, P. (1990). *What's your problem? Posing and solving mathematical problems, K-2.* Portsmouth, NH: Heinemann.

Srulowitz, F. (1992). Diary of a tree. *Science and Children, 29* (5), 19–21.

Stead, T., & Semple, C. (1992). Whole math in action. *Teaching K-8, 21* (4), 42–44.

Stiffler, L. A. (1992). A solution in the shelves. *Science and Children, 29* (6), 17, 46.

Thiessen, D., & Matthias, M. (Eds.) (1993). *The wonderful world of mathematics: A critically annotated list of children's literature in mathematics.* Reston, VA: National Council of Teachers of Mathematics.

Thrailkill, C. (1994). Math and literature: The perfect match. *Teaching PreK-8, 24* (4), 64–65.

Van Scoy, I. J., & Fairchild, S. H. (1993). It's about time! Helping preschool and primary children understand time concepts. *Young Children, 48* (2), 21–24.

Wadlington, E., Bitner, J., Partridge, E., & Austin, S. (1992). Have a problem? Make the writing-mathematics connection. *Arithmetic Teacher, 40* (4), 207–209.

Warm up to cooperative learning (1992). *Instructor, 102* (2), 52–55.

Wassermann, S. (1990). *Serious players in the primary classroom.* New York: Teachers College Press.

Welchman-Tischler, R. (1993). *How to use children's literature to teach mathematics.* Reston, VA: National Council of Teachers of Mathematics.

Whitin, D. J. (1994). Literature and mathematics in preschool and primary: The right connection. *Young Children, 49* (2), 4–11.

Whitin, D. J., & Gary, C. C. (1994). Promoting mathematical explorations through children's literature. *Arithmetic Teacher, 41* (7), 394–399.
Whitin, D., & Wilde, S. (1992). *Read any good math lately? Children's books for mathematical learning, K-6.* Portsmouth, NH: Heinemann.
Workman, S., & Anziano, M. C. (1993). Curriculum webs: Weaving connections from children to teachers. *Young Children, 48* (2), 4–9.

Children's Book References

Bare, C. S. (1985). *Guinea pigs don't read books.* New York: Crowell.
Cole, J. (1986) *The magic school bus at the waterworks.* New York: Scholastic.
Cummings, P. (1991). *Clean your room, Harvey Moon!.* New York: Bradbury.
de Paola, T. (1978). *The popcorn book.* New York: Holiday House.
de Regniers, B. S. (1985). *So many cats.* New York: Clarion Books.
Ehlert, L. (1988). *Planting a rainbow.* New York: HBJ.
Gibbons, G. (1985). *Playgrounds.* New York: Holiday House.
Hutchins, P. (1986). *The doorbell rang.* New York: Greenwillow.
Jonas, A. (1983). *Round trip.* New York: Greenwillow.
Kruskin, K. (1986). *The Philharmonic gets dressed.* New York: Harper-Collins.
Lobel, A. (1985). *Frog and toad are friends.* New York: Harper-Collins.
MacGill-Callahan, S., & Moser, B. (1991). *And still the turtle watched.* New York: Dial.
Morozumi, A. (1990). *One gorilla.* New York: Farrar, Straus, & Giroux.
Pienkowski, J. (1983). *Sizes.* Bergenfield, NJ: Puffin.
Slobofkins, R. (1968). *Caps for sale.* Reading, MA: Addison-Wesley.
Swift, J. (1983). *Gulliver's travels.* New York: William Morrow.
Yashima, T. (1955). *Crow boy.* New York: Viking Press.

9

Whole Language Portfolios: Assessment and Evaluation to Inform Children, Parents, and Educators

GARY AND MARYANN MANNING

Eight-year-old Claudio looks perplexed as he holds two revised and edited pieces of writing in front of him. Anna Wells, his teacher, stops by his table and asks if she can be helpful. Claudio responds by saying:

> I like both my stories, but I like the way I start this story better; my other story has a better ending. I like how I begin the story about going to sleep at night. How I ended my other story about my dog dying is sad but I like the way I wrote it. I don't know which story to put in my portfolio; I just want good stuff in my portfolio.

Anna listens and then takes out her ever-ready pad of post-its. She says, "Why don't you put both stories in your portfolio, and put a post-it on each that says just what you told me; that you especially like the beginning of one and the ending of the other."

Claudio gives a sigh of relief and begins writing on the post-its. His problem of deciding which piece, if any, to put in the portfolio has been resolved.

Anna is pleased about Claudio's dilemma for two reasons. First, he recognized that some parts of his stories were better than others, which indicates that he is developing as a critical reader of his own work. At the same time, she was able to help Claudio understand that not everything needs to be perfect to go into a portfolio.

There are 22 primary grade children in Anna's multiage, inner city classroom. It was January when this incident occurred; Claudio and the other children were making tremendous progress. They were making decisions about what they wanted to include in their portfolios and taking pride in the contents.

Anna knows that a portfolio is more than just a collection of "stuff." It includes a wide variety of data on a student's growth and development, such as work samples, descriptions of content and process, and reflections on work by the student, teacher, and parents.

Portfolios are fairly new to education, but not to other fields of endeavor. In fact, artists have long kept samples of their work to show their ability and versatility. Investors, too, keep portfolios that reflect the depth and diversity of various securities. Likewise, a child's portfolio demonstrates diversity and growth.

The actual containers for portfolios are created in a number of different ways. Some teachers prefer loose-leaf notebooks while others like pocketed folders or plastic containers. Some store portfolio materials in cardboard boxes, plastic crates, file cabinets, or cupboards.

Still other teachers, like Anna, are making the transition to computer portfolios. For example, Anna now has her children read from texts on the computer screen while their voices are recorded by the computer system. She later analyzes their reading; she can also use the recordings to compare their progress in oral reading skills over the year. Anna and the children save writing samples by scanning the pages and saving them in the computer filing system. When she wants to share children's writing samples with parents or others, she prints them out from the computer file. Anna's computer portfolio system even has the capability of filing a videotape of a child engaged in a literacy event or in some other worthwhile activity. Whatever system is used—from a file box to a computer—it's important that it be a manageable one, both for the teacher and the children.

This chapter will examine the classroom practices of three primary grade teachers, in addition to Anna Wells, who use portfolios in their teaching: Gayle Morrison, a first grade teacher in an inner city school; Ginny Hart, a second grade teacher in a school with a predominantly lower-middle-class population; and Carolyn Lytle, a third grade teacher in a school with a predominantly middle-class population. All four of these teachers use portfolios and value their use, although they are quick to point out that they constantly reassess their procedures in order to make the portfolio system work both more efficiently and more effectively.

WHOLE LANGUAGE NECESSITATES DIFFERENT EVALUATION

In the past, it was estimated that a basal reader approach, based on a skills-oriented view of reading, was used in over 90% of all classrooms in the nation (Goodman, Shannon, Freeman, & Murphy, 1988; Vacca, Vacca, & Gove, 1987). Skills-oriented reading teachers directed children to spend much of their time reading stories from basals and practicing skills isolated from meaningful contexts. This was general practice, even though experts in literacy education had shown that competent readers cannot necessarily demonstrate a mastery of isolated reading skills, and that no real hierarchy of reading skills exists (Downing, 1982; Goodman, 1976; McNeil, 1974). However, the situation is now changing. There is currently a movement toward whole language and this movement is gaining momentum as educators become more informed about theory and research on students' literacy development.

Goodman, Smith, Meredith, and Goodman (1987) describe whole language as "Curricula that keep language whole and in the context of its thoughtful use in real situations" (p. 6). In whole language classrooms children engage in purposeful reading activities and read children's books, rather than just stories from readers. The focus of teaching is on how to help readers attend to whole text, not merely to words, letters, and other bits and pieces of language. Reading materials for young children are meaningful, predictable, and authentic.

Whole language educators view reading and writing as interrelated processes, and believe that communication is the main aim of writing. Children need much practice and encouragement to become good communicators in writing. Teachers encourage children to develop as writers by letting them select their own topics for writing, accepting their attempts to express themselves, and giving them opportunities to share with others what they have written.

With new research and theoretical understandings, and the resulting innovative practices in literacy instruction, educators have directed their attention to the assessment and evaluation of literacy growth and development. Whole language educators are aware of the pressures exerted on school administrations to make sure children perform well on standardized tests; they realize that, for some, learning is still synonymous with achievement as measured by isolated bits and pieces of information on such tests. Whole language teachers, however, are anxious to end the tyranny of these tests.

Instead of relying on the single criterion of a standardized test, whole language teachers use appropriate and valid assessment procedures to make accurate evaluations of their children. Assessment is the beginning of the evaluation process: the collection of data on children. Evaluation, on the other hand, consists of describing, analyzing, and reflecting on the data. A careful evaluation of the data guides instructional decisions for whole language teachers. Portfolios enable teachers to use developmentally appropriate assessment techniques with young children, and to evaluate children's growth and development with an eye toward maintaining developmentally appropriate instructional practices.

This chapter will address portfolio assessment in the context of the individual classroom teacher, rather than in the context of large-scale assessment. It is important, however, to realize that portfolios hold much promise for the accurate assessment and evaluation of large groups of children. Simmons (1992), for example, has used large-scale writing assessment to compare the writing abilities of groups of students; he believes that portfolios can and should be used in large-scale settings.

ALL CHILDREN—INCLUDING SPECIAL NEEDS CHILDREN— PROFIT FROM PORTFOLIOS

All four teachers mentioned in this chapter teach children with special needs in their classes. They all indicate that these children benefit from having a portfolio. In fact, they say that special needs children often take more pride in their portfolios than the other children do. Since the children are active participants in their portfolios, it's not surprising that they view the process favorably.

It's not always readily apparent who is or isn't a special needs child. When we recently visited Ginny Hart's second grade classroom we had the opportunity to speak with Carolina, one of the children in the class. We were very impressed with her understanding of herself as a reader and writer, and how much she engaged in self-reflection as she reviewed several items in her portfolio with us. In talking with Carolina, we knew that English is a second language for her. However, we were surprised when Ginny later told us that Carolina has a learning disability.

Without question, portfolios are an asset for *all* children. All children can be portfolio keepers and can benefit greatly from the process as they, their parents, and their teachers gain insights into the strengths and needs of children with special needs.

INVOLVING PARENTS

Portfolios provide a way to involve parents in a child's learning. Teachers ask parents to contribute to their child's portfolio. Ginny, for instance, asks parents at the beginning of the year to share their insights about their child's literacy history. She sends home a form that includes several items (see Figure 9.1).

Carolyn Lytle also asks parents for information about their children at the beginning of the year, but does not use a formal list of questions. She writes a letter that invites parents to review their children's portfolio and to write something about their children's reading and writing that could be placed in the portfolio (see Figure 9.2).

During a recent open house at Carolyn's school, the children's portfolios were on their desks. When parents visited, they went to their child's desk and reviewed the portfolio with the child. Carolyn says this was a much better use of time than other activities she has planned at open house.

Sharing the portfolio with parents during a teacher–parent conference is the rule for the four teachers observed in this chapter. They can't imagine having a conference without using the portfolio as a main focal point. Gayle Morrison recalls an incident last year when a parent visited her in March and expressed great concern about her child's poor spelling. Gayle responded by saying that she, too, cared about good spelling. As usual during a teacher–parent conference, she got out the child's portfolio and pulled the writing samples from the beginning of the year to the present. The samples

Figure 9.1. *Literacy history of a child.*

At what age did your child first show an interest in books?
At what age did your child first show an interest in writing?
What was your child's favorite book before entering school?
How often did your child want you to read aloud?
Who selected the books you read aloud?
What family activities include reading?
What family activities include writing?
Who reads aloud children's books in your home?
How often does someone read aloud?
Who does your child see reading? How often? What?
Who does your child see writing? How often? What?
Does your child like to look at or read books?
Under what circumstances does your child willingly read independently for recreation?
Please write your thoughts about how I, as your child's teacher, can support your child's reading and writing this year.

Figure 9.2. *Letter to parents about portfolios.*

Dear Parents,

An important aspect in our third-grade classroom is the use of portfolios which will inform us of the growth and development of your child, especially in reading and writing. Your child's portfolio is a collection of items such as writing samples, oral reading samples, summaries or descriptions of books read, and sketches or photos of projects. The portfolio reveals your child's strengths and gives information on what is needed.

When you visit the class, please ask your child to show you his/her portfolio. On additional visits, you'll want to review entries that have been added since your last visit. Whenever we have a conference, we will use the portfolio to study the progress that has been made throughout the year.

I invite you to write something about your child's reading and writing, which could be included in the portfolio. During the year, you may see something that you'd like to add to your child's portfolio. When you visit our class, the portfolios are on the counter as you enter the classroom. Please feel free to look at your child's portfolio or better yet ask your child to show you.

Sincerely,
Carolyn Lytle

---

were dated and she put them on the table in chronological order. She and the mother then examined each paper, noting the changes in the child's spelling and other aspects of writing. At the end of the review, the mother sighed and said, "I forgot where he was at the beginning of the year. He has made a lot of progress." The mother went away with a renewed appreciation for her son's remarkable progress as a speller and writer.

CONTENTS OF LITERACY PORTFOLIOS

It's up to the students and the teacher to decide what goes into a portfolio. A number of variables—such as class size, grade level, type of student, and teacher experience—determine the number and types of entries. A few items that might be included in a portfolio are reviewed in the following sections.

ANECDOTAL RECORDS.   Teachers write anecdotal notes when they observe an important event in a student's literacy development. Gayle, for example, recalls a discussion she had recently with one of her first graders. Since this particular child is at a high level in spelling development, Gayle told her that, usually, *tion* represents the *shun* sound, as in *vacation* and *lotion*. As Gayle later observed this child writing, she noticed that the girl spelled *ocean* as *ohtion*. When she asked the child to explain why she had used that spelling, the child replied that she had learned about *tion* the week before. Needless to say, Gayle was impressed with this child's thinking ability, even though what she learned didn't apply with this particular word. Gayle made a note about the child's thinking on a post-it, and stuck it on a paper in the student's portfolio. Later, she helped the child correctly spell *ocean*.

However, if teachers do not work out a reasonable management system for anecdotal note taking, it could be the "straw that breaks the camel's back." The system Gayle uses works for her.

Ginny uses address labels to make anecdotal notes (see examples of this teacher's notes in Figure 9.3). To ensure that she records anecdotal remarks each week on her second graders, Ginny uses a grid on a sheet of paper. At the beginning of the year, she runs off enough copies of the grid so that she has one for each week of the year. On each sheet, she has a space to note the week and a cell in which to place one small address label for each of her 25 children. As the week progresses, she makes sure that she has made at least one remark for each child. At the end of the week, she transfers the labels to her file, which she might later place in the children's portfolios.

Figure 9.3. *Anecdotal notes for a second grade class.*

Happy Birthday Moon   9/3

—too difficult—meaning and structure break down. Overrelied on phonics to "sound out" words and stopped reading for meaning. Confused over some letter combinations.

Recommendations—
—Monitor levels carefully to avoid frustration
—Build supports to encourage risking

Rain, Rain, Rain   9/6

—better level—Uses some meaning cues—looks at picture (stream = flood). Becomes quickly frustrated if he doesn't know the word. A poor risker.

Recommendations—
—cloze activities
—watch for letter/sound confusions
—use as teaching point

At regular intervals during the year, Ginny refers to the notes on the address labels, summarizes them, and types them in on her computer.

ART SAMPLES.   Samples of children's artwork in a portfolio can provide a great deal of insight into children's intellectual development and interests. A small group of children in Anna Wells' classroom made a mural about a book they read. Although the mural was too big to put into a portfolio, the children took a picture of it and each child placed a copy of the picture in their portfolio, along with a brief description of the book activity.

CONFERENCE REPORTS.   Teachers make notes during and/or after a reading or writing conference with a child. Gayle and Carolyn, for example, write their notes on single sheets of paper, which they place in a separate conference folder for each child. Figures 9.4 and 9.5 show an example of conference notes these teachers wrote about their students. Other teachers make conference notes on index cards or in a notebook. The teachers then add selected conference notes, or summaries of the notes, to children's portfolios.

GOALS SET BY THE CHILD.   Children often set goals for themselves. Children in Ginny's and Carolyn's room set personal goals at the beginning of each 9-week term. They write a goal and list activities that will help them accomplish their goal. As shown in Figure 9.6, one of Ginny's children set a reading goal and listed activities. At the end of the 9-week term, she related how she thought she had done. She put her written goals and accompanying description in her portfolio. Figure 9.7 shows the goals listed by one of Carolyn's third graders.

Figure 9.4. *Gayle's conference notes (first grade).*

8/27	Uses beg. sounds—wrote 2 sentences. Not sure of some sounds yet. He likes to draw cars.
8/31	He self-corrected s/c himself when he started reading his story. He had—I S 9 Rot—. When he started reading the word "S" for saw, he remembered where it was on "Seekers' News," and he went and found it. His story read—"I saw 9 reaches."

What progress!!!

When putting the note on the door, he seems to lose some of his confidence in putting down his "best guess."   Y r at I (we are at lunch.)

Figure 9.5. *Carolyn's conference notes (third grade).*

11-7	Is copying from book into Log
11-8	Trying to read *The Boy on Third Base;* very committed; poor comprehension; doesn't use word skills; taught strategies
11-11	Listening to taped reading of book then reading to me; writing one sentence in Log.
11-14	Had trouble reading Log entry he had just written—very frustrated. Retold story he had just listened to w/details; said he enjoyed listening to stories;

We wrote a Log entry together about the story.

11-15	Read aloud *Frog and Toad Are Friends* very halting but he made it; he read it again; we recalled reading strategies that will help him read alone.
11-17	Reading *Class Clown* (he chose it) aloud to him at SSR; very interested in story; doesn't follow words even though I mark them when I call attention; can read some sentences alone in context; continue teaching strategies.
11-21	Read aloud several paragraphs in *Little House in Big Woods* after following while Sean and I read—Progress!

READING GOALS

To be a better reader.

Activities

To read more books. To know the words that I didn't know.

How I think I am doing   I read book at home.

I tink I am a better reader. I can read a Baby Sitter

Figure 9.6. *Reading goals and activities in Ginny's classroom.*

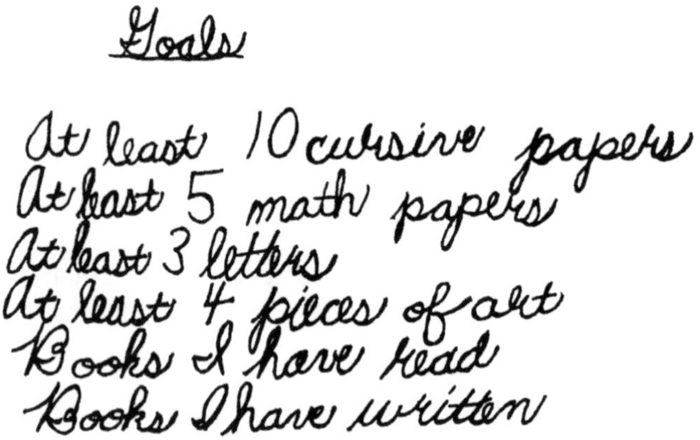

Goals

At least 10 cursive papers
At least 5 math papers
At least 3 letters
At least 4 pieces of art
Books I have read
Books I have written

Figure 9.7. *Reading goals in Carolyn's classroom.*

INTEREST INVENTORIES.   Teachers interview younger children to assess their interests, but children who are more proficient readers and writers can complete a written inventory. At the beginning of the year, Ginny interviews her second grade children using the interest inventory shown in Figure 9.8.

The wording and types of items will depend on the ages of the children and on what teachers want to know about them. We suggest using only a few items, so that children will not tire of the inventory.

JOURNAL ENTRIES.   The types of journal writing children engage in vary. In some classes, children write in a personal journal every day, while in others children write in a content journal, or learning log, divided into different content areas. In Carolyn's class, children write in a reading journal, recording their ideas about the books they read. Carolyn then corresponds with the children about books they're reading by writing comments in their reading journals, as suggested by Atwell (1987).

The children and Carolyn may refer to these journal entries in the portfolio, noting items that are of interest or that provide insights about a child's literacy development. Carolyn usually asks children to put three or four journal entries, written at different times of the year, into the portfolio in order to show growth over a period of time.

LETTER WRITING.   Children in whole language classrooms engage in a variety of authentic writing activities, including letter writing. They enjoy getting a response from a letter they've written to business or government offices, or to a favorite author. Letter writing takes a variety of forms.

Figure 9.8. *Interest inventory.*

What is your favorite book? Why?

Do you have a favorite author or illustrator? Why is he/she your favorite?

If someone says they will read to you, what books would you choose?

Do you have a poem that you like to hear or read? If so, what is it?

What do you enjoy doing outside of school?

If you could choose anything to do on the weekend, what would you do?

What is your favorite quiet activity?

Do you like to write?

What do you like to write best?

What's the best thing you ever wrote?

When you write for fun, what do you write?

What is a favorite TV show? Why?

Who is one of your best friends? Describe that person.

Gayle's first graders, for example, write letters to their parents each week. At the same time, she writes a group letter to the parents; both letters go into each child's three-ring notebook, which the child takes home on Friday. Gayle asks the parents to write a letter to their child and place it in the notebook, which is returned to the classroom on Monday (Manning, Manning, & Morrison, in press).

Children may want to place letters in their portfolio—letters they've written or received. Some of Gayle's children save all their letters in the portfolio, while others save photo copies of a selection.

LIST OF BOOKS.   Children in Gayle's classroom make a list of the books they read accompanied by an illustration of their comments on the book, as shown in Figure 9.9. In Ginny's classroom, children write a brief summary of the story along with the names of the books, as shown in Figure 9.10. Sometimes they add something about the book, but not always. It's fascinating to look over these portfolio entries and to see how many books, and what types of books, young children read. Most children in Ginny's and Gayle's rooms read well over 100 books each year.

In addition to revealing children's reading interests, a review of the book lists in the portfolios provides insights into the books a teacher may be emphasizing. For example, a look at the portfolios in Ginny's classroom will show that many children list books by Gail Gibbons. Each year Ginny conducts an author study on Gibbons and reads aloud from her books. The children become avid consumers of *Up Goes a Skyscraper* (Gibbons, 1986), *How a House Is Built* (Gibbons, 1990) and other Gibbons books.

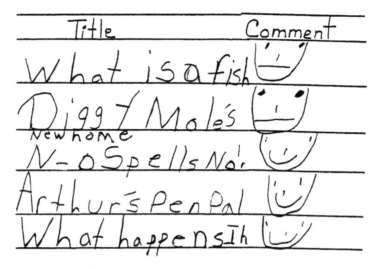

Figure 9.9. *List of books in Gayle's classroom.*

MISCUE ANALYSIS. A *miscue* is an unexpected response in oral reading. Reading the previous sentence aloud and saying "mistake" instead of "miscue" is, in fact, a miscue. An analysis of readers' miscues shows their strengths as well as their difficulties. A complete explanation of miscue analysis can be found in Goodman, Watson, and Burke's *Reading Miscue Inventory* (1987); whole language teachers are encouraged to administer a complete miscue analysis with readers who are having difficulty.

In most cases, with typical readers, however, teachers need only note miscues to determine if there is a change in meaning. Listening to a child read aloud, teachers ask themselves if the sentence makes sense with the miscue. If it does, the reader is probably focused on meaning, and there is no cause for concern because all readers make miscues. If the reader's miscues *do* change the meaning, the reader probably needs to become more focused on meaning.

In addition to miscue analysis for determining how children are developing as readers, teachers should also assess what meaning the children create from the text by asking them to retell what they've read. After the reader has retold the story, the teacher can ask more specific questions about what the student related. If the story retains most of its meaning in the retelling, the teacher will know that the reader understood the story.

After completing a miscue analysis, with an accompanying oral retelling, teachers place a copy of the results in the child's portfolio. Teachers should be aware of the fact that full miscue analyses are generally com-

Independent Reading

Date	Title, Author, Pages	Summary
Oct. 6 1993	Stringbean's Trip to the Shining Sea [31] Williams	It had different stamps, and some are colorful and some are funny looking stamps, Some of the post cards are fancy and are little picture's The End
Oct 6 1993	Max helps Out Linda Neilson 14	Max went out with his dad to a hardware store. When they got home they started painting the empty room.

Figure 9.10. *List of books in Ginny's classroom.*

pleted for very few children in a classroom—only for those who are troubled readers. Whole language teachers, however, always listen to a child read with a "miscue ear." As they note strengths and problems through such listening, they also often record their observations and place them in the child's portfolio.

A few children in Carolyn's room have conducted their own, modified miscue analyses. Under Carolyn's guidance, they audio-taped themselves reading, listened to the tapes, marked the miscues, and then discussed the results. This kind of activity offers children an opportunity to monitor their own reading.

PARENT COMMENTS. Teachers invite parents to write notes to or about their children and these are put in the portfolios. As stated earlier, teachers also invite parents at the beginning of the year to inform them about their children. This invitation can be reissued from time to time throughout the year. Teachers using a procedure like Gayle's, in which parents add a letter to a notebook each week, could refer to or make copies of some of those letters, and include them as well in the portfolios.

PHOTOS AND SKETCHES. Photos can capture important aspects of a child's literacy learning. A review of portfolios in Anna's multiage classroom shows photos of a group of children dramatizing a story they've just read, of an author from the area who visited her class to share her books and ideas about writing, and of big books that several children had written.

When a literacy-related project is too big to keep in the portfolio, Anna and her students often take a photo of it and place it in the portfolio. Other items that are too large to put into a portfolio, but that nevertheless are a source of information about a child's literacy, can be handled by making sketches that can then be put into the portfolio, together with an explanation of the project.

PUBLISHED PIECES.   Children in whole language classrooms select pieces of writing to publish after they have been revised and edited. In Carolyn's classroom, children set their own goals on how often to publish; many children publish at least one piece every month. She asks the children to place several published pieces, and drafts of their work, in their portfolio during the school year.

RETELLINGS.   In addition to oral retellings of stories as a part of the miscue analysis procedure, discussed above, written and oral retellings can also be utilized as specific activities. Teachers can learn about children's comprehension of a story by asking them to tell about the story, and then asking more specific questions on aspects told during the unaided retelling. Notes and analyses of these oral retellings can be placed in the portfolios.

In addition to oral retellings, teachers can ask children to engage in written retellings. Third graders in Carolyn's classroom, for example, complete written retellings of stories or of portions of nonfiction texts they've read in content areas. Some of these written retellings are placed in the children's portfolios.

RUNNING RECORDS.   Both Gayle and Anna take individual running records (Clay, 1993) of their emergent readers every month, which they place in the children's portfolios. The running record is a particularly effective way to assess the reading of young, beginning readers. In this process, teachers ask a child to read a selected text aloud. As the child reads, the teacher puts a check mark on a plain sheet of paper (or on a copy of the text), one mark for each word the child reads correctly. If the child makes an error, the teacher notes that also. Through an analysis of the running record, teachers get a clearer picture of the reading strategies that the child is using. By reviewing a child's running records in the portfolio over a period of several months, teachers are able to see a child's reading development.

SELF-EVALUATIONS.   Children in whole language classrooms evaluate the quantity and quality of their reading and writing, their attitudes toward reading and writing, and their ability to work with others in small and large group situations. These written self-evaluations reveal children's understandings. The self-evaluation of one of Carolyn's third graders, for example, shows an awareness of the relationship between reading and writing (see Figure 9.11). In other classes, students complete a self-evaluation checklist prepared by their teacher.

VIDEO AND AUDIO TAPES.   Perhaps the most obvious literacy event that can be recorded on an audio-tape is a child reading aloud. Asking a child to read a short story or passage at the beginning of the year, and then to read the same text and other texts at intervals throughout the year, is excellent documentation of growth in reading. Miscue analysis, running records, and retellings can be video- or audio-taped and then analyzed.

Other activities that can be video- or audio-taped include dramatic presentations, debates, oral reports, reading and writing conferences, poetry read-ins, book talks, literature set discussions, classroom talk, and small group discussions. A written entry in the portfolio about the taped events

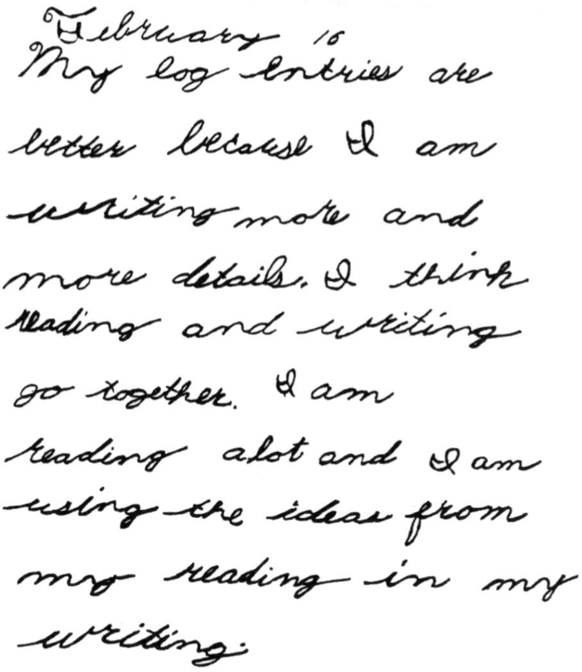

> February 16
> My log entries are better because I am writing more and more details. I think reading and writing go together. I am reading a lot and I am using the ideas from my reading in my writing.

Figure 9.11. *A third grader's self-evaluation.*

can briefly describe them and refer the reviewer to the separate locations where they are kept.

WRITING SAMPLES. Writing samples in a portfolio provide information about a child's literacy development. Older children are usually independent enough to make their own selections for the portfolio, and to analyze and reflect on their writing; however, younger children need more guidance from the teacher. A particularly impressive procedure for collecting writing samples comes from the example of a teacher observed in a New Zealand classroom of 5- and 6-year olds. The teacher collected all the writings of one or two of her students every school day—everything those children had written for the entire day. In this way, the teacher was able to acquire an all-day collection of writing from every one of her 30 students without being overwhelmed on any particular day with mountains of paper.

PORTFOLIOS AND OTHER AREAS OF THE CURRICULUM

In this chapter we focused on literacy portfolios, but portfolios can be kept for other areas of the curriculum as well. In fact, since reading and writing permeate all areas of the curriculum, the literacy portfolio naturally includes them. A child may include a written report of a research project as a part of an activity in science or social studies. In Gayle's classroom, for example, we recently saw a group of first graders conducting a research study on tadpoles (Manning & Manning, 1993). They observed two tadpoles in their classroom aquarium and made notes of their observations over a period of several days. They also made notes on information they found about tadpoles from books, magazines, and other sources. Later, they drafted their report, revised it, and made a bound copy with illustrations. Photo copies were made of the book and one was put into each of the children's portfolios. Some of the children also put their research notes on tadpoles into their portfolios.

EVALUATION OF STUDENT PERFORMANCE

As the year progresses, children's portfolios fill with information that can be used to assess their literacy learning. Teachers need to periodically review and sort the data in the portfolios so that they are more manageable for making evaluations. Any data that are removed from the portfolios can be stored in a file or sent home with the child.

As teachers review the information in a portfolio, literacy growth over a span of one or more years can be noted. Most importantly, teachers can use the information to assist them in determining developmentally appropriate instruction. The picture of a child's literacy development that emerges in a portfolio of this type is more complete than any other form of assessment and evaluation.

Whole language teachers spend time and effort in making assessments and evaluations using portfolios and then relating those evaluations to literacy instruction. Different teachers have their own ways of reviewing portfolios. Gayle, for example, studies no more than two or three portfolios at a time; she arrives at school very early each morning and, among other tasks, reviews portfolios while she is alert and can devote an uninterrupted amount of time to them. She places a small check next to each item she has reviewed. On a separate sheet of paper she writes the date of the review and any particular ideas she wants to note (see Figure 9.12). Her notes serve as a guide for planning future instruction; she also uses the notes when she conferences with a child or with parents.

The Portfolio Conference

Whole language teachers make a point of holding a portfolio conference with their children every few weeks, and they schedule these in different ways. Anna, for example, confers with one child each day on his/her portfolio. In this way she conducts a portfolio conference with each of her 22 students about once a month. The conferences usually last about 5–10 minutes. On one of our visits to her classroom, we listened to Anna confer with Mario, one of her students.

Figure 9.12. *Review notes on a child's portfolio.*

—Writes a letter using correct letter form.
—Spells 42/44 words conventionally.
—Uses phonetic spelling on "best guesses."
—Writes a 5 sentence letter.
—Uses periods correctly.
—Uses question marks correctly.
—Doubles final consonant before adding "ing."
—Uses proper names correctly with capital letters.
—Uses commas correctly.
—Uses word referents me, you, correctly.
—Uses correct subject/verb agreement.

ANNA: I'm so glad we have a few minutes to discuss your portfolio. Will you tell me how you feel about some of the items you've added since our last conference?

MARIO: I like my two new pieces of writing. It isn't very long, but I like the words I used to describe the house. You can see in your head how scary it is.

ANNA: I also like it. I'm pleased you're writing with your readers in mind.

MARIO: Did you see the giraffe that I drew for the animal theme?

ANNA: Yes, it makes you feel as though you're there in the jungle. I also noticed that you correctly spelled *giraffe* in the short description that accompanied the picture.

MARIO: My Dad gives me a hard time about some words that I don't spell right, but I tell him that I'm getting better. My Mom told him what you said about how I'm getting better at spelling.

ANNA: I also wanted to tell you how pleased I am that you're reading all of the Amelia Bedelia books by Peggy Parish. If you're interested in reading about Peggy Parish, I have an author file on her that tells a lot about her life and writing.

MARIO: Did you read the note I wrote to you on my book list? I read the book you told me about.

ANNA: Yes, I read it. I was impressed with the book you read about sharks. That's a difficult book and you seemed to understand it. Well, I have to move on. Thanks for sharing with me, Mario.

The Teacher's Portfolio

Most whole language teachers agree that they can't be effective in the use of portfolios with children unless they create their own portfolios. A teacher's portfolio serves at least two purposes: demonstration of the portfolio process and demonstration of themselves as readers and writers.

Demonstration is an important concept, both in school and in the world outside school; it is also a natural part of the learning process. All skilled craftsmen, for example, first undergo a period of apprenticeship during which they carefully observe their mentors and are finally engaged to work only under the strict supervision of the experts. Through demonstration and thoughtful engagement guided by experts, novices advance to becoming expert craftsmen.

Whole language teachers apply this same concept in their classrooms. It's difficult to imagine achieving much success in teaching reading and writing to children if the teachers themselves are not active readers and writers who demonstrate those skills to children. Similarly, it's difficult to imagine much success in getting children to be portfolio keepers if teachers themselves are not active portfolio keepers.

When teachers think aloud about their portfolios, it gives children insights into the processes they are using. In the following example, Ginny is thinking aloud to her classroom of second grade children:

> I want to put this poem in my portfolio; I've just realized that I haven't included any poetry.
> This story should go in my portfolio because it has a powerful beginning.
> I want to record a book I read over the weekend on my book list. I need to write a paragraph about it while it's still fresh in my memory.
> I don't have any art in my portfolio. Before I take apart this interest center, I'm going to make a sketch of it. I'm proud of the balance.
> I must clean out my portfolio because there are some pieces that don't represent me as well as I'd like. I have some new pieces to replace some of the old.

A teacher thinking aloud about her portfolio is demonstrating for the children the portfolio process.

FINDING TIME

Whenever we speak with whole language teachers about their portfolios, one resounding chord is always struck: It's difficult to find the time to engage in the portfolio process in a comprehensive way. Carolyn says, for example, that she gets frustrated with the time it takes to photocopy some of the children's work, like letters they write for mailing, before they go into a portfolio.

Ginny tries to review portfolios at least once a month to make sure they're updated. She says that there is usually also a stack of unfiled materials in her classroom that she and her less independent students must find the time to file.

When we asked Anna if she would like to have a file clerk, she quickly replied, "Oh, no! I learn so much when I work with the children to put items in the portfolio. I see things I didn't see before and I hear them give their reasons for including something in the portfolio." Creative teachers refine the necessary management aspects and get ideas from others engaged in similar processes. Gayle, for example, gets information and inspiration for portfolios from other teachers when she attends her local Teachers Applying Whole Language (TAWL) meetings.

Time, however, is an issue that teachers definitely have to confront, and there are no simple or "right" answers for everyone. However, when teachers value the process of portfolios, they will find the time and they will make the process work.

For all teachers who haven't begun to use portfolios in their classrooms, we encourage them to do so. As one of our mentors said to us years ago when we were thinking about initiating an individualized reading program in our classrooms, "Plant thy feet in mid-air and proceed!"

REFERENCES

Atwell, N. (1987). *In the middle.* Portsmouth, NH: Heinemann.

Clay, M. (1993). *An observation survey of early literacy achievement.* Portsmouth, NH: Heinemann.

Downing, J. (1982). Reading—Skill or skills? *The Reading Teacher, 35,* 534–537.

Goodman, K. (1976). Reading: A psycholinguistic guessing game. In H. Singer & R. Ruddell (Eds.), *Theoretical models and processes* (pp. 497–508). Newark, DE: International Reading Association.

Goodman, K., Shannon, P., Freeman, Y., & Murphy, S. (1988). *Report card on basal readers.* New York: Richard C. Owen.

Goodman, K., Smith, E. B., Meredith, R., & Goodman, Y. (1987) (3rd ed.). *Language and thinking in school—A whole language curriculum.* New York: Richard C. Owen.

Goodman, Y., Watson, D., & Burke, C. (1987). *Reading miscue inventory.* New York: Richard C. Owen.

Manning, M., & Manning, G. (1993). Remarkable researchers in first grade. *Teaching K-8, 23,* 54–56.

Manning, M., Manning, G., & Morrison, G. (in press). Home school connections: A teacher, first graders, and their parents write letters. *Young Children.*

McNeil, J. (1974). False prerequisites in the teaching of reading. *Journal of Reading Behavior, 4,* 421–427.

Simmons, J. (1992). Portfolios for large-scale assessment. In D. Graves & B. Sunstein (Eds.), *Portfolio portraits* (pp. 96–113). Portsmouth, NH: Heinemann.

Vacca, J., Vacca, R., & Gove, M. (1987). *Reading and learning to read.* Boston: Little, Brown.

Children's Book References

Gibbons, G. (1986). *Up goes a skyscraper.* New York: Winds Press.

Gibbons, G. (1990). *How a house is built.* New York: Holiday House.

10

Epilogue:
Challenges for Whole Language
Primary Teachers

SHIRLEY C. RAINES

William Katzenmeyer, former Dean of the College of Education at the University of South Florida, has written a working paper entitled, *Improving the Schools of Today and Inventing the Schools of Tomorrow* (1991). Dean Katzenmeyer postulated five key strategies we must embrace to accomplish the formidable task expressed in the title of his paper.

* Provide a continuity of caring for children
* Reinvent the learning environment
* Create a "high-option" environment
* Infuse technology
* Reinvent the teaching profession

Dean Katzenmeyer's paper, and the preface to this book, express similar philosophies. In the preface, I described my philosophy of teaching and teacher education as a process of "perceiving, behaving, becoming." The process of becoming a whole language teacher means perceiving the roles, behaving as the best examples of teachers in our profession, and trusting that worthy challenges can be met. "Perceiving, behaving, becoming" describes the change process.

The teachers described throughout *Whole Language Across the Curriculum: Grades 1, 2, 3* are reinventing the teaching profession. They personify Dean Katzenmeyer's challenge "to improve the schools of today and invent the schools of tomorrow." They do not have recipes or formulas for change; they are reflective practitioners who are examining what they teach, how they teach, with whom they teach, and even who they teach.

In some whole language schools, the process of change has been led by thoughtful administrators who create supportive climates in which to change traditional methods and curriculum structures. In most schools, the process of change has been initiated as a grass roots effort, teacher-to-teacher, and the results have been sustainable.

As with all departures from standard practice, critics and nay-sayers abound. Yet, the ground swell of support for whole language as a means of reinventing the learning environment has grown. Teachers have become researchers, organizers of conferences, and keynote speakers. They have opened their classroom doors and their own wallets. They have purchased children's books when library funds were inadequate or when textbook publishers had a stranglehold on instructional materials accounts. They have tutored one another, mentored neophytes, and challenged the authorities. Teachers have also questioned theorists who tell us that teachers must know the theory first and then change their practice. We have seen teachers who changed their practice first, saw the results, and *then* examined their theories of teaching and learning.

"Continuity of caring" is the motto of continuous progress teachers, and whole language teachers everywhere could adopt it as our credo because it reflects the developmental perspective we have long embraced. According to Loris Malaguzzi (Gandini, 1994), the thinker behind the great Reggio Emilia approach, schools must be amiable environments. Reading the descriptions of the teacher-to-child interactions and the child-to-child interactions permeating the chapters of this book we can sense the amiable environments these teachers have created. Our challenge remains to create whole language classrooms: places where "continuity of caring" is the description that reaches from home to school, and from home to community.

"Reinventing the learning environment" for primary grade children must mean that our classrooms become amiable environments for children. The contributors to this book have been "reinventors," as we pushed the interpretation of whole language from a view of literacy learning to a view of learning environments. We see reinventions of the learning environments in classrooms where children sing, dance, chant, graph, map, measure, compare, contrast, play, and design representations of what they are learning. Teachers are reinventing the learning environments and engaging children in real-life problem solving. Instruction has become more authentic and assessments more meaningful. Teachers are inventing portfolios, computer programs, and video-reports, and reaching out to parents to communicate.

The "high-option" environment Dean Katzenmeyer proposes is alive in early childhood and primary grade classrooms. Centers, computers, outdoor research stations, playgrounds, musical theaters, and community projects are just a few of the children's choices. Children are given more choices in what they read, in the topics to write about, in studies to investigate, and in ways to represent what they learn and how they learn.

Teachers request "high-option" environments, as well. We want more freedom to teach the curriculum in our way, to work with parents in different ways, to interpret the children's needs based on our understandings. We want to choose not to participate in one-shot staff development exercises. We want to choose not to buy exactly the same set of supplies the grade-level team selected. We want to choose not to follow the pattern, but to redesign our own pattern. We want to visit other teachers' classrooms, observe, reflect, try, and be supported in the process. Loris Malaguzzi calls for a profession which does not think small.

In our "reinvention of the learning environment," whole language teachers are transforming the teaching profession.

The challenge is to continue . . . perceiving, behaving, becoming.

REFERENCES

Gandini, L. (1994). History, ideas, and basic philosophy of Loris Malaguzzi. In C. Edwards, L. Gandini, & G. Forman (Eds.), *The hundred languages of children: The Reggio Emilia approach to early childhood education* (pp. 41–89). Norwood, NJ: Ablex.

Katzenmeyer, W. (1991). *A working paper: Improving the schools of today and inventing the schools of tomorrow.* Tampa, FL: University of South Florida, College of Education.

Index

About the Contributors

DR. SHIRLEY C. RAINES, author of Chapters 1–4 and 10 and book editor, is Professor of Education and Chairperson of the Department of Childhood/Language Arts/Reading at the University of South Florida in Tampa. With her husband, Dr. Robert J. Canady, Shirley is the author of *The Whole Language Kindergarten* from Teachers College Press. With Rebecca Isbell, she has written *Stories: Children's Literature in Early Education* from Delmar Publishers. She is also the author of the *Story S-t-r-e-t-c-h-e-r* series of teacher resource books from Gryphon House. Shirley is member-at-large on the executive board of the Association for Childhood Education International and is active in the National Association for the Education of Young Children and various teacher educator professional associations. Her research interests are in developing teaching cases for reflective practice and young children's literature interests.

DR. LINDA LEONARD LAMME, author of Chapter 5, is Professor of Education at the University of Florida in Gainesville, where she teaches courses in children's literature and language arts. Her most recent book, *Literature-Based Moral Education,* is published by Oryx Press of Phoenix, Arizona. Dr. Lamme's research interests are in authentic multicultural literature and children's responses to literature. Dr. Lamme is active in the National Council of Teachers of English and the International Reading Association.

DR. JOAN P. ISENBERG, author of Chapter 6, is Professor of Education and Coordinator of Early Childhood Programs at George Mason University in Fairfax, Virginia. Two of her recent co-authored books are *Creative Expression and Play in Early Childhood* from Merrill/Macmillan and *Teachers' Stories: From Personal Narrative to Professional Insights* from Jossey-Bass. She is on the NCATE Board of Examiners and holds leadership roles in the Association for Childhood Education International and the National Association of Early Childhood Teacher Educators. Her research interests are in teacher development and children's creativity.

DR. CAROL SEEFELDT, author of Chapter 7, is Professor of Human Development at the Institute for Child Study, University of Maryland. She is the author of *Social Studies for the Preschool and Primary Child* and co-author of *Early Childhood Education: An Introduction* from Merrill/Macmillan. Dr. Seefeldt is the editor of *Continuing Issues in Early Childhood Education* from Teachers College Press. Her research emphasizes early childhood curriculum, intergenerational attitudes, and the effects of competition on child growth and development.

DR. ROSALIND CHARLESWORTH, co-author of Chapter 8, is Professor of Early Childhood Education and Development in the Department of Child and Family Studies at Weber State University in Ogden, Utah. She is the author of *Understanding Child Development* and co-author with Karen K. Lind of *Math and Science for Young Children* from Delmar Publishers. Her major research effort, with Diane C. Burts and Craig H. Hart, is focused on a longitudinal study of the effects on academic achievement and classroom behavior of children who attended kindergartens identified as having classroom practices that were predominantly developmentally appropriate or inappropriate.

DR. KAREN K. LIND, co-author of Chapter 8, is Associate Professor of Curriculum and Instruction at the University of Louisville, where she teaches courses in early and middle childhood science education. Dr. Lind's work in inservice teacher education and curriculum development is funded by the National Science Foundation. She is co-author of *Math and Science for Young Children* from Delmar Publishers. She edits the early childhood column for *Science and Children,* is past president of the Council for Elementary Science International, and is an active member of the National Science Teachers Association.

DRS. GARY MANNING AND MARYANN MANNING, co-authors of Chapter 9, are Professors of Education at the University of Alabama, Birmingham, where they teach courses in literacy development. Former classroom teachers and administrators, Gary and Maryann collaborate on research, co-author journal articles and books, and present their research data to audiences at the International Reading Association and other literacy and language development conferences. Their most recent book is *Theme Immersion: Inquiry-Based Curriculum in Elementary and Middle Schools* from Heinemann. Maryann and Gary are teaching editors and write a monthly column for *Teaching K-8.*